COMPUTER NETWORKS

NETWORK PROTOCOLS

COMPUTER NETWORKS

Additional books in this series can be found on Nova's website under the Series tab.

Additional E-books in this series can be found on Nova's website under the E-book tab.

COMPUTER NETWORKS

NETWORK PROTOCOLS

GENG LIANG
EDITOR

Nova Science Publishers, Inc.
New York

For permission to use material from this book please contact us:
Telephone 631-231-7269; Fax 631-231-8175
Web Site: http://www.novapublishers.com

Library of Congress Cataloging-in-Publication Data

Network protocols / [edited by] Geng Liang.
p. cm.
Includes index.
ISBN 978-1-61470-821-6 (hardcover)
1. Computer network protocols. I. Liang, Geng.
TK5105.55.N48 2011
004.6'2--dc23

2011026734

Published by Nova Science Publishers, Inc. †New York

CONTENTS

PREFACE

Network and communication is something that indeed is changing the world of automatic control system in the most dramatic way. Concept and architecture of automation is updated. Network related methods of automation and control represent a broad research topic with applications in many disciplines and fields such as information technology, industrial engineering, manufacturing, instrumentation and many others based on the sophistication, flexibility and brought by network and communication.

The great interest in network model led manufactures to implement their own communication protocols, to enable communication among their devices, and during the last two decades, some criteria were defined in order to standardize the communication model, and enable communication among different models of devices, developed by different manufacturers. There are several standard and widespread network protocols and their components quite often used in industrial engineering, such as TCP/IP, fieldbus and Web based ones. The combination of two or more protocols on integrated hybrid systems, as well as the use of such systems on process or equipment with fast dynamic responses, motivates networked protocol related research. Such studies result in advances and optimization of transmission media technologies, communication methods, new proposals of network based architecture of systems, as well as advanced industrial control schemes. Furthermore, some layers in the corresponding network protocol also find their important uses in the fields mentioned above. Improvement in the design, re-design and combination of these sub-layer protocols contributes more robustness, flexibility and better performance to industrial engineering. Although being standardized, there are complex concepts and architectures behind these systems and, therefore, it necessitate the deeper understanding and more practical application of these protocols.

This book intends to focus on network protocol and communication in the area of information and industrial control. In this book, various research on sub-layer protocols including Data Link Layer (DLL), Application Layer (AL) and User Layer (UL) in instrumentation network and TCP/IP, Web based protocol for industrial and informatic network and control problems involving network communication, along with the design of corresponding system are presented explicitly. The main objective of this book is to provide information on some latest research on some mainstream network protocols used in industry, including fundamental concepts and principles, latest technological developments, and as the main part, theoretical and practical research results ever accomplished. It incorporates research, development, tutorials, case studies. The motivation comes from the fact that the research and development on new network protocols, refining of some sub-layers protocols and finding more powerful application of these protocols in industry are being carried out at many academic institutions and industrial sectors around the world. The technology trend is necessary to be disseminated so that the knowledge can be better and quickly put into use. The principles and methodologies in research, design and development of system dealing with various types of protocol, such as control, communication and simulation system, are the main topics of this book.

The book will undoubtedly enable the readers to understanding the underlying technology, philosophy, concepts, ideas and principles with regards to not only the network protocol itself but to instrumentation control system, automation, industrial network system, integration of data and control network, web based supervision and control. The readers can also benefit more from intuitive learning by the explicitly presented case studies and application examples included in every chapter of this book. This book includes comprehensive, general and also specific description of current research and technological developments and can meet the requirements of readers from different field. Fundamentals, principles, research results along with references for further study has been presented. Both novices and advanced practitioners can use this book as a guide in their learning, design and development. Since the book contains not only fundamentals but also sophisticated expertise, a wide range of reader can use it as reference. This book can serve as medium of information and ideas. It can also be a reference book at the research level for many engineering and technological disciplines. Wide range of researchers can find many useful methodologies and potential knowledge from it. All the contributions have been reviewed, cited and processed appropriately to guarantee the reader can get the most out of it. This book covers many interdisciplinary subjects and knowledge, the importance of this book within the industrial control, instrumentation and information technology is significant.

Geng Liang

ACKNOWLEDGMENT

This book is supported by Beijing Municipal Natural Science Foundation (4122074), the Fundamental Research Funds for the Central Universities (11MG12) and the National Natural Science Foundation of China (61174116).

In: Network Protocols
Editor: Geng Liang
ISBN 978-1-61470-821-6

Chapter 1

Function Block in User Layer Protocol of a Distributed Control Network: Concept and Design

Geng Liang[1] and Wen Li[2]
[1]School of Control and Computer Engineering, North China Electric Power University, Beijing, China
[2]Beijing GUODIANZHISHEN Control Technology Co. Ltd, Beijing, China

Abstract

Configuration platforms based on function blocks and links such as Function Block Diagram (FBD) are used widely in design and implementation of distributed intelligent control network (DICN). Traditionally, FBD and Ladder Diagram (LD) are two completely different programming languages with different data models and compilation algorithms to generate different data and instructions for field intelligent nodes. Essential difference exists between implementation methods of control strategies with the two programming languages for data exchange within and between different nodes, which make it difficult for unification of programming languages in configuration platform, hybrid programming and improvement of control systems' openness and compliancy. A kind of generalized FBD model for distributed intelligent control network is proposed. Scheme for implementing the model in field intelligent node is presented in detail. Transformation models for language elements in LD are presented based on the proposed model. The proposed model is flexible and widely applicable. Application of the proposed model in design and development of configuration platform software for distributed intelligent system show the effectiveness of the model.

1. INTRODUCTION

In recent years, distributed intelligent control networks (DICN) symbolized by fieldbus technology and fieldbus control system (FCS), wireless communication network, sensors network developed fast to become the development trend for larg-scale measurement and control system. These systems are characterized by parallel computation and complete danger-distribution with their control and measurement function in these systems are distributed in each field node. Implementation of DICN are mainly based on upper-level configuration platform whose principal programming languages are Function Block Diagram (FBD) and ladder diagram (LD) conformed to norm IEC61131-3, remote communication between field intelligent nodes and local control function. All or parts of the 5 programming languages are to be supported by upper-level configuration platform according to norm IEC61131. FBD and LD are more widely used in DICN [1-5]. Completely different data model and compilation algorithm are used in traditional FBD and LD that are 2 completely different and independent languages in user's configuration. In the meantime, implementation methods for data exchange locally and between nodes dealing with control strategies written in the 2 programming languages are different essentially [6], which make it very difficult to realize uniform in the programming languages and hybrid programming in a same programming platform. In this paper, a kind of Generalized Function Block Diagram (GFBD) model and implementation scheme for the model in field intelligent nodes is proposed. The transform model for Ladder Diagram based on the GFBD is also presented. The proposed model is with strong flexibility and wide application range and independent of sorting algorithms in compilation of configuration written in GFBD, which resolved the above mentioned problems. Based on the proposed GFBD model, traditionally different programming languages can be used together in a same configuration platform and the same compiler and compilation algorithm can be used to compile user's program written in the both FBD and LD languages, which improved the re-usage and production efficiency of software and shorten the time in configuration software development and programming in configuration platform. In the meantime, the related thought can be extended, expanded and used in the capsulation of configuration modules written in other programming languages such as instruction list (IL) and structured text (ST).

2. OSI/ISO Reference Model, User Layer and Function Blocks

2.1. OSI/ISO Reference Model and User Layer

2.1.1. History of OSI

After 1970, rapid development has been seen in computer industry. Different computer products including hardware and software were put into market by their respective manufacturers. Some of them began to develop their own network products to meet the ever-increasing demands for network communication. The products were proved capable in the communication inside the enterprises. However, it came to a big problem when different network products were interconnected to exchange information between different groups. They are not compliant for each other. Essentially, the manufacturer-tailored network was a closed system. Heterogeneous network was unable to interconnected for short of a unified communication norm.

It was expected that there were an open, ideal system independent of any manufacturers, that is to say, of any constraint or limitations in protocols and technologies.

The drive from demands facilitates the creation of OSI reference model. A international standard organization ISO found a OSI technological committee in 1978. The Open Systems Interconnection Reference Model (OSI Reference Model or OSI Model) is an abstract description for layered communications and computer network protocol design. It was developed as part of the Open Systems Interconnection (OSI) initiative. In its most basic form, it divides network architecture into seven layers which, from top to bottom, are the Application, Presentation, Session, Transport, Network, Data-Link, and Physical Layers. It is therefore often referred to as the OSI Seven Layer Model. A layer is a collection of conceptually similar functions that provide services to the layer above it and receives service from the layer below it. For example, a layer that provides error-free communications across a network provides the path needed by applications above it, while it calls the next lower layer to send and receive packets that make up the contents of the path. All aspects of OSI design evolved from experiences with the CYCLADES network, which also influenced Internet design. The new design was documented in ISO 7498 and its various addenda. In this model, a networking system is divided into layers. Within each layer, one or more entities implement its functionality. Each entity interacts directly only with the layer immediately beneath it, and provides facilities for use by the layer above it.

Protocols enable an entity in one host to interact with a corresponding entity at the same layer in another host. Service definitions abstractly describe the functionality provided to an (N)-layer by an (N-1) layer, where N is one of the seven layers of protocols operating in the local host.

2.1.2. Description of OSI Reference Model

The Content of OSI Model can be described as Table 1.

Table 1. Content of OSI Model

	Data unit	Layer	Function
Host layers	Data	7. Application	Network process to application
		6. Presentation	Data representation and encryption
		5. Session	Interhost communication
	Segment	4. Transport	End-to-end connections and reliability
Media layers	Packet	3. Network	Path determination and logical addressing
	Frame	2. Data Link	Physical addressing
	Bit	1. Physical	Media, signal and binary transmission

Layer 7: Application Layer

The application layer is the OSI layer closest to the end user, which means that both the OSI application layer and the user interact directly with the software application. This layer interacts with software applications that implement a communicating component. Such application programs fall outside the scope of the OSI model. Application layer functions typically include identifying communication partners, determining resource availability, and synchronizing communication. When identifying communication partners, the application layer determines the identity and availability of communication partners for an application with data to transmit. When determining resource availability, the application layer must decide whether sufficient network resources for the requested communication exist. In synchronizing communication, all communication between applications requires cooperation that is managed by the application layer. Some examples of application layer implementations include Telnet, Hypertext Transfer Protocol (HTTP), File Transfer Protocol (FTP) , and Simple Mail Transfer Protocol (SMTP).

Layer 6: Presentation Layer

The Presentation Layer establishes a context between Application Layer entities, in which the higher-layer entities can use different syntax and semantics, as long as the Presentation Service understands both and the mapping between them. The presentation service data units are then encapsulated into Session Protocol Data Units, and moved down the stack. This layer provides independence from differences in data representation (e.g., encryption) by translating from application to network format, and vice versa. The presentation layer works to transform data into the form that the application layer can accept. This layer formats and encrypts data to be sent across a network, providing freedom from compatibility problems. It is sometimes called the syntax layer. The original presentation structure used the Basic Encoding Rules of Abstract Syntax Notation One (ASN.1), with capabilities such as converting an EBCDIC-coded text file to an ASCII-coded file, or serializing objects and other data structures into and out of XML.

Layer 5: Session Layer

The Session Layer controls the dialogues (connections) between computers. It establishes, manages and terminates the connections between the local and remote application. It provides for full-duplex, half-duplex, or simplex operation, and establishes checkpointing, adjournment, termination, and restart procedures. The OSI model made this layer responsible for "graceful close" of sessions, which is a property of TCP, and also for session checkpointing and recovery, which is not usually used in the Internet Protocol Suite. The Session Layer is commonly implemented explicitly in application environments that use remote procedure calls (RPCs).

Layer 4: Transport Layer

The Transport Layer provides transparent transfer of data between end users, providing reliable data transfer services to the upper layers. The Transport Layer controls the reliability of a given link through flow control, segmentation/desegmentation, and error control. Some protocols are state and connection oriented. This means that the Transport Layer can keep track of the segments and retransmit those that fail.

Although not developed under the OSI Reference Model and not strictly conforming to the OSI definition of the Transport Layer, the best known examples of a Layer 4 protocol are the Transmission Control Protocol (TCP) and User Datagram Protocol (UDP). Of the actual OSI protocols, there are five classes of connection-mode transport protocols ranging from class 0 (which is also known as TP0 and provides the least error recovery) to class 4 (which is also known as TP4 and is designed for less reliable networks, similar to the Internet). Class 0 contains no error recovery, and was designed for use on network layers that provide error-free connections. Class 4 is closest to TCP, although TCP contains functions, such as the graceful close, which OSI assigns to the Session Layer. Also, all OSI TP connection-mode protocol classes provide expedited data and preservation of record boundaries, both of which TCP is incapable. Perhaps an easy way to visualize the Transport Layer is to compare it with a Post Office, which deals with the dispatch and classification of mail and parcels sent. Do remember, however, that a post office manages the outer envelope of mail. Higher layers may have the equivalent of double envelopes, such as cryptographic presentation services that can be read by the addressee only. Roughly speaking, tunneling protocols operate at the Transport Layer, such as carrying non-IP protocols such as IBM's SNA or Novell's IPX over an IP network, or end-to-end encryption with IPsec. While Generic Routing Encapsulation (GRE) might seem to be a Network Layer protocol, if the encapsulation of the payload takes place only at endpoint, GRE becomes closer to a transport protocol that uses IP headers but contains complete frames or packets to deliver to an endpoint. L2TP carries PPP frames inside transport packet.

Layer 3: Network Layer

The Network Layer provides the functional and procedural means of transferring variable length data sequences from a source to a destination via one or more networks, while maintaining the quality of service requested by the Transport Layer. The Network Layer performs network routing functions, and might also perform fragmentation and reassembly, and report delivery errors. Routers operate at this layer—sending data throughout the extended network and making the Internet possible. This is a logical addressing scheme – values are chosen by the network engineer. The addressing scheme is hierarchical.

The best-known example of a Layer 3 protocol is the Internet Protocol (IP). It manages the connectionless transfer of data one hop at a time, from end system to ingress router, router to router, and from egress router to destination end system. It is not responsible for reliable delivery to a next hop, but only for the detection of errored packets so they may be discarded. When the medium of the next hop cannot accept a packet in its current length, IP is responsible for fragmenting the packet into sufficiently small packets that the medium can accept.

A number of layer management protocols, a function defined in the Management Annex, ISO 7498/4, belong to the Network Layer. These include routing protocols, multicast group management, Network Layer information and error, and Network Layer address assignment. It is the function of the payload that makes these belong to the Network Layer, not the protocol that carries them.

Layer 2: Data Link Layer

The Data Link Layer provides the functional and procedural means to transfer data between network entities and to detect and possibly correct errors that may occur in the Physical Layer. Originally, this layer was intended for point-to-point and point-to-multipoint media, characteristic of wide area media in the telephone system. Local area network architecture, which included broadcast-capable multiaccess media, was developed independently of the ISO work, in IEEE Project 802. IEEE work assumed sublayering and management functions not required for WAN use. In modern practice, only error detection, not flow control using sliding window, is present in modern data link protocols such as Point-to-Point Protocol (PPP), and, on local area networks, the IEEE 802.2 LLC layer is not used for most protocols on Ethernet, and, on other local area networks, its flow control and acknowledgment mechanisms are rarely used. Sliding window flow control and acknowledgment is used at the Transport Layer by protocols such as TCP, but is still used in niches where X.25 offers performance advantages.

The ITU-T G.hn standard, which provides high-speed local area networking over existing wires (power lines, phone lines and coaxial cables), includes a complete Data Link Layer which provides both error correction and flow control by means of a selective repeat Sliding Window Protocol.

Both WAN and LAN services arrange bits, from the Physical Layer, into logical sequences called frames. Not all Physical Layer bits necessarily go into frames, as some of these bits are purely intended for Physical Layer functions. For example, every fifth bit of the FDDI bit-stream is not used by the layer.

WAN Protocol Architecture

Connection-oriented WAN data link protocols, in addition to framing, detect and may correct errors. They also are capable of controlling the rate of transmission. A WAN Data Link Layer might implement a sliding window flow control and acknowledgment mechanism to provide reliable delivery of frames; that is the case for SDLC and HDLC, and derivatives of HDLC such as LAPB and LAPD.

IEEE 802 LAN Architecture

Practical, connectionless LANs began with the pre-IEEE Ethernet specification, which is the ancestor of IEEE 802.3. This layer manages the interaction of devices with a shared medium, which is the function of a Media Access Control sublayer. Above this MAC sublayer is the media-independent IEEE 802.2 Logical Link Control (LLC) sublayer, which deals with addressing and multiplexing on multiaccess media.

While IEEE 802.3 is the dominant wired LAN protocol and IEEE 802.11 the wireless LAN protocol, obsolescent MAC layers include Token Ring and FDDI. The MAC sublayer detects but does not correct errors.

Layer 1: Physical Layer

The Physical Layer defines the electrical and physical specifications for devices. In particular, it defines the relationship between a device and a physical medium. This includes the layout of pins, voltages, cable specifications, Hubs, repeaters, network adapters, Host Bus Adapters (HBAs used in Storage Area Networks) and more. To understand the function of the Physical Layer in contrast to the functions of the Data Link Layer, think of the Physical Layer as concerned primarily with the interaction of a single device with a medium, where the Data Link Layer is concerned more with the interactions of multiple devices (i.e., at least two) with a shared medium. The Physical Layer will tell one device how to transmit to the medium, and another device how to receive from it (in most cases it does not tell the device how to connect to the medium). Standards such as RS-232 do use physical wires to control access to the medium. The major functions and services performed by the Physical Layer are:

- Establishment and termination of a connection to a communications medium.
- Participation in the process whereby the communication resources are effectively shared among multiple users. For example, contention resolution and flow control.
- Modulation, or conversion between the representation of digital data in user equipment and the corresponding signals transmitted over a communications channel. These are signals operating over the physical cabling (such as copper and optical fiber) or over a radio link.

Parallel SCSI buses operate in this layer, although it must be remembered that the logical SCSI protocol is a Transport Layer protocol that runs over this bus. Various Physical Layer Ethernet standards are also in this layer; Ethernet incorporates both this layer and the Data Link Layer. The same applies to other local-area networks, such as Token ring, FDDI, ITU-T G.hn and IEEE 802.11, as well as personal area networks such as Bluetooth and IEEE 802.15.4.

The structure of data frame reflecting the OSI/ISO model can be described as Figure 1.

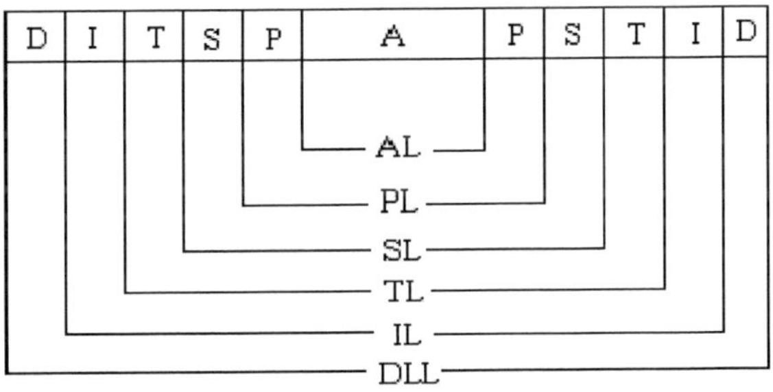

Figure 1. Structure of data frame mapping to the OSI/ISO model. D: Data link layer (DLL). I: IP layer (IL). T: TCP layer (TL). S: Session layer (SL). P: Presentation layer (PL). A: Application layer (AL). U: User layer (UL).

2.1.3. User Layer Protocol out of OSI Model

Generally, OSI model can meet most of the demands for information exchange and sharing. However, the disadvantage of the model lies in its complexity. The more layers the model have, the more time system need to resolve the information packaged in frames. Therefore, the OSI model is not fully suitable for a time-critical network that is always running real-time tasks. Besides, not all the information included in the OSI model is needed for such time-critical network for the data load transmit over the network can not be compared with that over Internet . Only several necessary layers, such as physical layer, DLL and application layer, are adopted in some time-critical network such as FF and WorldFIP fieldbus network. To increase flexibility, one more layer named User layer is added on the top of Application layer in OSI model. In practice, the user layer is constructed inside the application layer. Construction of user layer in application layer is described as Figure2. That is to say, parts of the data packaged in the application layer with a frame is used to be treated as user layer information and resolved according to user layer protocol correspondingly. Interface models for user layer service decide the function and meaning of user layer message based on the header in this layer.

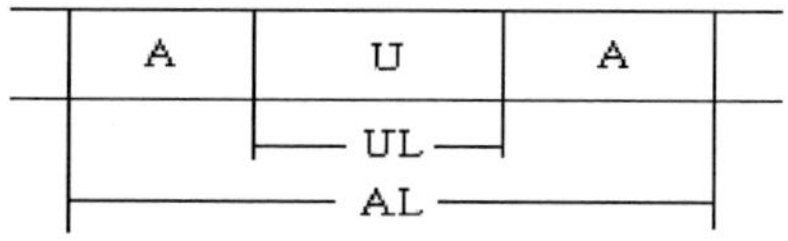

Figure 2. Construction of user layer in application layer.

2.2. Function Blocks

Function block (FB) is the most important and active element in user layer. It is a graphical programming element and can be described as "soft integration circuit". The structure of FB is shown in Figure 3.

FB presents the fundamental automation function implemented by function block application (FBA). Three elements are included in the structure. Input signal is processed by FB according to specific control algorithm. Meanwhile, the output of a FB can be used by other FBs in the same FBA or other FBAs.

FB controls the functions of control system. Its input and output parameters can be interconnected over network and the execution of FB is scheduled time-precisely .FB is a complete combination of parameters, algorithm and events. The execution of FBs is activated by events. Input parameters are used by specified algorithm. Output is produced by algorithm. Control function is implemented by this mechanism. Input and output FBs are concerned with I/O function of specific devices. The input and output parameters can be inter-connected over fieldbus network.

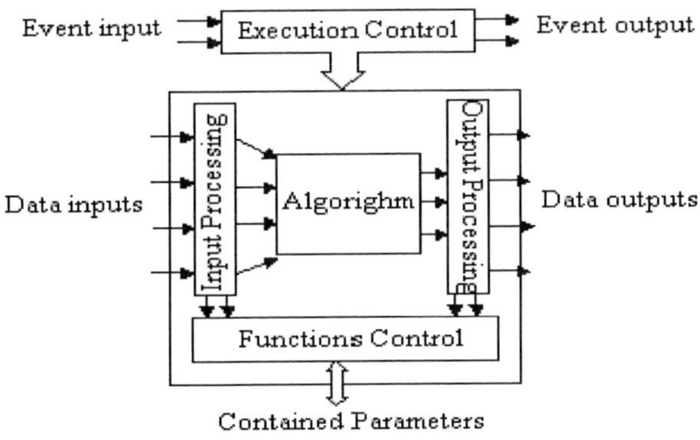

Figure 3. Structure of FB.

The outside structure of FB is general-purposed whatever the algorithm inside it is and the function it implements, as shown in figure 1. Input parameters and output parameters are assigned to the either sides of FB and represent the information to be exchanged with other FBs and the output is produced by input parameters, algorithm inside and the contained parameters.

The algorithm inside is independent of the structure and frame of FBs by adopting this general-purposed structure. Users need not concern the concrete implementation of the function and algorithm of FBs which is helpful in the interconnection between different FBs , the update of algorithm inside the FBs and the crossing-revoking and configuring between devices made by different manufactures.

This kind of general-purposed structure for FBs is the foundation for the implementation of a really open system and network function and automation. Definition of a FB is concerned with input parameters, output parameters , contained parameters and execution algorithm.

3. Generalized Function Block Diagram Model

The fundamental thought in constructing GFBD is that any a kind of diagram system composed of “block” and “link” can be discomposed into 2 fundamental elements, i.e. generalized function blocks (GFB) and links. Therefore, the applicable premise for the proposed is loose, which makes the model more flexible and wider in usage. In this model, execution of a GFB and a link is relatively independent. It can make the execution of the two kind of elements asynchronized, increasing the flexibility of design greatly.

In the proposed GFB model, all characteristics in standard FB specified by IEC61131-3 are included. Furthermore, number in inputs and outputs specified by the norm are extended, which means the number of inputs and outputs can be 0~n (n >=1).

GFBD can be described as:

(1) GFBD is composed of multiple GFBs and links. Multiple starting and ending GFBs are allowable in GFBD. Starting GFB is defined as a GFB without input, with more than 1 output and linked with other GFBs. Ending GFB is defined as a GFB without output, with more than 1 input and linked with other GFBs;
(2) Each GFB can be viewed as a module including input and output terminals, contained parameters and instruction operation;
(3) Each Link can be viewed as "copy" operation to copy the data from output terminal of one GFB to input terminal of the other GFB;
(4) GFB and Link are independent from each other in operation and function. Operational field of GFB is within the function block itself and has nothing to do with Link. Data are drawn out from the input terminal of GFB and processed with certain algorithm and written out to the output of the GFB. Data transmission between different GFBs are handled by Link. The location information for both upper-reach GFB and lower-reach GFB are stored in a Link which linking the starting GFB and ending GFB. Only location information for output terminals are stored in starting GFB. Only location information for input terminals are stored in ending GFB.

The proposed GFB model is illustrated with Figure 4.

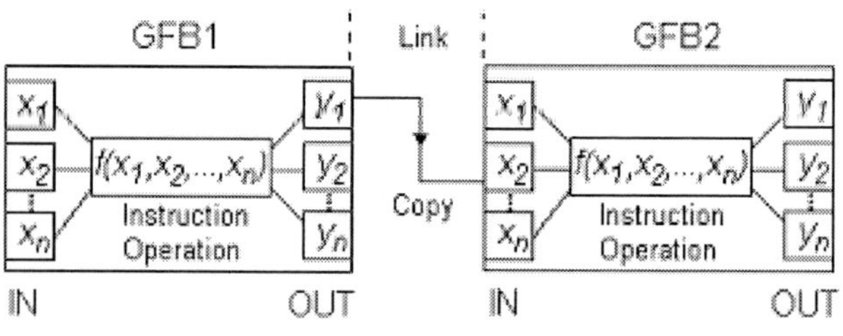

Figure 4. Generalized Function Block Diagram Model.

4. Construction and Implementation of GFBD Model in Field Intelligent Nodes in DICN

Form and structure of field intelligent nodes are relatively simple and with small-sized memory. In the meantime, the performance of processors in them is lower than that in a PC. These facts make it necessary that the data storage are to be continuous and can be accessed quickly.

In the proposed GFBD model, data after compilation of GFBD are stored into 4 segments which are GFB instruction codes segment, GFB input terminals segment,GFB output terminals segment, GFB contained parameters segment. All GFB instruction codes are stored in the GFB instruction codes segment. All GFB input terminals are stored in the GFB input terminals segment. All GFB output terminals are stored in the GFB input terminals segment. All GFB contained parameters are stored in GFB contained parameters segment. Data storage structures in 4 segments are different from each other.

The execution process of GFBD can be described as Figure5, in which the number 1,2 and 3 represents the execution order as follows.

- Step 1: read input data (maybe including events) from input area in data segment;
- Step 2: execute control algorithms or logics
- Step 3: write output data to output area in data segment

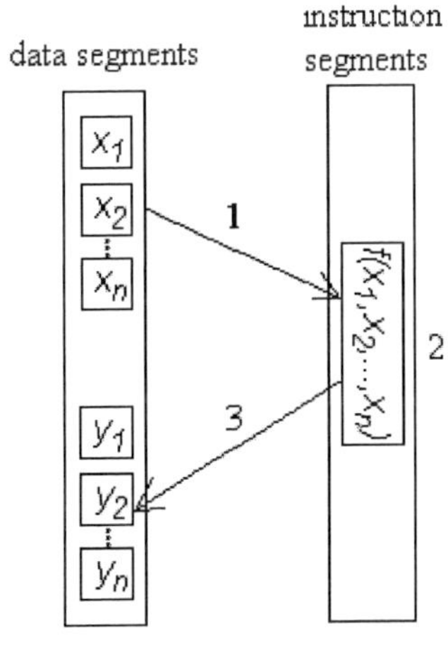

Figure 5. Execution process of GFBD.

The execution process of 'Link' can be described as Figure 6.

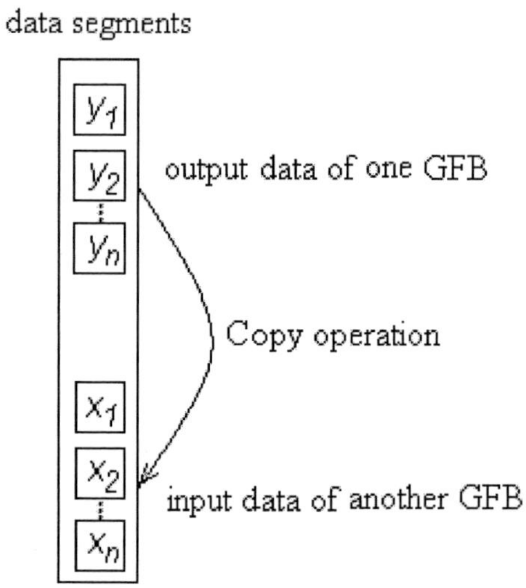

Figure 6. Execution process of 'Link'.

4.1. Data Storage Structure in GFB Instruction Codes Segments

Two kinds of instruction code, which are GFB and Link instruction respectively, are stored in GFB instruction segment in field intelligent node. The structure of GFB instruction code is shown in Figure7. Meaning of each field are as following:

- Flag: instruction flag;
- GFB_type: GFB types indicating algorithms or functions implemented with the GFB, such as PID control function;
- In_index: starting index for input terminals of the GFB in input terminal segment;
- Out_index: starting index for output terminals of the GFB in output terminal segment;
- Offset: offset in number of byte of contained parameters in the FB in contained parameters segment.

flag	GFB_type	in_index	out_index	offset

Figure 7. Structure of GFB instruction code in field intelligent node.

The structure of Link instruction code is shown in Figure 8. Meaning of each field are as following:

- Flag: instruction flag;
- Out_index: starting index in FB output terminal segment in local node for the output terminal of upper-reach FB linked by starting point of Link instruction;
- Addr: physical address of the remote field intelligent node in which the lower-reach GFB linked by ending point of Link instruction. The field value is 255 if the GFB is local;
- In_index: starting index of input terminal of FB linked by Link instruction in FB input terminal segment in object node.

flag	out_index	addr	in_index

Figure 8. Structure of Link instruction code in field intelligent node.

Each GFB instruction and Link instruction are stored together with the same memory size. The first byte of each instruction is instruction flag. When the instruction is scanned with the instruction segment by the intelligent node, the instruction is differently interpreted and processed and pointer in instruction segment is moved backwards with different memory size span. The whole process is repeated continuously until the flag in current instruction indicates the end of the segment.

4.2. Data Storage Structure in GFB input/output Segments

Four-byte unit are used universally as input/output storage structure for that operations dealing with float number are mainstream in field intelligent nodes and the uniform in data storage. The numbers of Four-byte units in memory for the input/output segment are generated in time of compilation of user's configuration in upper-level computer. Initialization of input/output segments in memory are done by field intelligent nodes autonomously when configuration downloads are finished.

4.3. Data Storage Structure in GFB Contained Parameter Segments

It is difficult even impossible to construct a universal data storage unit which is economic and flexible for many variety of GFB contained parameters. Therefore, 1-byte unit is chosen as the data storage unit for GFB contained parameters segment. Each parameter are aligned adjacently and offset in bytes and data length are used in identification of each parameter.

To summarize, the data storage segmentation and linkage orienting field intelligent nodes are shown as Figure9, in which a PID control is set as an example.

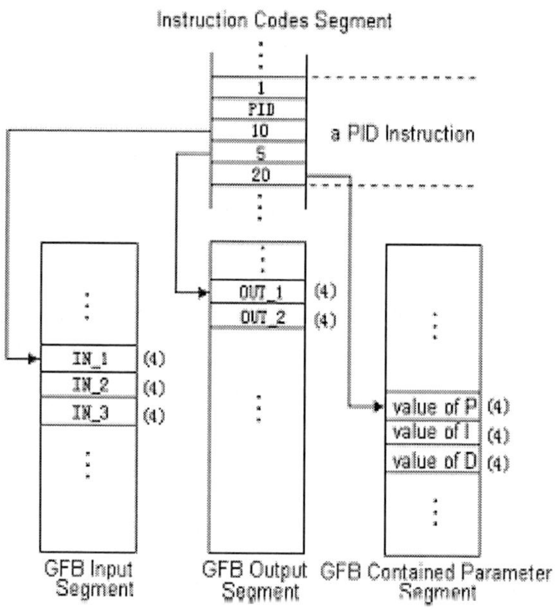

Figure 9. Data storage segmentation model in field intelligent nodes.

Data in each segment is stored compactly in field intelligent nodes. Array is used as the storage forms for all data in each segment except data in contained parameters segments in which byte-unit is used to store data. Array elements in input/output segment are of double-word type. Instruction codes in instruction segment is stored with the same memory size using following data structure [8]:

```
typedef union COMMAND_FOR_DEVICE
{
FBINFO_FOR_DEVICE fbinfo_for_device;
LINKINFO_FOR_DEVICE linkinfo_for_device;
};
typedef struct FBINFO_FOR_DEVICE
{
BYTE flag ;
BYTE fb_type;
WORD in_index;
WORD out_index;
WORD offset;
};
typedef struct  LINKINFO_FOR_DEVICE
{
BYTE flag;
WORD out_index;
BYTE addr;
WORD in_index;
};
```

5. Ladder Diagram Model Derived from GFBD Model

5.1. Ladder Diagram

Ladder Diagram (LD) is widely used in Programmable Logic Controller (PLC). It is also a standardized language specified in IEC61131-3.Generally, there are 3 kinds of elements in LD as:

1)Tracks/Bars
2)Contacts and coil
3)Links

Besides, more often than never, a typical function block is also used in a LD to execution some specified logic or algorithms, e.g. a counter block. A typical application with LD elements and function blocks mixed together is shown in Figure 10.

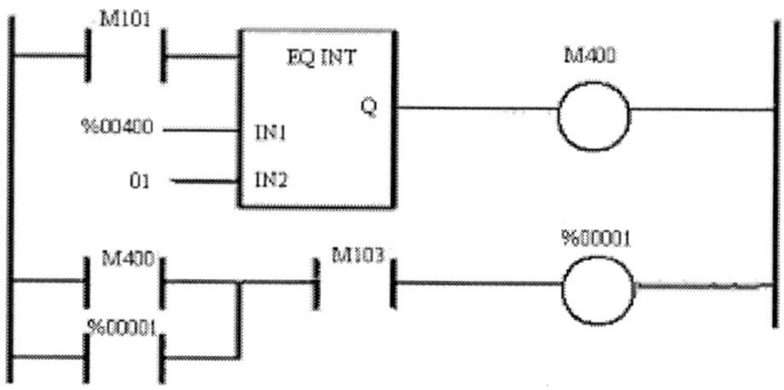

Figure 10. A typical application with LD elements and function blocks mixed together.

It can be seen that the compilation of a LD can become much easier if LD elements and function blocks used in it can be understood and resolved with a universal rule. To make it more clear, one compilation algorithm can be used to compile FBD and LD at the same time, which improves the re-usage of software greatly. This is the very point of derivation of LD elements to GFB elements. It can make them universal in semantic.

Semantically, there are also two elements in LD, i.e. block and link though their graphical display may be beyond the shape or form of the a block or a link. Therefore, transformation between LD elements and GFB elements is necessary.

5.2. Transformation of LD Elements to GFB Elements

LD conforms to the application condition for GFBD model. Therefore, LD diagram elements can be analysed and transformed into GFB elements. The transformation is as followed:

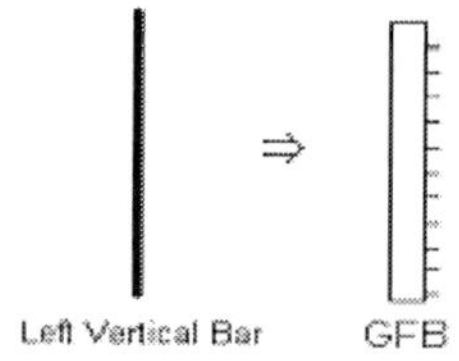

Figure 11. Equivalent transformation from left vertical bar to GFB.

1. Left vertical bar: equivalent to a kind of GFB with 0 input and multiple outputs. Its operational logic can be described as that the output value of each equivalent GFB is constant 1. Equivalent transformation is shown in Figure 11.

2. Contact and coil: equivalent to a kind of GFB with 1 input and 1 output. Their operational logics are dependent on the types of specified diagram elements. For example, equivalent transformation from normally open contact/ normally closed contact to a GFB is shown in Figure 12.

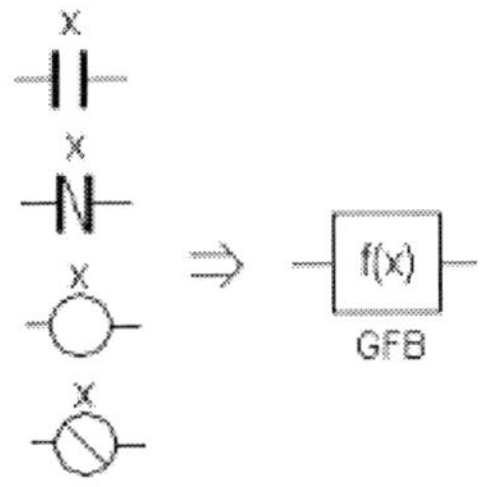

Figure 12. Equivalent transformation from contacts and coils to GFB.

The flow chart of operational logic of normally open contact is shown in Figure 13.

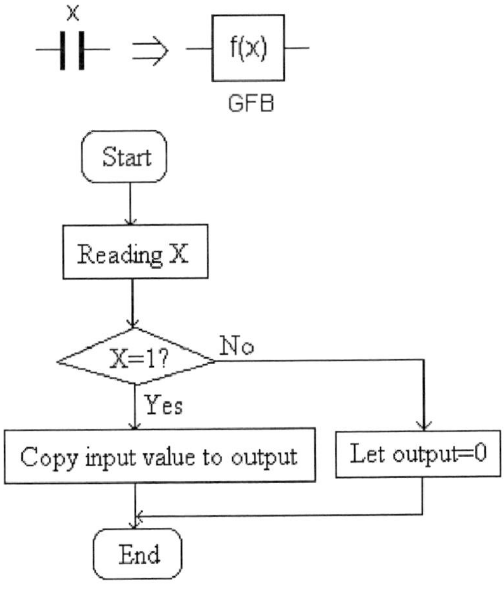

Figure 13. Flow chart of operational logic of normally open contact.

The flow chart of operational logic of normally closed contact is shown in Figure 14.

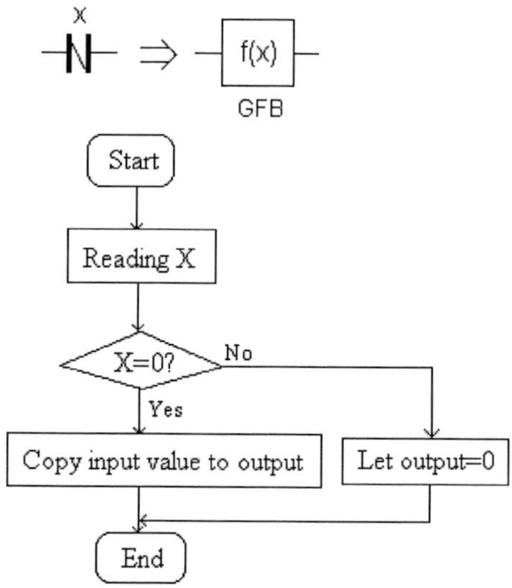

Figure 14. Flow chart of operational logic of normally closed contact.

The flow chart of operational logic of normally open coil is shown in Figure 15.

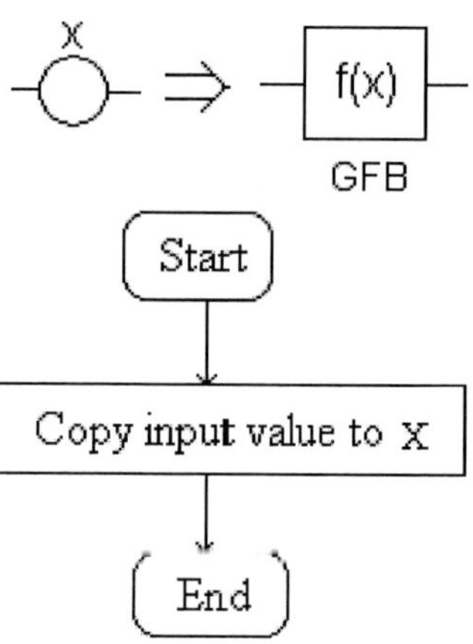

Figure 15. Flow chart of operational logic of normally open coil.

The flow chart of operational logic of normally closed coil is shown in Figure 16.

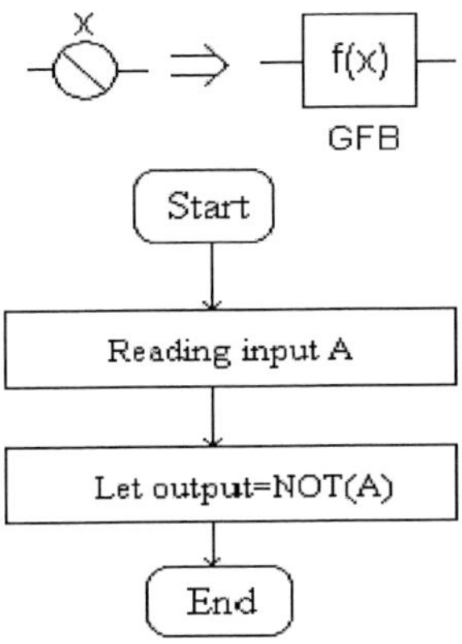

Figure 16. Flow chart of operational logic of normally closed coil.

3. Horizontal link: equivalent to a kind of GFB with 1 input and multi outputs. Its operational logic can be described as logical operation "OR", as shown in Figure 17.

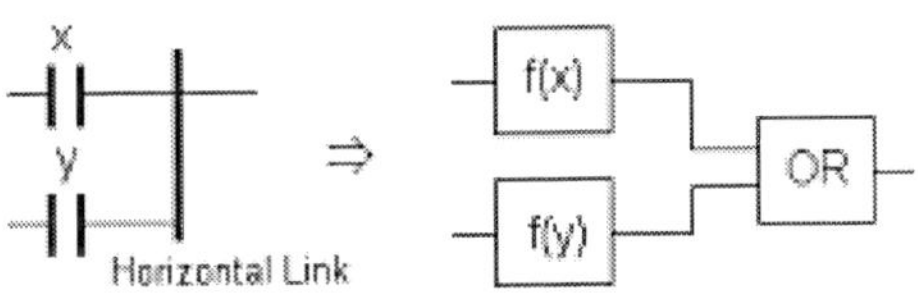

Figure 17. Equivalent transformation from horizontal link to GFB.

4. Links in LD: equivalent to link element in GFBD.

5.3. Examples

Example 1:

A LD is shown as Figure 18.

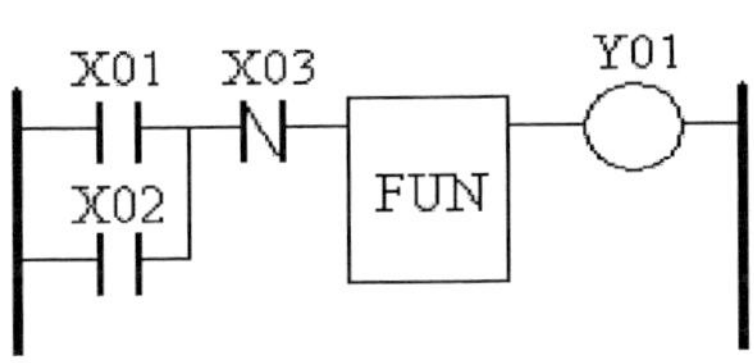

Figure 18. LD example 1.

The code list of the LD in a PLC is as follows.

LD X01
OR X02
AND NOT X03
FUN
OUT Y01

The transformation of the LD to GFBD is shown as Figure 19.

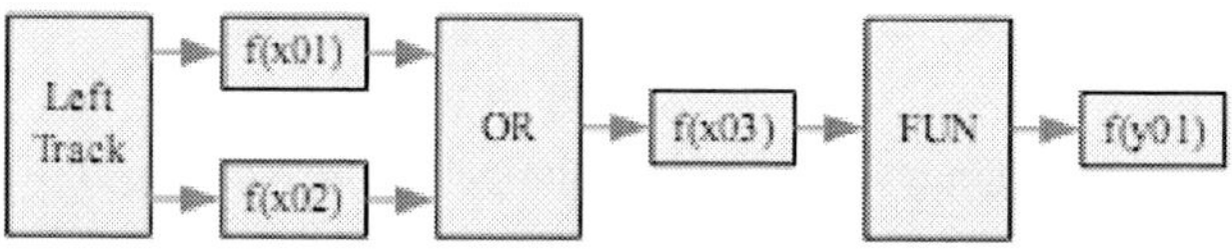

Figure 19. Transformation of the LD to GFBD.

The execution order of the GFBD is shown in Figure 20.

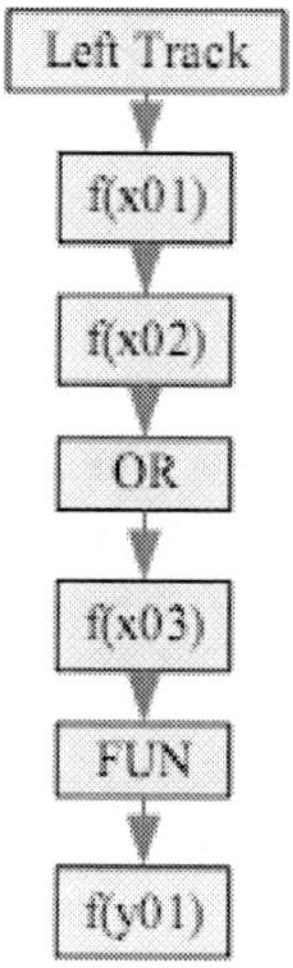

Figure 20. The execution order of the GFBD in Figure 13.

Example 2:

A LD is shown as Figure 21.

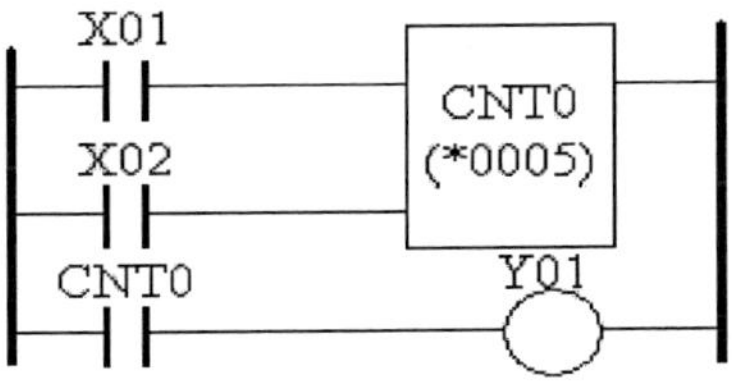

Figure 21. LD example 2.

The code list of the LD in a PLC is as follows.

LD X01
LD X02
CNT0 #0005
LD CNT0
OUT Y01

The transformation of the LD to GFBD is shown as Figure 22.

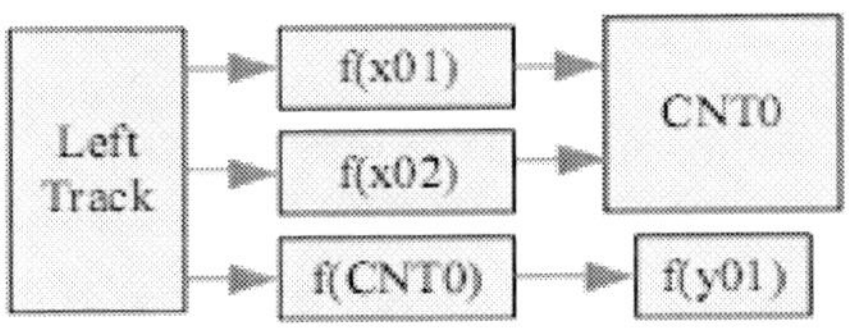

Figure 22. Transformation of the LD to GFBD.

The execution order of the GFBD is shown in Figure 23.

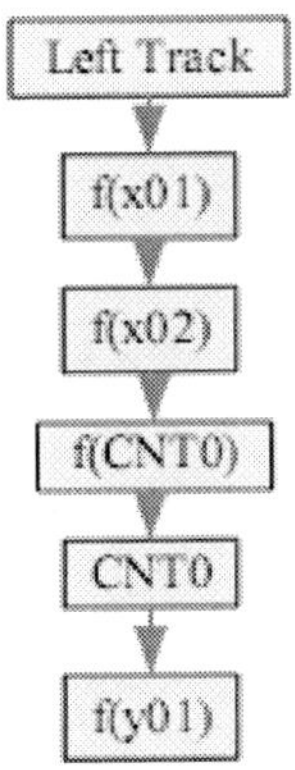

Figure 23. The execution order of the GFBD.

From the transformation, it can be seen that phase delay of one GFB in execution is introduced compared with the PLC code list.

CONCLUSION

In this chapter, a kind of Generalized Function Block Diagram (GFBD) model and implementation scheme for the model in field intelligent nodes is proposed. The transformation model for Ladder Diagram based on the GFBD is also presented. The proposed model is with strong flexibility and wide application range and independent of sorting algorithms in compilation of configuration written in GFBD, which resolved the above mentioned problems. Based on the proposed GFBD model, traditionally different programming languages can be used together in a same configuration platform and the same compiler and compilation algorithm can be used to compile user's program written in the both FBD and LD languages, which improved the re-usage and production efficiency of software and shorten the time in configuration software development and programming in configuration platform. In the meantime, the related thought can be extended, expanded and used in the capsulation of configuration modules written in other programming languages such as instruction list (IL) and structured text (ST)[9-12]. The proposed GFBD model has been applied in design and development of configuration software platform conforming to norm IEC61131-3 for DICN. The developed configuration platform is stable, efficient, flexible and extensible, which showed great effectiveness of the proposed model.

REFERENCES

[1] Laihua Fang, Research on the Key Technology of Configuration Software, *Control and instruments in chemical industry*, Vol.31, No.3, 33-38,2004.

[2] Shuyu Sun, Researching And Realization Of Embed Intelligent Control Software In Man Machine Interface Software, *Journal of Tianjin Science and Technology University*, Vol.15, No.4, 45-46,2002.

[3] Guangqing Xi, Visual System Simulation Method, *Journal of System Simulation*, Vol.10, No.1, 27-32,1998.

[4] Zhenhua Hu, An Algorithm Of Graphics Configuration Based On Distributed Control System, *Computer Application and Software*, Vol.14, No.7, 10-11,2002.

[5] Fuzhen Xu, Simulation Software of Control System Diagram Configuration Based on Elements, *Journal of System Simulatio*n, Vol.14, No.7, 855-857,2002.

[6] Chen Yang, Development of Visual Configurating Simulation Software for DCS, *Journal of System Simulat*ion, Vol.11, No.4, 261-264,1999.

[7] Geng Liang, Design And Implementation Of Control Strategy Configuration SOFTWARE FOR Worldfip FIELDBUS CONTROL SYSTEM, *Proceedings of CSEE*, Vol.24, No.2, 150-156, 2005.

[8] Geng Liang, *Research and development of function block application of the fieidbus intelligent device based on WorldFIP fieldbus*, Vol.27, No.6 (suppl), 902-904,2006.

[9] Xia, Feng, Function block oriented architecture for open distributed automation, *Proceedings of the World Congress on Intelligent Control and Automation (WCICA)*, Vol.3, 2706-2710, 2004.

[10] Zhang, Wei ,Specification of function block applications with UML, *Proceedings of the 2005 IEEE International Conference on Robotics and Automation*, Vol.1,4002-4007, 2005.

[11] Diedrich, Christian, "Function block applications in control systems based on IEC 61804", *ISA Transactions*, vol.43, no.1, , pp.123-131, 2004.

[12] Hagge, Nils, A new function block modeling language based on petri nets for automatic code generation, *IEEE Transactions on Industrial Informatics,* Vol.1, No.4, 226-237,2005.

In: Network Protocols
Editor: Geng Liang
ISBN 978-1-61470-821-6

Chapter 2

FUNCTION BLOCK APPLICATION IN USER LAYER PROTOCOL OF WORLDFIP NETWORK: DESIGN AND IMPLEMENTATION

***Geng Liang*[1] *and Wen Li*[2]**
[1]School of Control and Computer Engineering, North China Electric Power University, Beijing, China
[2]Beijing GUODIANZHISHEN Control Technology Co. Ltd, Beijing, China

ABSTRACT

Products and systems developed based on WorldFIP technology are all above control level. No fully distributed intelligent control system based on field intelligent nodes is implemented. Function Block Application (FBA) is the kernel part in implementation of distributed intelligent control network. Concept of user layer is not proposed in WorldFIP communication model and the specification of user layer is not presented so far. Based on independently developed WorldFIP distributed intelligent control network developed, a practical and general-purposed FBA model is proposed. Data storage segmentation model orienting field intelligent nodes are expounded in detail. Concept of user layer in WorldFIP communication model is proposed and data model for user layer is defined. The schedule algorithms for the proposed FBA model are presented in detail. Guided by the proposed FBA model, design and implementation of distributed intelligent system based on Function Block and FBA was achieved. The proposed FBA model is easy in implementation and with good real time property, good real-time property in control and transplantability. Operational practice of the distributed intelligent control network shows effectiveness of the proposed model.

1. INTRODUCTION

In recent years, fieldbus technology and distributed intelligent system are widely used in process control. With the increasing complexity and capacity of controlled objects, demands for reliability of control system are higher and tougher [1]. Non-redundancy in field level is the main obstacle in application of fieldbus into control system. WorldFIP, one of the international norm for fieldbus, is industrial control oriented [2]. It is unparalleled in various kinds of fieldbus with its unique double-bus redundancy architecture, which makes it very suitable in control of process control with high reliability and have been paid increasing attention to [3]. WorldFIP fieldbus have been applied successfully in Lingao Power Plant and Junliangcheng Power Plant in China showing strong developmental momentum. Now, products and systems developed based on WorldFIP are above control level and Fully Distributed Intelligent Control Network (FDICN) based on intelligent nodes are not implemented yet. Function Block (FB) and Function Block Application (FBA) [4], which are the most important means to implement fully distributed intelligent control network based on field intelligent nodes and communication in field, are the kernel parts in the implementation of FDICN. A kind of practically feasible FBA model is proposed in this paper based on independently developed WorldFIP FDICN. Field intelligent nodes oriented data segmentation and structure for data segments in the proposed model are expounded. Concept of user layer in WorldFIP communication model is proposed and data sub-model in user layer in WorldFIP communication model, which serving as the base for implementation of the proposed FBA model in WorldFIP communication protocol. The proposed model is easy to implement and with good real time, certainty and transplantation in control. Good validity of the proposed FBA model is shown by operational practice of the developed intelligent network control system.

The proposed FBA deals with 2 important parts in system structure, which are field intelligent nodes and network communication including data segmentation model in field intelligent nodes and FBA schedule algorithms for control network scheduler and intelligent nodes [5-7].

2. Function Block Model

Function block (FB) is the most important and active element in user layer. It is a graphical programming element and can be described as "soft integration circuit". The structure of FB is shown in Figure 1.

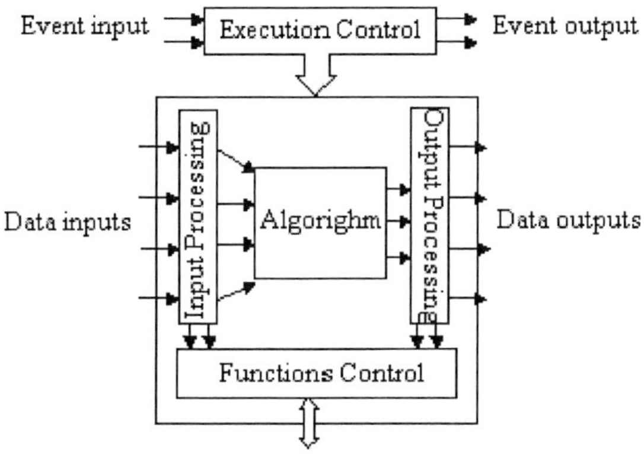

Figure 1. Structure of FB.

FB presents the fundamental automation function implemented by function block application (FBA). Three elements are included in the structure. Input signal is processed by FB according to specific control algorithm. Meanwhile, the output of a FB can be used by other FBs in the same FBA or other FBAs.

FB controls the functions of control system. Its input and output parameters can be interconnected over network and the execution of FB is scheduled time-precisely .FB is a complete combination of parameters, algorithm and events. The execution of FBs is activated by events. Input parameters are used by specified algorithm. Output is produced by algorithm. Control function is implemented by this mechanism. Input and output FBs are concerned with I/O function of specific devices. The input and output parameters can be interconnected over fieldbus network.

The outside structure of FB is general-purposed whatever the algorithm inside it is and the function it implements, as shown in figure 1. Input parameters and output parameters are assigned to the either sides of FB and represent the information to be exchanged with other FBs and the output is produced by input parameters, algorithm inside and the contained parameters.

The algorithm inside is independent of the structure and frame of FBs by adopting this general-purposed structure. Users need not concern the concrete implementation of the function and algorithm of FBs which is helpful in the interconnection between different FBs, the update of algorithm inside the FBs and the crossing-revoking and configuring between devices made by different manufactures.

This kind of general-purposed structure for FBs is the foundation for the implementation of a really open system and network function and automation. Definition of a FB is concerned with input parameters, output parameters , contained parameters and execution algorithm.

3. Data Storage Segmentation in Field Intelligent Nodes for General Purpose

It is relatively simple in structure for field intelligent nodes in distributed intelligent control network. Memory in the nodes is small-sized; furthermore, performance of processor in the nodes is much lower than that in the PC. These facts make it necessary that the data storage are to be continuous and can be accessed quickly [8-10].

In the proposed FBA model, the memory in field intelligent nodes is divided into 4 segments, which are FB instruction codes segment, FB input terminals segment, FB output terminals segment, FB contained parameters segment, to store the compiled and downloaded users' configuration data. All FB instruction codes are stored in the FB instruction codes segment. All FB input terminals are stored in the FB input terminals segment. All FB output terminals are stored in the FB input terminals segment. All FB contained parameters are stored in FB contained parameters segment. Data storage structures in 4 segments are different from each other.

3.1. Data Storage Structure in FB Instruction Codes Segments

Two kinds of instruction code, which are FB and link instruction respectively, are stored in FB instruction segment in field intelligent node. The structure of FB instruction code is shown in Figure 2. Meaning of each field are as following:

- Flag: instruction flag;
- FB_type: FB types indicating algorithms or functions implemented with the FB, such as PID control function;
- In_index: starting index for input terminals of the FB in input terminal segment;
- Out_index: starting index for output terminals of the FB in output terminal segment;
- Offset: offset in number of byte of contained parameters in the FB in contained parameters segment.

flag	FB_type	in_index	out_index	offset

Figure 2. Structure of FB instruction code in field intelligent node.

The structure of Link instruction code is shown in Fig3. Meaning of each field are as following:

- Flag: instruction flag;
- Out_index: starting index in FB output terminal segment in local node for the output terminal of upper-reach FB linked by starting point of Link instruction;
- Addr: physical address of the remote field intelligent node in which the lower-reach FB linked by ending point of Link instruction. The field value is 255 if the FB is local;
- In_index: starting index of input terminal of FB linked by Link instruction in FB input terminal segment in object node.

flag	out_index	addr	in_index

Figure 3. Structure of Link instruction code in field intelligent node.

Each FB instruction and Link instruction are stored together with the same memory size. The first byte of each instruction is instruction flag. When the instruction is scanned with the instruction segment by the intelligent node, the instruction is differently interpreted and processed and pointer in instruction segment is moved backwards with different memory size span. The whole process is repeated continuously until the flag in current instruction indicates the end of the segment.

3.2. Data Storage Structure in FB input/utput Segments

Four-byte unit are used universally as input/output storage structure for that operations dealing with float number are mainstream in field intelligent nodes and the uniform in data storage. The numbers of Four-byte units in memory for the input/output segment are generated in time of compilation of user's configuration in upper-level computer. Initialization of input/output segments in memory are done by field intelligent nodes autonomously when configuration downloads are finished.

3.3. Data Storage Structure in FB Contained Parameter Segments

It is difficult even impossible to construct a universal data storage unit which is economic and flexible for many variety of FB contained parameters. Therefore, 1-byte unit is chosen as the data storage unit for FB contained parameters segment. Each parameter are aligned adjacently and offset in bytes and data length are used in identification of each parameter.

To summarize, the data storage segmentation and linkage orienting field intelligent nodes are shown as Figure3, in which a PID control is set as an example. In Figure4, number "(4)" indicates number of bytes.

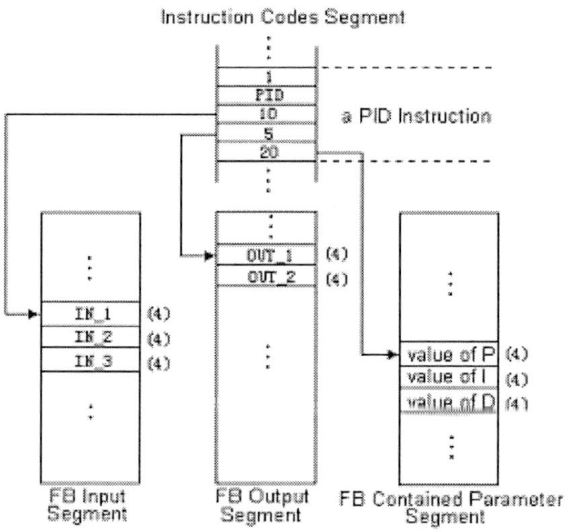

Figure 4. Data storage segmentation model in field intelligent nodes.

Data in each segment is stored compactly in field intelligent nodes. Array is used as the storage forms for all data in each segment except data in contained parameters segments in which byte-unit is used to store data. Array elements in input/output segment are of double-word type. Instruction codes in instruction segment is stored with the same memory size using following data structure:

```
typedef union COMMAND_FOR_DEVICE
{
FBINFO_FOR_DEVICE fbinfo_for_device;
LINKINFO_FOR_DEVICE  linkinfo_for_device;
};
typedef struct FBINFO_FOR_DEVICE
{
BYTE flag ;
BYTE fb_type;
WORD in_index;
WORD out_index;
WORD offset;
};
typedef struct  LINKINFO_FOR_DEVICE
{
BYTE flag;
WORD out_index;
BYTE addr;
WORD in_index;
};
```

Meaning of each variable can be referred to Figure 1 and Figure 2.

4. Data Model in User Layer in WorldFIP Communication

4.1. WorldFIP Protocol

4.1.1. General Introduction

WorldFIP is a single consistent technology for all levels of the fieldbus system, combining the worlds of closed-loop control and information-technology on one bus. WorldFIP is accepted technology for international contracts, and is a European Standard (EN50170). This guarantees its stability and openness, and ensures that WorldFIP is a preferred technology for all applications in the public sector and utility industries throughout the European Union. With the fastest growing user base in the world and a complete answer in a single technology, WorldFIP offers the most practical and proven solution [11].

WorldFIP differs from all other fieldbus systems in a number of respects -- one of them being its use of a single simple protocol to cover both the real-time and background information needs of a control or instrumentation system.

- A Single Protocol
  In plain words this means that, no matter what you intend to use your fieldbus for, there is only one protocol to learn. Some other bus systems require two or even three different protocols to cover the range of tasks, which makes them harder to learn as well as requiring extra interfaces and conversions within the system.
- A Simple Protocol
  WorldFIP protocol is also simple to learn. There are no lengthy vocabularies of specialised terms, and maximum use is made of existing International Standard formats such as the Manufacturing Message Specification (MMS). You can confidently expect that any work you carry out with WorldFIP will align very easily to full International Fieldbus standards when they ultimately emerge.

4.1.2. Description of Protocol Layer

Physical layer, data linkage layer and application layer in ISO/OSI 7-layer reference model are adopted in reference model for WorldFIP fieldbus communication.

Composition of WorldFIP communication protocol is shown in Figure 5.

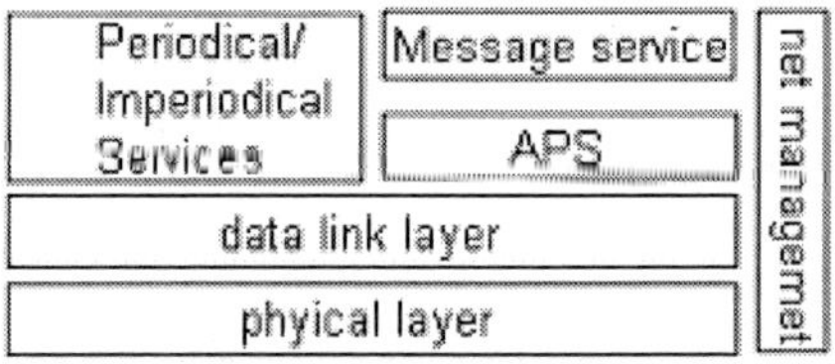

Figure 5. Composition of WorldFIP communication protocol.

- Physical Layer
  - Bus topology to IEC 1158-2.
  - Data rates of 31.25kbit/sec, 1 Mbit/sec or 2.5 Mbit/sec via twisted pair copper cable, overall screen.
  - Data rate of 5 Mbit/sec via optical fibre.
  - 64 nodes per cable segment, up to 4 segments through repeaters.
  - Segment length: 1 Km or more depending on data rate, cable and number of nodes.
  - Redundant cable as an option.
- Data Link Layer
  - Uses "producer-consumer" model (described later in this module) with centralized bus-scheduler (redundant bus-schedulers can be used if required).
  - Supports time-critical "variables" and "messages" (described later in this module).
  - Time-critical "variables" can be "cyclic" or "event" variables.
  - Up to 64000 message identifiers. Up to 64000 variable identifiers. (A few identifiers are reserved).
  - Size of variables from 2 bytes to 127 bytes. Message size up to 256 bytes.
- Application Layer
  - Variables accessible through MPS interface.

Messages accessible via sub-MMS interface. Maximum size of message 64kBytes using sub-MMS.

4.1.3. Producer-Consumer Model

WorldFIP's producer/consumer model is central to the effectiveness of WorldFIP's protocol.

Why Producer/Consumer?

Many networks are based upon protocols developed for long-distance communications. They were developed to transmit messages from point to point, with built-in re-try mechanisms to cope with the high risk of data corruption on public message routes.

Though well-suited to their original application, such protocols are quite unsuitable for time-critical data-transfer between devices on a fieldbus, since:

- The possibility of re-try prevents a deterministic response.
- Data must be re-sent to each node which requires it.

The "producer/consumer" model gives deterministic high-speed response, by allowing the data produced by one node to be consumed at the same time by any or all other nodes on the network.

How It Works?

The "producer" node does not need to know which nodes are consuming the data. The Bus Arbiter function controls the "producers" rather like the conductor of an orchestra, so transmission of data at known time intervals (equivalent to the conductor's "beat") is guaranteed. Data integrity is guaranteed by status flags, which show the "timeliness" and the "freshness" of data. There is no re-transmission in the event of corrupted data, the next value simply overwrites the previous value.

"The "producer/consumer" mechanism is very effective for time-critical data and event data. It allows easy construction of a distributed real-time database in a WorldFIP-connected system.

As a simple example, imagine a PLC using WorldFIP cyclic data to communicate with its distributed I/O system.

You may add a PC into that network, set up to consume all the data that is already passing; the PC is effectively invisible to the PLC. The PC might be supporting SCADA or other packages, and thus be able to provide links into the information networks onthat site, all without requiring any change to the program in the PLC and with no effect on the data-traffic across the fieldbus.

4.1.4. Coding the Data Frame

All WorldFIP frames (frame_question, response, message, etc.) are composed of three parts:

- Frame Start Sequence (FSS)
- Control and Data field(CAD)
- Frame End Sequence (FES)

1) Frame Start Sequence (FSS)

This contains two fields:

- Preamble (PRE)

This series of 8 "1" bits is used by receivers to synchronize themselves with the transmitter's clock.

- Frame Start Delimiter (FSD)
  This series of bits indicates to the data link layer the beginning of useful information (CAD).

2) Control and Data Field

This field contains only the logical information ("0" and "1") from the data link layer.

3) Frame End Sequence (FES)

This series of bits is used by the data link layer as a delimiter, to locate the end of the CAD field.

4) The User May Define the Data Field

The above description explains the way in which each frame is encoded for secure transmission. This is interesting for a product developer -- but it is largely "invisible" to a user, who is far more interested in the information which he can send and receive via the frames.

The Control and Data Field (CAD) has three parts:

- Control Field: Contains control and address information used by the protocol
- Data Field: Contains the user data
- Check Field: Contains a 16-bit CRC computed and checked by the protocol

All the "real-life" data is transmitted within the Data field defined above, and the user (or his system builder) can define exactly how the Data field is built up, according to the needs of his specific system. The definition of the contents of the Data field is part of the system-builder's task when he builds the system.

The Application Layer of WorldFIP provides both time-critical and non-critical (or messaging) services.

Time-critical services are managed via WorldFIP's distributed database (functionally identical with those in the draft IEC Standard). Non-critical services are provided by a sub-set of the Manufacturing Message Specification (MMS).

Time-Critical Data

Time-critical data (eg control-loop variables) are passed around the network using "MPS" real-time periodic/aperiodic services.

Cyclic variables are sent to the network using the periodic services. The repetition rate may be fixed (down to 2msec) or free-running. Such variables always have absolute priority, and are typically used to transmit data used in fast speed-control loops etc.

Event variables are sent only if requested, using the aperiodic service -- for instance, to respond to a change of state (eg alarm) or a demand for an operator display. Use of event variables is very appropriate in systems where change is normally infrequent but there are occasional cascades of alarms, such as gas/water/electricity industries.

Non-Critical Data

Less time-dependent data (such as diagnostic reports), is sent via the message service. This may be typically used for:

- Installing and setting up an application
- Network supervision and diagnosis
- Integration with higher-level systems.

5) How It All Works

Network time is split into "macro-cycles" -- usually based on the update time of the slowest periodic variable in the system. These are further divided into "elementary cycles" each of the same length (min. 2 msec).

Data is allocated to the cycles in the following priority order:

- Cyclic variables
- Event variables
- Messages (non critical)

Cyclic variables always travel on time, regardless of other network traffic. Any Event requests are serviced next, and only then are messages handled. If network traffic is heavy, Messages are placed in a queue.

Unlike token-passing systems, WorldFIP leaves no doubts about transmission time and regularity for cyclic data variables.

6) Frame Format

WorldFIP communication is master-slave typed. The whole network is composed of bus schedulers serving as master and field intelligent nodes which are subordinate. Value exchange between periodical and non-periodical variables and messages exchange are scheduled with bus schedulers. Two types of data exchange are used in network: data exchanges based on variable exchanges, which are usually used to transmit real-time and periodical data, and message exchange based on physically addressing. Detailed information can be referred to related reference. The following types of frames are used to exchange data over WorldFIP network.

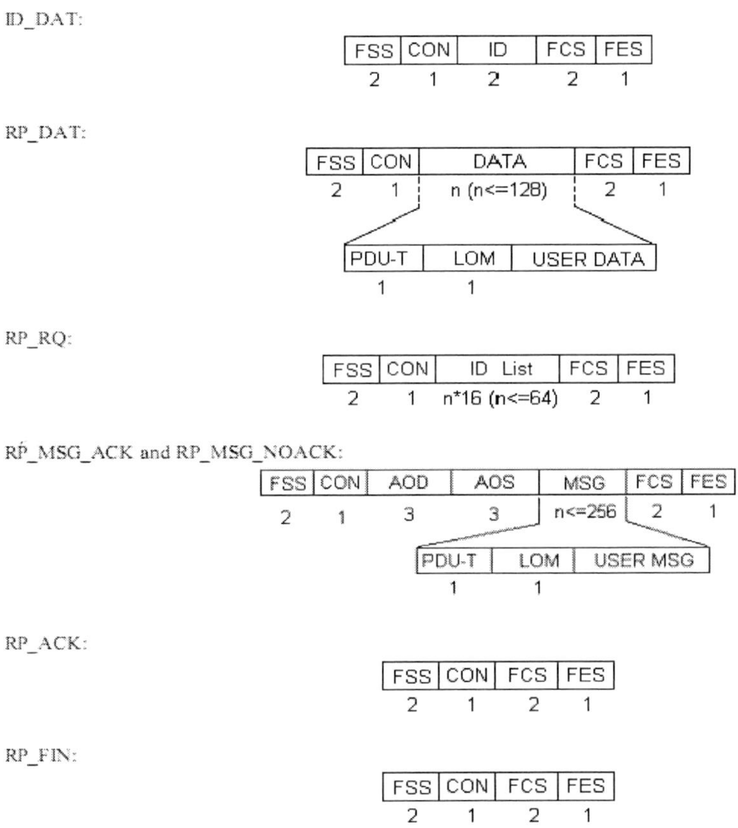

Figure 6. Format of WorldFIP frames. FSS: frame starting series; CON: control. PDU_T: type of protocol data unit; LOM: length of message; AOD: address of destination; AOS: address of source; MSG: user's message; FCS: frame check series: FES: frame ending series.

The following is based on variables exchange:

ID_DAT: sent by bus scheduler and used to initialize a variable exchange process;

RP_DAT: sent by a field intelligent node and used to respond to ID_DAT to realize the data transmission based on variable exchange.

The following is based on message transmission:

ID_MSG: sent by bus scheduler and used to initialize a message transmission process;

RP_MSG: sent by a field intelligent node and used to respond to ID_MSG to realize the message transmission.

RP_MSG_ACK: sent by bus scheduler and used to acknowledge the data sent by field intelligent node;

RP_FIN: sent by a field intelligent node and used to respond to RP_MSG_ACK to finalize a message transmission process.

In the proposed model, RP_MSG_ACK is used to assure the reliable data transmission.

Format of WorldFIP frame is shown in Figure 6. The numbers under the frame figures represent bytes used by the corresponding segment in frames.

In above frame format, all fields except "MSG" field are specified by WorldFIP protocol and have nothing to do with user layer in WorldFIP protocol. Therefore, "MSG" are the only field users can control use freely.

4.2. Proposed Data Model in User Layer in WorldFIP Protocol

Although physical layer, data link layer and application layer in WorldFIP communication reference model are standard, it is noted that there is no concept of user layer in the reference model. Norm for user layer is not specified in WorldFIP protocol, that is to say, no universal norm is specified for user's data wrapped by application layer. A kind of user layer model in WorldFIP communication protocol is proposed according to "USER MSG" field in Figure6 with process control as its application object.

For those field intelligent nodes using WorldFIP FULLFIP2 chips in communication, the maximum length of message is 256 bytes; for those using MICROFIP chips, the maximum length of message is 128 bytes. In the proposed user layer model, user's data are divided into several sub-fields illustrated by Figure 7, which relates closely to the data storage segmentation model in field intelligent nodes.

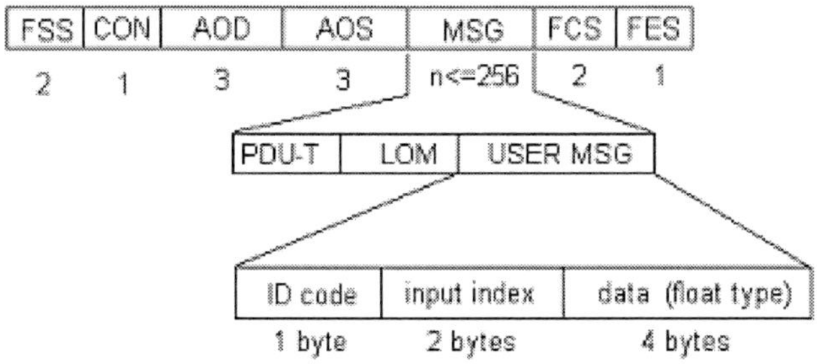

Figure 7. User layer model in WorldFIP communication protocol.

ID code: the field is set for system extension in future. Currently, ID code bears only 1 value that means "link operation" corresponding to the data transmission between FBs in different field intelligent nodes;

Input_index: index for the input terminal in input segment of lower-reach FB in remote linkage between FBs in different field intelligent nodes.

Data (float type): data wrapped in message.

5. FBA Schedule Algorithm

5.1. "Passive Schedule" Based on Compel Data

Control strategies specified by users through configuration are executed in field intelligent nodes. Data and instructions are downloaded from users' PC to field nodes over network link scheduler. A "passive" schedule algorithm are used, which is different from "active" schedule algorithm in local nodes. In this mode, only compel data (CD) are transmitted between bus scheduler and element intelligent nodes. The compel data can be defined as a constant instruction execution in element nodes is scheduled by bus scheduler. Current instruction pointed by instruction pointer is to be executed only after receipt of compel data from bus scheduler. Field element nodes wait until the next compel data are received after finishing executing current instruction. The data, which are not constant, transmitted between different field intelligent nodes are those needed by remote FBs in FBA. FBs are executed repeatedly. Each repetition is a macro cycle. Any instruction executions within field intelligent nodes are under full-time schedule in each macro cycle. The "passive" schedule algorithm based on compel data are described as followed:

Bus scheduler sends compel data to field element intelligent nodes over network in periodical variable exchange form at certain time-tick specified by schedule table. Instructions are executed in the element nodes after the compel data are received. Detailed implementation is described as followed.

(1)production variables corresponding to each element node are established in bus scheduler before startup of the whole control system. For example, 0x0501 is a consuming variable in element node N1, 0x0502 is a consuming variable in element node N2. Then 2 production variables 0x0501 and 0x0502 corresponding to the 2 consuming variables are established in bus scheduler;
(2)CD are written into the production variables in bus scheduler;
(3)scheduling item dealing with variable exchange , which are {0x0501,ID_DAT}and {0x0502,ID_DAT} in this example, are added to bus schedule table.

Thus, variable exchange can be implemented conforming to the time-tick specified by the schedule table over WorldFIP network, illustrating in Figure8. After the CD is received as a consuming variable by element node, current instruction pointed by a pointer in FB instruction segment are executed. The pointer is moved backwards to next instruction after the execution of current instruction.

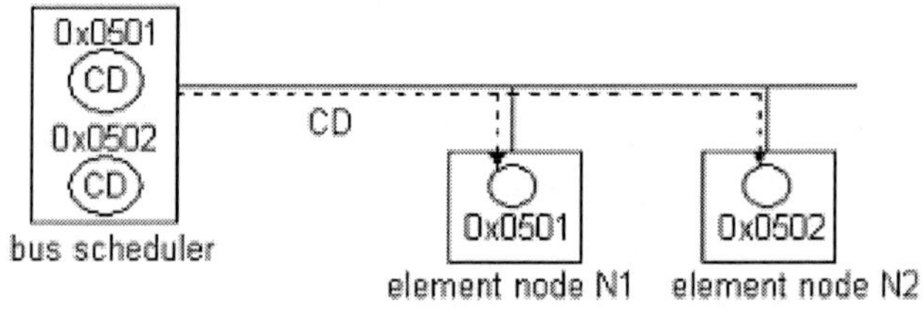

Figure 8. “Passive Schedule” based on compel data.

When MicroFIP chips are used in field intelligent nodes, data exchange can not be implemented between field intelligent nodes and can only be implemented by forwarding of bus scheduler, which make the communication less efficient. In the proposed model, periodical message exchanges between nodes are chosen to solve the problem. The data to be transmitted are wrapped in a message frame based on the above mentioned “data model in user layer ”, which ensures direct data exchange between element nodes and real-time in communication.

There are 2 types of FBA that are single-task FBA, which means that only one set of linkage from starting FB to ending FB, named FB task here, is included in whole FBA, and multi-task FBA which means 2 or more sets of linkage from starting FB to ending FB is included in whole FBA and each task is executed nearly at the same time. Unlinked FBs are not treated as a valid FBA. in single-task FBA. Unlinked FBs are not treated as a valid FBA. FBA schedule for single-task FBA and multi-task FBA are included in FBA schedule under "passive" schedule mode. Any FBA can be classified as the following 4 types:

5.2. Single-Task FBA Schedule

1. FB schedule for local linkage

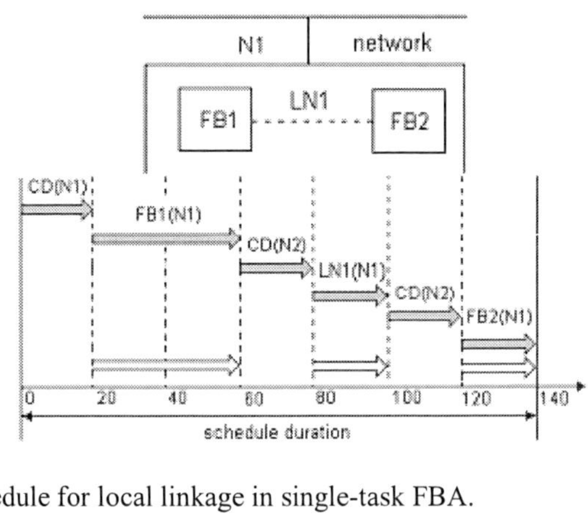

Figure 9. FB schedule for local linkage in single-task FBA.

Horizontal coordinate does not indicate time but the offset to absolute starting time in bus schedule. CD(N1) indicates bus scheduler sends CD to element node N1; FB1(N1) indicates execution of FB instruction FB1 in node N1; LN(N1) indicates execution of Link instruction in node N1, i.e. the output value of FB1 is sent to the input of FB2. In Figure9, white empty arrows indicate schedule for non-periodical variable exchange or message transmission.

2. FB schedule for remote linkage

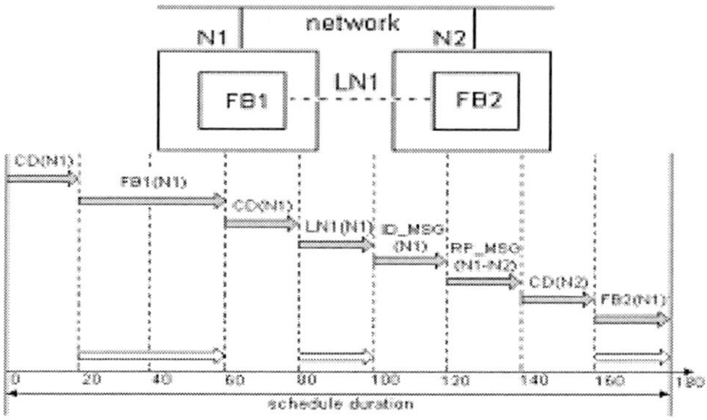

Figure 10. FB schedule for remote linkage in single-task FBA.

In Figure10 the Link instruction is identified as remote link by node N1 when LN(N1) is executed. The value of output of local FB FB1 is wrapped in the response frame FR1 according to the above mentioned "data model in user layer" to prepare for the transmission of the response frame; ID_MSG(N1) indicates bus scheduler sends ID_MSG frame to node N1 to initialize message transmission between node N1 and N2 in order to transmit output of FB1 to input of FB2; RP_MSG(N1-N2) indicates responding message frame FR1 is sent by node N1 to N2.

5.3. Multi-Task FBA Schedule

1. FB schedule for local linkage

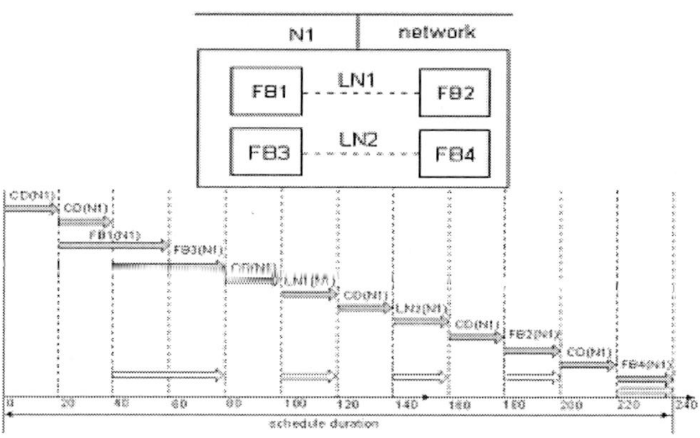

Figure 11. FB schedule for local linkage in multi-task FBA.

2. FB schedule for remote linkage

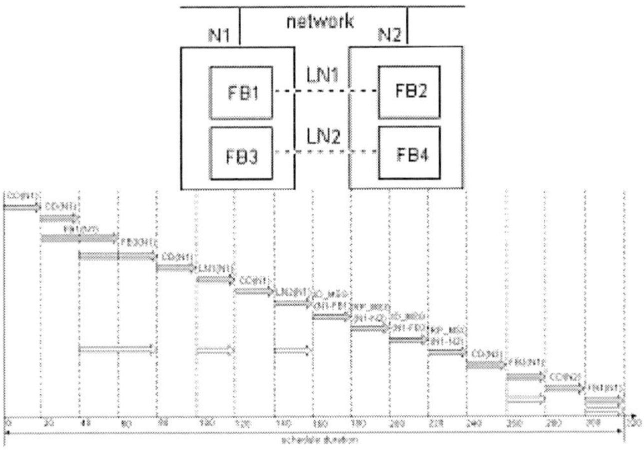

Figure 12. FB schedule for remote linkage in multi-task FBA.

In Figure 12, ID_MSG(N1-FB1) indicates bus scheduler sends frame ID_MSG to node N1 to prepare for message transmission between N1 and N2 in order to put value of output of FB1 in N1 into input of FB2 in N2.

Example: Data transmission process between node N1 and N2 illustrated by Figure9 can be described as followed:

(1)In time of periodical communication, CD is sent to node N1 by bus scheduler by means of production variable ox0501; instruction is executed in N1 on its receipt of CD; value of output of FB1 is wrapped in responding frame to prepare for frame transmission if current instruction in N1 is a "remote Link";

(2)Frame (ID_MSG, 0x0601) is sent to N1 by bus scheduler to initialize a message transmission;

(3)N1 identifies itself with variable 0x0601 as its producer and respond to the frame (ID_MSG, 0x0601) by sending frame (RP_MSG, 2, 1) which includes the wrapped data over network. In the frame, 2 is for the physical address of N2, 1 is for source address, i.e. address of node N1;

(4)Frame (RP_MSG, 2, 1) is received by node N2 and data is drawn out frame the frame and put the data into the specified input terminal of FB2.

CONCLUSION

Now, products and systems developed based on WorldFIP are above control level and FDICN based on intelligent nodes are not implemented yet. FBA is the kernel parts in FDICN. Concept of user layer and norm for user layer in WorldFIP protocol are not proposed yet. A kind of practically feasible FBA model is proposed in this paper based on independently developed WorldFIP FDICN. Guided by the propose model, main problems in design and implementation of FDICN based on FB and FBA in field control network can be resolved effectively and FDICN with high reliability and good real-time property can be realized. Operational practice of the developed FDICN by author's research team shows the effectiveness of the propose model and algorithms.

REFERENCES

[1] Xianhui Yang, *Fieldbus Technology and Application*, Tsinghua University Press, Beijing, China, 1999.

[2] Yaping Wu, WorldFIP fieldbus communication protocol, *WorldFIP Technology promotion center,* Beijing, 2001.

[3] Xia, Feng, Function block oriented architecture for open distributed automation, *Proceedings of the World Congress on Intelligent Control and Automation (WCICA),* vol.3, 2706-2710, 2004.

[4] Diedrich, Christian, Function block applications in control systems based on IEC 61804, *ISA Transactions*, vol.43, no.1, 123-131, 2004.

[5] Geng Liang, Development of Scheme Configuration Software for WorldFIP FCS Based on Object Model, *Journal of Scientific Instruments,* Vol.26, No.12, 1293-1297, 2005.

[6] Geng Liang, Design And Implementation Of Control Strategy Configuration Software For Worldfip Fieldbus Control System, *Proceedings of CSEE*, Vol.24, No.2, 150-156, 2005.

[7] Geng Liang, *Research and development of function block application of the fieldbus intelligent device based on WorldFIP fieldbus,* Vol.27, No.6 (suppl), 902-904,2006.

[8] D. Z. Cheng, Controllability of switched bilinear systems, *IEEE Trans. on Automatic Control,* Vol.50, No.4, 511-515, 2005.

[9] Neumann, Habil P, "Free configurable function block application software in distributed control systems", *IEEE International Symposium on Industrial Electronics,* Vol.1, No.1, 293-298,1996.
[10] Yu Zhang, Performance Analysis of Distributed Function Block Control Application, *Computer Science*, Vol.34, No.4, 265-269,2007.
[11] www.worldFIP.org.

In: Network Protocols
Editor: Geng Liang
ISBN 978-1-61470-821-6

Chapter 3

DATA LINK LAYER TRANSMISSION SERVICES WITH ITS PERFORMANCE ANALYSIS IN WORLDFIP NETWORK

Geng Liang,[1] Wen Li,[2] Hong Wang,[4] and Dazhong Li[3]

[1]School of Control and Computer Engineering, North China Electric Power University, Beijing, China

[2]Beijing GUODIANZHISHEN Control Technology Co. Ltd, Beijing, China

[3]Automation Department, North China Electric Power University, Baoding, China

[4]Control System Center, the University of Manchester, UK

ABSTRACT

Data exchange patterns between nodes in WorldFIP fieldbus network are quite important and meaningful in improving communication performance of WorldFIP network. Based on the basic communication ways supported in WorldFIP protocol, there are two DLL transmission services for data exchange between peer nodes over WorldFIP network. Effects on communication performance of WorldFIP network in terms of some network parameters, such as number of bytes in user's data and turn-around time, in both proposed services, are analyzed at length when different network speeds are applied. Such effects with the services of periodic messages transmission using acknowledged and non-acknowledged messages, are also studied. Communication performance in both services are analyzed and compared. Practical applications of the research are presented. Through the study, it can be seen that different transmission services make a great difference in improving communication efficiency with different network parameters, which is quite useful and helpful in practical design of distributed systems based on WorldFIP network.

Keywords: WorldFIP, Fieldbus, Variable exchange, Message transmission, Bus communication efficiency, Performance analysis

1. INTRODUCTION

WorldFIP protocol is one of the profiles that constitute the European fieldbus standard EN-50170. It is particularly well suited to be used in distributed computer-controlled systems where process variables and information must be shared among network devices. WorldFIP fieldbus is increasingly applied in process control, manufacturing industry, power system automation and traffic information integration. It is unparalleled with its dual-bus redundancy techniques ensuring high communication reliability in process control [1-2]. Distributed intelligent control network based on WorldFIP technology is completely distributed in function, high in reliability and intelligence. Bus schedule algorithms and patterns for data exchange between nodes in WorldFIP network are quite important and meaningful in improving communication performance of the network. As for previous research work, almost all the studies on improving WorldFIP network performance and communication efficiency, dealt with WorldFIP network scheduling algorithms and designs of BAT (Bus Arbitrator Table) or ST (Schedule Table). More attentions are paid to algorithms on scheduling of periodic or aperiodic data frames. Luís Almeida presented response-time-based schedulability analysis for WorldFIP real-time traffic and used a fixed-priorities-based policy to schedule the periodic traffic [3]. Zhi Wang investigated real-time traffic of aperiodic messages using WorldFIP and analyzed the worst-case responding time of aperiodic message in order to improve scheduling methods [4]. Jiming Chen compares performance under various traffic loads of aperiodic messages in WorldFIP and FF fieldbus [5]. Control performance and schedule issues for periodic message with sequence constrain are also investigated [6,7]. Methodology ensuring real-time constrain for aperiodic message in FF fieldbus, which is technologically similar to WorldFIP, is researched and approaches to improve the protocol is given as well [8]. Some important research results dealing with function blocks (FB) and their applications (FBA) for WorldFIP network to check and improve the communication efficiency of WorldFIP network are presented in our previous work [9,10,11] and Y. Pang's research [12]. Simulation-related problems for different layers in WorldFIP and Foundation Fieldbus protocols were investigated in our previous research [11], and also studied by Zhou [13] as well as E.A. Mossin [14]. Some devices development and practical applications based on WorldFIP are also reported [15-17].

In addition to the scheduling related issues, other issues on data exchange between nodes in WorldFIP network also have great effects on communication performance of WorldFIP network. Data exchange between nodes in WorldFIP networks can be implemented by different means. Two kinds of basic data exchange fashion, which are variable exchange and message transmission, are supported in WorldFIP protocol. In this chapter, rather than focusing on scheduling related problems, we investigate the methodologies to improve communication efficiency from a different perspective. Based on the basic ways, two patterns for data exchange between nodes in WorldFIP network are presented. The relationship between some important network parameters, such as number of bytes in user data and the communication efficiency, is analyzed and compared. Effects of both patterns on communication performance of WorldFIP network in terms of number of bytes in user's data and turn-around time, are analyzed when different network speeds are applied. Such effects of periodic message transmission pattern using acknowledged and non-acknowledged message approaches are analyzed respectively. Communication performance of WorldFIP network is analyzed and compared when the proposed patterns applied. The study demonstrates that different data exchange patterns make a significant difference in improving communication efficiency with different network parameters. Furthermore, the two proposed patterns are related closely with hardware chips used in WorldFIP system design, namely WorldFIP communication controllers including MICROFIP and FULLFIP2. Practically, it is more meaningful and helpful in the design of distributed intelligent systems based on fieldbus network.

This chapter is organized as follows: In section 2, the two DLL transmission services for data exchange between nodes in WorldFIP network supported in WorldFIP protocol are briefly introduced. The relationship between the two services and two different WorldFIP communication controllers, namely MICROFIP and FULLFIP2, is presented. Then, based on the basic communication ways, we propose two kinds of pattern for data exchange between nodes with MICROFIP chips. In section 3, we present the proposed pattern Ⅰ for data exchange over WorldFIP network, namely by means of variable exchange and LAS forwarding at length. Then, analysis of network communication performance under circumstance of single data exchange and maximum communication cycles between nodes respectively when pattern Ⅰ is applied is given at length. In section 4, we present the proposed pattern 2 for data exchange over WorldFIP network, namely by means of WorldFIP periodic message to achieve direct data exchange. Analysis of network communication performance under circumstance mentioned in section 3 when pattern 2 is applied is given in detail. In section 5, we conduct comparison of network communication performance under circumstance mentioned in section 3 when pattern Ⅰ and Ⅱ are applied respectively. Two practical applications of the research to design logic and process control systems based on WorldFIP network are presented in Section 6. Some conclusions, which are useful in system design to improve communication efficiency, are given and opportunities for future work are pointed out in the last part of the chapter.

2. WORLDFIP PROTOCOL

2.1. General Introduction

WorldFIP is a single consistent technology for all levels of the fieldbus system, combining the worlds of closed-loop control and information-technology on one bus. WorldFIP is accepted technology for international contracts, and is a European Standard (EN50170). This guarantees its stability and openness, and ensures that WorldFIP is a preferred technology for all applications in the public sector and utility industries throughout the European Union. With the fastest growing user base in the world and a complete answer in a single technology, WorldFIP offers the most practical and proven solution [11].

WorldFIP differs from all other fieldbus systems in a number of respects - - one of them being its use of a single simple protocol to cover both the real-time and background information needs of a control or instrumentation system.

- A Single Protocol
  In plain words this means that, no matter what you intend to use your fieldbus for, there is only one protocol to learn. Some other bus systems require two or even three different protocols to cover the range of tasks, which makes them harder to learn as well as requiring extra interfaces and conversions within the system.
- A Simple Protocol
  WorldFIP protocol is also simple to learn. There are no lengthy vocabularies of specialised terms, and maximum use is made of existing International Standard formats such as the Manufacturing Message Specification (MMS). You can confidently expect that any work you carry out with WorldFIP will align very easily to full International Fieldbus standards when they ultimately emerge.

2.2. Description of Protocol Layer

Physical layer, data linkage layer and application layer in ISO/OSI 7-layer reference model are adopted in reference model for WorldFIP fieldbus communication.

Composition of WorldFIP communication protocol is shown in Figure 1.

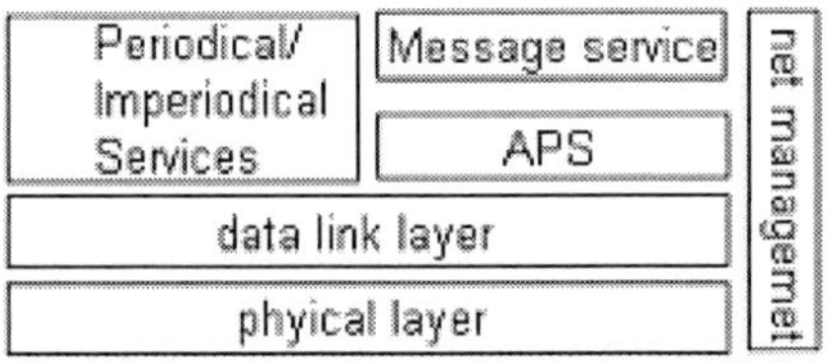

Figure 1. Composition of WorldFIP communication protocol.

- Physical Layer
  - Bus topology to IEC 1158-2.
  - Data rates of 31.25kbit/sec, 1 Mbit/sec or 2.5 Mbit/sec via twisted pair copper cable, overall screen.

- Data rate of 5 Mbit/sec via optical fibre.
- 64 nodes per cable segment, up to 4 segments through repeaters.
- Segment length: 1 Km or more depending on data rate, cable and number of nodes.
- Redundant cable as an option.

- Data Link Layer
  - Uses "producer-consumer" model (described later in this module) with centralized bus-scheduler (redundant bus-schedulers can be used if required).
  - Supports time-critical "variables" and "messages" (described later in this module).
  - Time-critical "variables" can be "cyclic" or "event" variables.
  - Up to 64000 message identifiers. Up to 64000 variable identifiers. (A few identifiers are reserved).
  - Size of variables from 2 bytes to 127 bytes. Message size up to 256 bytes.
- Application Layer
  - Variables accessible through MPS interface.

Messages accessible via sub-MMS interface. Maximum size of message 64kBytes using sub-MMS.

2.3. Producer-Consumer Model

WorldFIP's producer/consumer model is central to the effectiveness of WorldFIP's protocol.

Why Producer/Consumer?

Many networks are based upon protocols developed for long-distance communications. They were developed to transmit messages from point to point, with built-in re-try mechanisms to cope with the high risk of data corruption on public message routes.

Though well-suited to their original application, such protocols are quite unsuitable for time-critical data-transfer between devices on a fieldbus, since:

- The possibility of re-try prevents a deterministic response.
- Data must be re-sent to each node which requires it.

The "producer/consumer" model gives deterministic high-speed response, by allowing the data produced by one node to be consumed at the same time by any or all other nodes on the network.

How It Works?

The "producer" node does not need to know which nodes are consuming the data. The Bus Arbiter function controls the "producers" rather like the conductor of an orchestra, so transmission of data at known time intervals (equivalent to the conductor's "beat") is guaranteed. Data integrity is guaranteed by status flags, which show the "timeliness" and the "freshness" of data. There is no re-transmission in the event of corrupted data, the next value simply overwrites the previous value.

"The "producer/consumer" mechanism is very effective for time-critical data and event data. It allows easy construction of a distributed real-time database in a WorldFIP-connected system.

As a simple example, imagine a PLC using WorldFIP cyclic data to communicate with its distributed I/O system.

You may add a PC into that network, set up to consume all the data that is already passing; the PC is effectively invisible to the PLC. The PC might be supporting SCADA or other packages, and thus be able to provide links into the information networks onthat site, all without requiring any change to the program in the PLC and with no effect on the data-traffic across the fieldbus.

2.4. Coding the Data Frame

All WorldFIP frames (frame_question, response, message, etc.) are composed of three parts:

- Frame Start Sequence (FSS)
- Control and Data field(CAD)
- Frame End Sequence (FES)

1) Frame Start Sequence (FSS)

This contains two fields:

- Preamble (PRE)

This series of 8 "1" bits is used by receivers to synchronize themselves with the transmitter's clock.

- Frame Start Delimiter (FSD)
  This series of bits indicates to the data link layer the beginning of useful information (CAD).

2) Control and Data Field

This field contains only the logical information ("0" and "1") from the data link layer.

3) Frame End Sequence (FES)

This series of bits is used by the data link layer as a delimiter, to locate the end of the CAD field.

4) The User May Define the Data Field

The above description explains the way in which each frame is encoded for secure transmission. This is interesting for a product developer -- but it is largely "invisible" to a user, who is far more interested in the information which he can send and receive via the frames.

The Control and Data Field (CAD) has three parts:

- Control Field: Contains control and address information used by the protocol
- Data Field: Contains the user data
- Check Field: Contains a 16-bit CRC computed and checked by the protocol

All the "real-life" data is transmitted within the Data field defined above, and the user (or his system builder) can define exactly how the Data field is built up, according to the needs of his specific system. The definition of the contents of the Data field is part of the system-builder's task when he builds the system.

The Application Layer of WorldFIP provides both time-critical and non-critical (or messaging) services.

Time-critical services are managed via WorldFIP's distributed database (functionally identical with those in the draft IEC Standard). Non-critical services are provided by a sub-set of the Manufacturing Message Specification (MMS).

Time-Critical Data

Time-critical data (eg control-loop variables) are passed around the network using "MPS" real-time periodic/aperiodic services.

Cyclic variables are sent to the network using the periodic services. The repetition rate may be fixed (down to 2msec) or free-running. Such variables always have absolute priority, and are typically used to transmit data used in fast speed-control loops etc.

Event variables are sent only if requested, using the apcriodic service -- for instance, to respond to a change of state (eg alarm) or a demand for an operator display. Use of event variables is very appropriate in systems where change is normally infrequent but there are occasional cascades of alarms, such as gas/water/electricity industries.

Non-Critical Data

Less time-dependent data (such as diagnostic reports), is sent via the message service. This may be typically used for:

- Installing and setting up an application
- Network supervision and diagnosis
- Integration with higher-level systems.

5) How It All Works

Network time is split into "macro-cycles" -- usually based on the update time of the slowest periodic variable in the system. These are further divided into "elementary cycles" each of the same length (min. 2 msec).

Data is allocated to the cycles in the following priority order:

- Cyclic variables
- Event variables
- Messages (non critical)

Cyclic variables always travel on time, regardless of other network traffic. Any Event requests are serviced next, and only then are messages handled. If network traffic is heavy, Messages are placed in a queue.

Unlike token-passing systems, WorldFIP leaves no doubts about transmission time and regularity for cyclic data variables.

6) Frames Format

WorldFIP communication is master-slave typed. The whole network is composed of bus schedulers serving as master and field intelligent nodes which are subordinate. Value exchange between periodical and non-periodical variables and messages exchange are scheduled with bus schedulers. Two types of data exchange are used in network: data exchanges based on variable exchanges, which are usually used to transmit real-time and periodical data, and message exchange based on physically addressing. Detailed information can be referred to related reference. The following types of frames are used to exchange data over WorldFIP network.

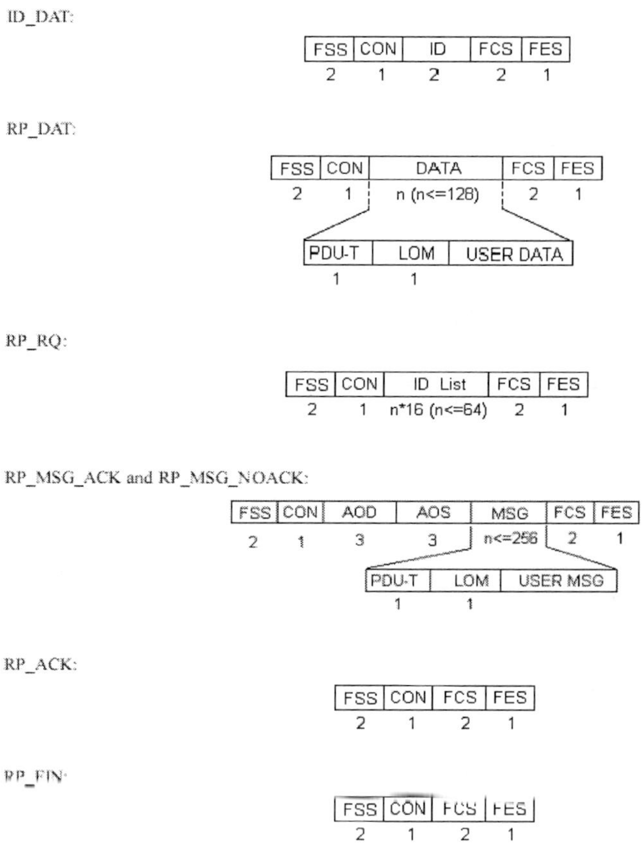

Figure 2. Format of WorldFIP frames. FSS: frame starting series; CON: control. PDU_T: type of protocol data unit; LOM: length of message; AOD: address of destination; AOS: address of source; MSG: user's message; FCS: frame check series: FES: frame ending series.

The following is based on variables exchange:

ID_DAT: sent by bus scheduler and used to initialize a variable exchange process;

RP_DAT: sent by a field intelligent node and used to respond to ID_DAT to realize the data transmission based on variable exchange.

The following is based on message transmission:

ID_MSG: sent by bus scheduler and used to initialize a message transmission process;

RP_MSG: sent by a field intelligent node and used to respond to ID_MSG to realize the message transmission.

RP_MSG_ACK: sent by bus scheduler and used to acknowledge the data sent by field intelligent node;

RP_FIN: sent by a field intelligent node and used to respond to RP_MSG_ACK to finalize a message transmission process.

In the proposed model, RP_MSG_ACK is used to assure the reliable data transmission.

Format of WorldFIP frame is shown in Figure2. The numbers under the frame figures represent bytes used by the corresponding segment in frames [23].

In above frame format, all fields except "MSG" field are specified by WorldFIP protocol and have nothing to do with user layer in WorldFIP protocol. Therefore, "MSG" are the only field users can control use freely.

3. DLL Transmission Services for Data Exchange in WorldFIP Network

Centralized medium control strategy is used in WorldFIP network, which is a schedule-based communication system. Two kinds of network nodes, which are Link Activity Scheduler (LAS) and elementary nodes respectively, are included in WorldFIP fieldbus network. Variable exchange and message transmission, both supported in WorldFIP protocol, are the two basic patterns for data exchange between nodes in the network [1,18].

Variable exchange is a more effective way for communication among nodes over WorldFIP network, by which data transmission from 1 node to n nodes simultaneously can be achieved. In a data transmission cycle, all nodes requiring the data of the same produced variable can obtain the value of the data as consumed variables. Addressing is used in message transmission to implement data exchange between any two peer nodes. The data can be transmitted in m cycles of message transmission if required by m nodes, which makes it less efficient than variable exchange in communication performance [1,18]. The two basic patterns supported by WorldFIP protocol are shown in Figure 3 and Figure 4.

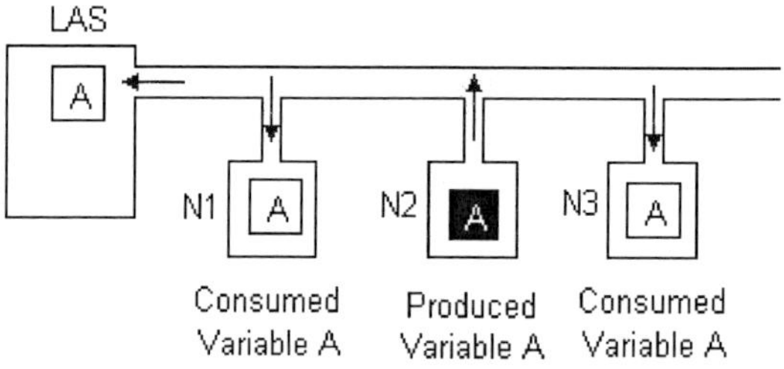

Figure 3. Data exchange between nodes by means of Produced/Consumed variable exchange.

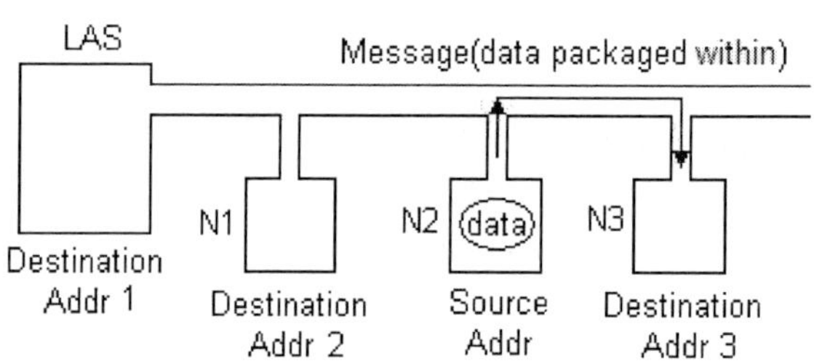

Figure 4. Data exchange between peer nodes by means of message transmission.

Patterns for data exchange between nodes are related closely to the type of communication controller used in nodes. Two types of communication controller, including FULLFIP2 and MICROFIP chips [19, 20], are widely used in WorldFIP network. FULLFIP2 supports periodical/non-periodical variables exchange and messages transmission with direct addressing and can be used to implement scheduling of communication over the fieldbus. FULLFIP2 provides interface between data link layer and application layer and user. By contrast, MICROFIP cannot serve as bus communication scheduler. It is often applied to elementary nodes, which have no bus schedule function. MICROFIP supports periodical/non-periodical variables exchange between LAS, elementary nodes and direct addressing messages transmission. Generally, FULLFIP2 is used in LAS while MICROFIP is used in elementary nodes in practice [1,19,20].

As far as functions are concerned, MICROFIP and FULLFIP2 are quite different in terms of data communication over WorldFIP network. Limited by the number of identifiers, network nodes with the chip MICROFIP as their communication controller cannot exchange data directly. Namely, direct data exchange between peer nodes, just as described in the basic pattern of variable exchange, cannot be achieved if MICROFIP chips are applied to them. Instead, it is achievable with FULLFIP2 chips [21,22]. However, cost of nodes with FULLFIP2 chips is much higher than that with MICROFIP chips. In practice, MICROFIP chips are more widely used in design of elementary nodes, which can lower the cost of system to great extent.

Based on the basic communication ways supported in WorldFIP protocol, here we propose two kinds of pattern in data exchange between nodes with MICROFIP chips, which can be described as follows:

- Pattern Ⅰ : Variable exchange - LAS forward. Since nodes with MICROFIP cannot exchange data directly in the basic pattern of variable exchange, LAS with FULLFIP2 can get the data from source node and forward it to destination node, both by means of direct data exchange. Therefore, 2 times of direct variable exchanges take place during this process: ①source node N sends the data to LAS by means of direct variable exchange ②LAS sends the data to destination node M by means of direct variable exchange.
- Pattern Ⅱ : Periodic message transmission for peer-to-peer data exchange as described before in the basic pattern of message transmission.

Periodic message transmission for data exchange between 2 peer nodes is supported both by MICROFIP and FULLFIP2. Therefore, direct data exchange between peer nodes can be achieved over the network.

The assumed condition of variable exchange application in the proposed pattern I is that the number of destination nodes is 1. Namely, data in produced variable is consumed by only one node.

4. MICROFIP AND FULLFIP2

4.1. Microfip

4.1.1. General Description

MICROFIP is an ASIC solution implementing the WorldFIP protocol, to be used in field devices able to communicate at the three standard speeds: 31.25 kbits/s, 1 Mbit/s, 2.5 Mbits/s. In addition its static implementation guarantees low power consumption. MICROFIP is a low–cost and easy–to–use solution which supplies a subset of the WorldFIP services, in particular it can be configured as a station, without being able to run the bus arbitrator. The frame delimiters and control sequence can be selected in compliance with the NFC46–604 FIP original standard or IEC11586–2. Network management facilities are directly embedded in the chip, such as the presence and identification variables. The identification contains a 32–bit tag. MICROFIP is able to operate with or without associated microcontroller, using various MAUs such as FIELDRIVE, CREOL for copper twisted pairs and others kind of supports (optical fiber, etc.). The two ways to run the MICROFIP, with or without microcontroller, are respectively identified Standalone and Microcontrolled, and offer benefits from dedicated features [24].

4.1.2. Standalone

MICROFIP operating in Standalone mode allows direct interfacing with the process inputs and outputs through two 8–bit bi–directional ports. The port states are directly mapped on the network using one produced variable (identifier: 06xy) for inputs, and one consumed variable (identifier: 05xy) for outputs. MICROFIP operating in Standalone mode can be automatically started after power up initialization or after having received a start command from the configuration variable (identifier: 03xy). The configuration variable which is a consumed variable contains, in addition, bits dedicated to I/O port configuration. MICROFIP operating in Standalone mode takes the xy subscriber number from a dedicated port, and the promptness and refreshment statuses are managed on the MPS variables and tuned by dedicated pins.

4.1.3. Microcontrolled

MICROFIP operating with a microcontroller doesn't require any external logic glue for many of them (8051, 68HC11, etc.). The use of microprocessors (80186, 68000, etc.) is also simplified. MICROFIP communication resources are accessed by the microcontroller through an embedded dual port memory which is shared with the protocol machine. MICROFIP can be configured with 0 to 4 produced MPS variables, and 0 to 4 consumed MPS variables, using a global resource capability of 15 blocks of 8 bytes. The variable identifiers are allocated in the physical space (00xy to 07xy, with xy as subscriber number), with the possibility for one of the consumed variables to modify the identifier number, and to assign a number from the global addressing space (16 encoded bits), in a user interface register. A MICROFIP memory of 120 bytes can be extended using another MICROFIP chip installed in "cascade" with the first one. The promptness and refreshment statuses are managed for all the MPS variables and the period can be selected from several possible values. MICROFIP takes its subscriber number directly from the dedicated pins during chip set–up, and can be modified later by the microcontroller. MICROFIP is fitted with a full duplex (transmit and receive) messaging channel allowing message exchanges with maximum size 128 bytes. The message exchanges may or may not be acknowledged according to user needs. MICROFIP provides an interrupt mechanism attached to one produced variable (06xy identifier), to the four consumed variables, and to the messaging transmit and receive channels. Seven different factors may be at the origin of an interrupt.

4.1.4. Functional Description

1) Block Partition

MICROFIP is composed of the following block units:

- Control,
- Dual Port Memory,
- User Interface,
- Two parallel Input/Output Ports PIA an PIB ,and an input Port for Subscriber Number,
- Protocol Machine,
- UART,
- Medium Redundancy Management.

2) Control

This block manages the initialization and clock signals used inside the chip.

It also handles the operating mode selections:

- Operations with or without microcontroller,
- Selection of the microcontroller used, ifany,
- Direction for the two ports PIA and PIB.

3) Dual Port Memory

This block contains the communication data base (variables and message contents) which is shared between the MICROFIP protocol machine and between the microcontroller and the I/O peripheral.

4) User Interface

This block allows a microcontroller to configure the MICROFIP component with a set of dedicated control and status registers. It also handles the exchange between the microcontroller and the internal dual port memory which contains the communication data base (messages and variable contents). Lastly this block handles the interrupt mechanism towards the microcontroller. The interrupts, when configured, are initiated upon network event recognition.

5) PIA and PIB input/output Ports and Subscriber Number Input Port

The PIA and PIB 8–bit ports can be configured by dedicated external input pins of the circuit in write or read direction mode. When MICROFIP is operating without a microcontroller, these ports are linked to the corresponding network variables (produced variable for the port configured in input, consumed variable for the port configured in output).

6) Protocol Machine

This block manages network communication element exchanges, and is able to handle the following sequence:

- ID_DAT+RP_DATfor up to 8 MPS variables,
- ID_DAT+RP_DAT for the presence anidentification variables,
- ID_DAT + RP_DAT_MSG for one MPS variable (with identifier 06xy anwhen handling the associate aperiodic messaging channel),
- ID_MSG+RP_MSG_NOACK+RP_FIN for a broadcasting message,
- ID_MSG+RP_MSG_NOACK+RP_FIN for a point–to–point unacknowledge message,

- ID_MSG+RP_MSG_ACK+RP_ACK+/–+RP_FIN for an acknowledged message.

The protocol machine can be considere as a crossroaD between the following elements:

- the UART input and output parallel ports,
- the PIA and PIB ports,
- the dua lport memory which contains the database.

7) Uart

This block is derived from the FULLFIP2 chip. It allows management framing and FCS calculation with the possibility to be compliant with NFC or IEC standardization.

The structure of MICROFIP is shown in Figure 5.

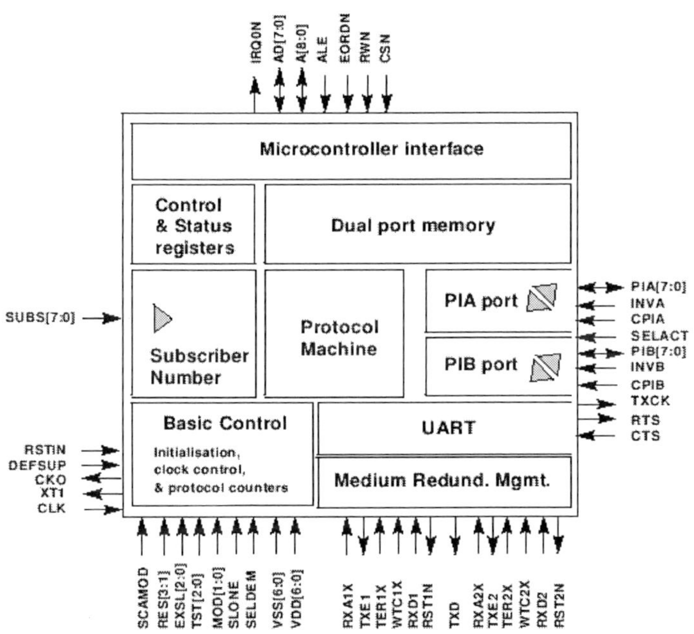

Figure 5. structure of MICROFIP.

4.1.5. Variable Structure and Addressing

When MICROFIP operates in Standalone mode, since its initialization it works as a station handling the following variables addressed by:

- ID_DAT = 14xy. For the presence variable with a content described in Section 4.
- ID_DAT = 10xy. For the identification variable with a content described in Section 5.
- ID_DAT = 03xy. If SELDEM input pin is active high, this variable is consumed and contains a start/reset order on 1 byte, 3 bytes dedicated to the station configuration, and the MPS status. If SELDEM is inactive low, this variable is not handled by the station.
- ID_DAT = 06xy. The station produces a 2–byte data and 1–byte MPS status variable. The 2–byte data contains the parallel ports
- PIA and PIB, whatever the port direction selected.
- ID_DAT = 05xy. The station consumes a 2–byte and 1–byte MPS status variable. The 2–byte data can drive the parallel ports PIA and PIB for those configured as outputs. For ports configured as inputs, the corresponding byte of the consumed variable is not used.

4.2. FULLFIP2

4.2.1. General Description

The FULLFIP2 component is a communication coprocessor implementing most of the link and application protocols of the WorldFIP fieldbus. It has been designed with VLSI TECHNOLOGY silicon compiler tools. The FULLFIP2 chip is the second generation of the FULLFIP integrated circuit; it enhances communication performances by integrating the possibility to operate at the physical layer in conformance with the IEC standard and by increasing the network transmission rate. This circuit is intended to equip any field device having a certain intelligence level such as PLC, I/O mux, Drive, Console,... capable of managing a great number of variables, including intelligent sensors and actuators. It implements a set of periodic and aperiodic buffer transfer and messaging services of the data link layer, as well as for a station supporting the arbitrator function as for a slave station. It also supports the MPS application layer services including promptness, refreshment, and synchronization mechanisms. It can process up to 4096 identifiers among the 65536 possible on the network. For this purpose it must have a private memory which can reach a size of 2 Mbytes. The objects handled by the circuit which constitutes the local data base are stored in this memory address space. The circuit is micro-programmed. A part of the micro-program is located in an internal ROM while the remaining part is loaded into the internal RAM from the external private memory. It is interfaced through a bus of type '8–bit peripheral device' with the 'user' processor in charge of running the application software. The user requests and the network events may be totally asynchronous as any database access conflict is solved by internal algorithms. On the network side, FULLFIP2 is connected to the WorldFIP bus by a line driver which can be doubled to ensure medium redundancy. The circuit implements a FIP standardized full–duplex UART whose transmission rate is selectable among the following values: 31.25 Kbit/s, 1 Mbit/s, 2.5 Mbit/s and 5 Mbit/s. Signals on the network interface are encoded data sequence (Manchester Biphase L). The circuit principle of FULLFIP2 is shown as Figure6.The integration of FULLFIP2 into a microcomputer system is shown as Figure 7.

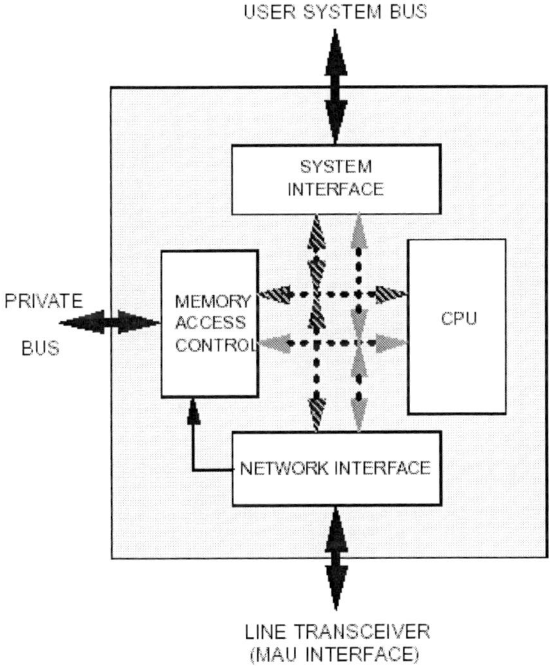

Figure 6. Circuit principle block diagram of FULLFIP2.

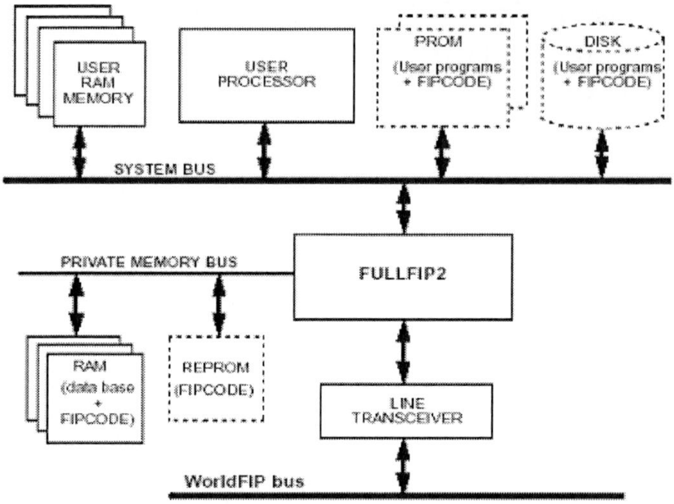

Figure 7. Integration of FULLFIP2 into a microcomputer system.

4.2.2. Features

- Compatible with standards AFNOR UTE NFC 46–601–7; CENELEC EN 50170 and IEC 1158,
- Configurable as simple station, as well as, Bus Arbitrator and station
- Handles up to 4096 identifiers
- Bit rate from 31.25 Kbit/s to 5 Mbit/s
- Clock frequency operation up to 80 MHz
- 8–bit Data Bus User Interface
- Direct interface with the line transceiver
- Private memory up to 2 Mbytes
- Extended temperature range –40°C + 85°C
- Available as a 84 PLCC or 100 MQFP

4.2.3. Memory Access Control

The memory access controller is the interface between the core of the FULLFIP2 circuit and the external private memory. It handles three access channels: the A and B channels are under the control of the central unit, the C channel is reserved for the identifier search device of the network manager. The electrical interface of FULLFIP2 with the memory bus is shown in Figure 8.

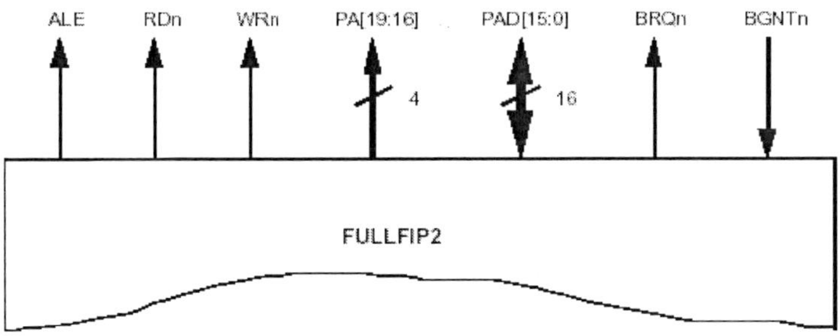

Figure 8. Electrical interface with the memory bus.

The external private memory may be sized between 32 K word and 1M word of 16–bit words (external private memory address bus width sized to 20 bits).

The external private memory is used to store:

- FULLFIP2 microcode (FIPCODE)
- Database management structures
- Database contents

The external private memory may be composed of RAM memory chip only, but in some implementations, the microcode may be kept permanently in a REPROM memory chip and the remaining information located in RAM memory. In any case, it is recommended to design the RAM private memory with static RAM chips without wait state for which microcode operating is guaranteed.

5. Data Link Layer Transmission Service: Variable Exchange with Its Communication Performance Analysis

5.1. Variable Exchange and LAS Forward

Assumed that number of intelligent nodes in field, which MICROFIP chips are applied to, is *n*. FULLFIP2 is used in LAS with physical address *0x*a. Source node *N* with address *0x*n is required to transmit periodic data to destination node *M* with address *0x*m. Proposed pattern I is used in data transmission. Addressing of LAS and evaluation of *N*, *M* conform to the relational expression (1).

$$a < N, a < M \tag{1}$$

A produced variable *0x*06n is configured in *N*; a consumed variable *0x*01m is configured in *M*; a consumed variable *0x*02n is configured in LAS to receive data from *N*; a produced variable *0x*01m is configured in LAS to forward data, which is received from *N*, to *M*. Corresponding communication flow is described as followed.

1)Periodic data inquiry frame ID_DAT(*0x*02n) is broadcast by LAS;

2)Response frame RP_DAT(*data*) is sent by *N* as response to frame ID_DAT(0x02n). After this step, data in N denoted as data here is transmitted to variable 0x02n in LAS;

3)Data in consumed variable *0x*02n in LAS is copied to produced variable *0x*01m by internal program of LAS;

4)Periodic data inquiry frame ID_DAT(*0x*01m) is broadcast by LAS;

5)Reply frame RP_DAT(*data*) is sent by LAS itself as response to frame ID_DAT(*0x*01m) since LAS is the producer of variable *0x*01m. After this, data in produced variable *0x*01m in LAS is transmitted to consumed variable *0x*01m in *M*.

Formats for the related frames in the data transmission cycle are shown in Figure 9 [1,18].

ID_DAT frame：

FSS	Control	Identifier	FCS	FES
(2)	(1)	(2)	(2)	(1)

RP_DAT frame：

FSS	Control	User Data	FCS	FES
(2)	(1)	(1~128)	(2)	(1)

Figure 9. Format of frames used in the pattern of variable exchange.

In the process mentioned above, the cycle time for the data transmission is different when different network speed is applied even if the number of bytes in user data is the same. To make it convenient, the number of bytes in user data, instead of the time consumed in data transmission, is used here to analyze and compare the communication performance of the network under such circumstances. Therefore, bus efficiency, a newly defined concept, is introduced here.

Bus efficiency λ is defined as: the proportion of number of bytes in user data, which is denoted as N_{data} here, to the number of bytes in all the frames within a data transmission cycle, which is denoted as N_{all} here.

Namely,

$$\lambda = \frac{N_{data}}{N_{all}} \tag{2}$$

As a matter of fact, λ indicates the efficiency of data transmission between nodes over WorldFIP network in terms of user data packaged in various frames, which is the ultimate valid data for system users. During a data transmission with frame ID_DAT and RP_DAT involved, N_{data} is user data packaged in RP_DAT. According to WorldFIP protocol, it conforms to $N_{data} \leqslant 128$. N_{all} is the number of bytes in frame ID_DAT and RP_DAT, i.e.

$$N_{all} = N_{ID\_DAT+RP\_DAT} \tag{3}$$

5.2. Performance Analysis for A Single Data Exchange between Nodes in Pattern I

In the case of a single data exchange between peer nodes,

$$\begin{aligned} N_{all} &= N_{ID\_DAT(0x02n)} + N_{RP\_DAT(data)} + N_{ID\_DAT(0x01m)} + N_{RP\_DAT(data)} \\ &= 8 + (6+n) + 8 + (6+n) = 2n + 28 \end{aligned} \tag{4}$$

where, n is the number of bytes in user data packaged in frame RP_DAT, $n \leqslant 128$.

Then the bus efficiency

$$\lambda = \frac{n}{2n+28} \tag{5}$$

Turn-around time T_r, which represents the time span between the time instant when prior frame is received and that when next frame is sent over WorldFIP network, is taken into account and converted into number of bytes of data during communication equivalently, i.e.

$$N_{tr} = \frac{T_r \times \beta}{8} \tag{6}$$

where β in *bps*, denotes the speed of WorldFIP network.

Therefore, expression (4) is transformed as

$$\begin{aligned} N_{all} &= N_{ID\_DAT(0x02n)} + N_{RP\_DAT(data)} + N_{ID\_DAT(0x01m)} + N_{RP\_DAT(data)} + 4N_{tr} \\ &= 8+(6+n)+8+(6+n)+4N_{tr} = 2n+28+4N_{tr} \end{aligned}$$

Then bus efficiency

$$\lambda = \frac{n}{2n+28+4N_{tr}} \tag{7}$$

Relationship between network speed β and turn-around time T_r can be chosen as

$$T_r = \begin{cases} 0.18 \sim 2.5ms, \beta = 31.25Kbps \\ 80 \sim 560\mu s, \quad \beta = 1Mbps \\ 30 \sim 220\mu s, \quad \beta = 2.5Mbps \end{cases} \tag{8}$$

Then we can obtain

$$N_{tr} = \begin{cases} 0.7 \sim 10, \beta = 31.25Kbps \\ 10 \sim 70, \quad \beta = 1Mbps \\ 10 \sim 70, \quad \beta = 2.5Mbps \end{cases} \tag{9}$$

For N_{tr} must be integer, expression (9) is transformed as

$$N_{tr}=\begin{cases} 1\sim 10, & \beta=31.25Kbps \\ 10\sim 70, & \beta=1Mbps \\ 10\sim 70, & \beta=2.5Mbps \end{cases} \tag{10}$$

Then bus efficiency is analyzed in different cases as follows.

Case 1: $\beta=31.25Kbps$, number of bytes in user data $n\in[1,128]$, $N_{tr}\in[1,10]$. The relationship curves of bus efficiency λ and n are shown in Figure 10.

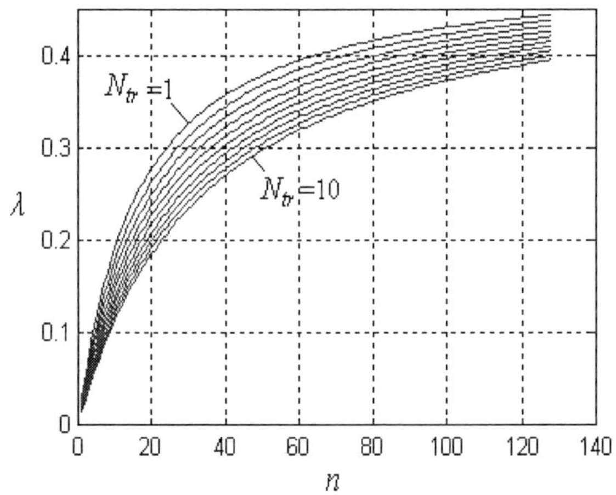

Figure 10. A single data exchange between nodes in Pattern I : λ -n relationship curves, n∈[1,128], $N_{tr}\in[1,10]$, $\beta=31.25Kbps$.

When $N_{tr}=1$ and $n\in[1,128]$, λ takes the maximum value, namely $\lambda_{\max}$ = 0.44; when $N_{tr}=10$, $n\in[1,128]$, λ takes the minimum value, namely $\lambda_{\min}$ = 0.395.

Case 2: $\beta=1Mbps,2.5Mbps$, $n\in[1,128]$, $N_{tr}\in[10,70]$. λ -n relationship curves are shown in Figure 11.

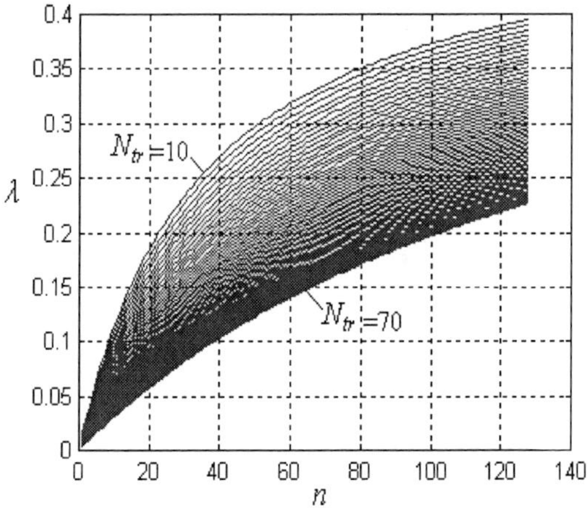

Figure 11. A single data exchange between nodes in Pattern I : λ -*n* relationship curves, $N_{tr} \in [10,70]$, $\beta = 1Mbps, 2.5Mbps$.

When $N_{tr} = 10$ and $n \in [1,128]$, λ takes maximum value $\lambda_{max} = 0.395$; when $N_{tr} = 70$, $n \in [1,128]$, λ takes minimum value $\lambda_{min} = 0.227$.

Therefore, in the case of a single data exchange between nodes, bus communication efficiency λ is in inverse proportion to network speed β . When lower network speed is applied, bus efficiency is higher. Meantime, number of bytes in user data also has prominent effects on bus efficiency. Bus efficiency varies greatly with $n \leqslant 50$; Increment in bus efficiency becomes less prominent gradually with $n > 50$. Bus efficiency takes linear relationship with turn-around time equivalent N_{tr} when higher network speed is applied, such as $\beta = 1Mbps, 2.5Mbps$.

5.3. Performance Analysis for Data Exchange between Nodes with Maximum Communication Cycles in Pattern I

Assume that the total number of nodes over the network is *m*. Each of *m* nodes requires data from one of the (*m*-1) nodes.

Then m communication cycles, here we name it as the maximum cycles, are needed to implement all the required data transmission tasks, i.e.

$$N_{all} = \sum_{a=1}^{m} D_{ij} = \sum_{a=1}^{m} (2n_{ij} + 28 + 4N_{tr}) \tag{11}$$

$$i \neq j, \quad D_{ij} \neq D_{ji}$$

where N_{all} denotes the number of bytes of all data transmission in the m communication cycles; D_{ij} denotes the data sent from node i to j; n_{ij} denotes the number of bytes of user data packaged in various frames. Therefore, the number of all the bytes in user data in various frames can be denoted as $\sum_{a=1}^{m} n_{ij}$

Then the bus efficiency in this case is

$$\lambda = \frac{\sum_{a=1}^{m} n_{ij}}{N_{all}} = \frac{\sum_{a=1}^{m} n_{ij}}{\sum_{a=1}^{m} (2n_{ij} + 28 + 4N_{tr})} = \frac{\sum_{a=1}^{m} n_{ij}}{2 \times \sum_{a=1}^{m} n_{ij} + 28m + 4mN_{tr}} \tag{12}$$

where $\sum_{a=1}^{m} n_{ij}$ is the sum of number of bytes in user data during m communication cycles.

Therefore, bus efficiency λ is a function of variable $m, \sum_{a=1}^{m} n_{ij}$ and N_{tr}.

Obviously, here $\lambda \propto \frac{1}{m}$ holds. Relation of λ and $\sum_{a=1}^{m} n_{ij}$, N_{tr} is analyzed as follows.

Case 1: $\beta = 31.25Kbps$, let m = 1 to simplify the computation, $N_{tr} \in [1,10]$. λ - $\sum_{a=1}^{m} n_{ij}$. The relationship curves are shown in Figure 12.

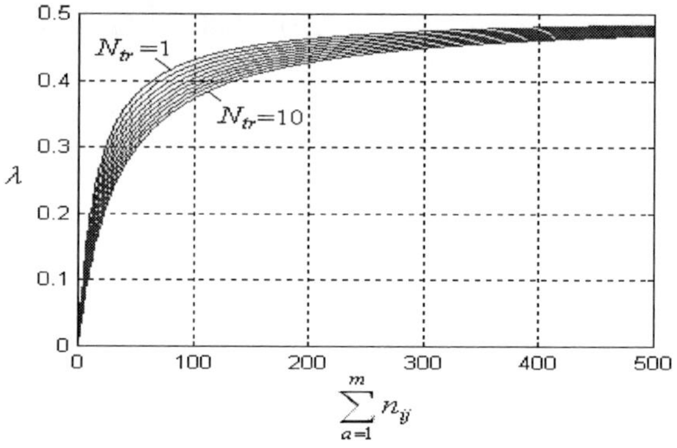

Figure 12. Data exchange between nodes with maximum communication cycles in Pattern I : λ - $\sum_{a=1}^{m} n_{ij}$ relationship curves, N_{tr} ∈[1,10], $\beta = 31.25Kbps$.

It can be seen that bus efficiency is affected greatly by $\sum_{a=1}^{m} n_{ij} \in [40,100]$; bus efficiency kept roughly unchanged and is much less affected by N_{tr} on the whole when $\sum_{a=1}^{m} n_{ij} > 400$.

Case 2: $\beta = 1Mbps, 2.5Mbps$, m=1, N_{tr} ∈[1,10]. λ - $\sum_{a=1}^{m} n_{ij}$. The relationship curves are shown in Figure 13.

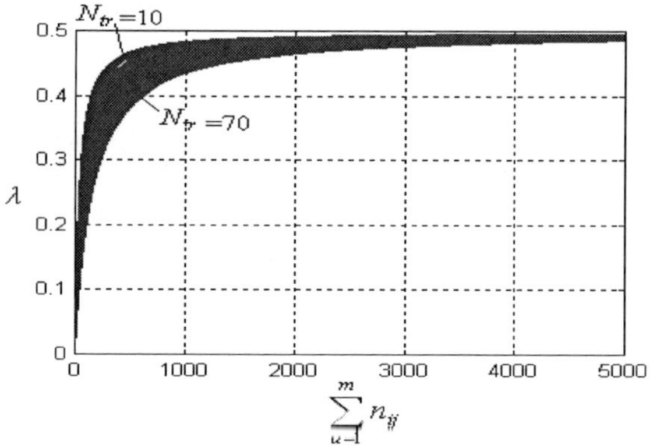

Figure 13. Data exchange between nodes with maximum communication cycles in Pattern I : λ - $\sum_{a=1}^{m} n_{ij}$ relationship curves, N_{tr} ∈[10,70], $\beta = 1Mbps, 2.5Mbps$.

It can be seen that bus efficiency is affected greatly by $\sum_{a=1}^{m} n_{ij} \in [20,2000]$; bus efficiency kept roughly unchanged and is much less affected by N_{tr} on the whole when $\sum_{a=1}^{m} n_{ij} > 5000$.

6. Data Link Layer Transmission Services: Periodic Message with Communication Performance Analysis

6.1. Direct Data Exchange between Nodes by Means of WorldFIP Periodic Message

Assume that number of field intelligent nodes, all of which MICROFIP chips are applied to, is n. FULLFIP2 chip is applied in LAS with physical address 0xa. Node N with address 0xn is required to transmit periodic data to node M with address 0xm. Direct data exchange between N and M by means of WorldFIP periodic message is used to implement the task. A produced variable needs to be configured in N. No configuration of variables is needed for M. User data is packaged in WorldFIP message frames and addressing is used to implement the data transmission between the two peer nodes. Communication flow can be described as follows.

1) When Non-Acknowledged Message is Used

(1)LAS sends the periodic message inquiry frame ID_MSG(*0x*02n);

(2)Node *N* responds to frame ID_MSG(*0x*02n) by sending frame RP_MSG_NOACK(*msg*) over the network. User data is packaged in the WorldFIP message segment of the frame, denoted as *msg* here. After this step, data in *N* is transmitted to *M* directly;

(3)*N* sends frame RP_FIN() to terminate the whole message transmission process.

2) Acknowledged Message Used

(1)LAS sends periodic message inquiry frame ID_MSG(*0x*02n);

(2)Node *N* responds to frame ID_MSG(*0x*02n) by sending frame RP_MSG_ACK(*msg*). User data is packaged in *msg*. After this step, data in *N* is transmitted to *M*;

(3)Node *M* sends message response frame RP_ACK() if the message is received;

(4)Node *N* sends frame RP_FIN() to terminate the whole process of message transmission.

Formats of the frames mentioned in the message transmission process above are shown in Figure 14.

ID_MSG :

FSS	Control	Identifier	FCS	FES
(2)	(1)	(2)	(2)	(1)

RP_MSG_NOACK and RP_MSG_ACK :

FSS	Control	Source_Addr	Dest_Addr	Message	FCS	FES
(2)	(1)	(3)	(3)	(1~256)	(2)	(1)

RP_ACK and RP_FIN

FSS	Control	FCS	FES
(2)	(1)	(2)	(1)

Figure 14. Format of frames used in the pattern of message transmission.

6.2. Performance Analysis for a Single Data Exchange between Nodes

1) When Non-Acknowledged Message is Used

$$N_{all} = N_{ID\_MSG(0x02n)} + N_{RP\_MSG\_NOACK(msg)} + N_{RP\_FIN()} \\ = 8 + (12 + n) + 6 = n + 26 \quad (13)$$

Where $n \in [1,256]$ is the number of bytes in user data N_{data}, which constitutes *msg* that is packaged in frame RP_MSG_NOACK as WorldFIP message.

Then bus efficiency

$$\lambda = \frac{N_{data}}{N_{all}} = \frac{n}{n+26} \tag{14}$$

Taking N_{tr} into account, we revise (13) as

$N_{all} = N_{ID\_MSG(0x02n)} + N_{RP\_MSG\_NOACK(msg)} + N_{RP\_FIN()} + 4N_{tr} = 8+(12+n)+6+4N_{tr} = n+26+4N_{tr}$ Therefore, the revised bus efficiency is

$$\lambda = \frac{n}{n+26+4N_{tr}} \tag{15}$$

Case 1: $\beta = 31.25Kbps$, $n \in [1,256]$, $N_{tr} \in [1,10]$. λ -n relationship curves are shown in Figure15.

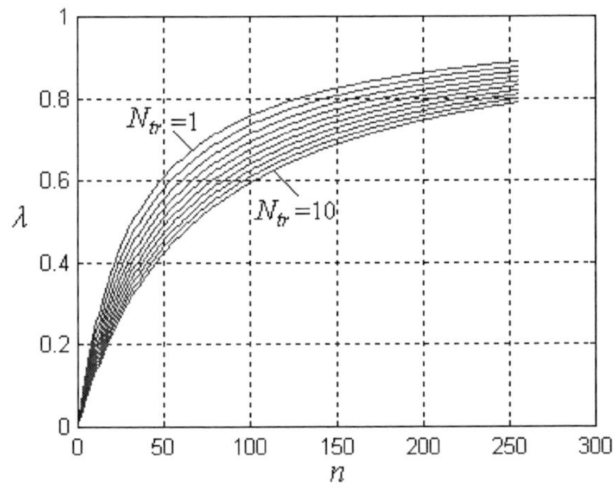

Figure 15. A single data exchange between nodes in Pattern II with non-acknowledged message used: λ -n relationship curves with $N_{tr} \in [1,10]$, $n \in [1,256]$, $\beta = 31.25Kbps$.

Case2: $\beta = 1Mbps, 2.5Mbps$, $n \in [1,256]$, $N_{tr} \in [10,70]$. λ -n relationship curves are shown in Figure16.

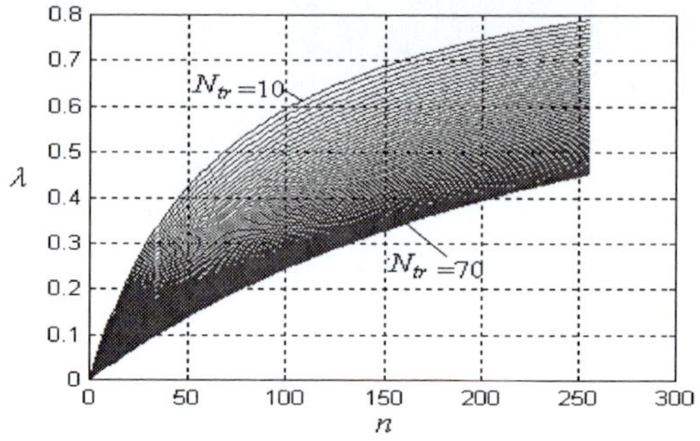

Figure 16. A single data exchange between nodes in Pattern II with non-acknowledged message used: λ -*n* relationship curves with N_{tr} ∈[10,70], *n*∈[1,256] , $\beta = 1Mbps, 2.5Mbps$

2) When Acknowledged Message is Used

$$N_{all} = N_{ID\_MSG(0x02n)} + N_{RP\_MSG\_ACK(msg)} + N_{RP\_ACK()} + N_{RP\_FIN()} \\ = 8 + (12+n) + 6 + 6 = n + 32 \tag{16}$$

The revised bus efficiency is

$$\lambda = \frac{n}{n + 32 + 4N_{tr}} \tag{17}$$

Case 1: $\beta = 31.25Kbps$, n∈[1,256], N_{tr} ∈[1,10]. λ - n relationship curves are shown in Figure 17.

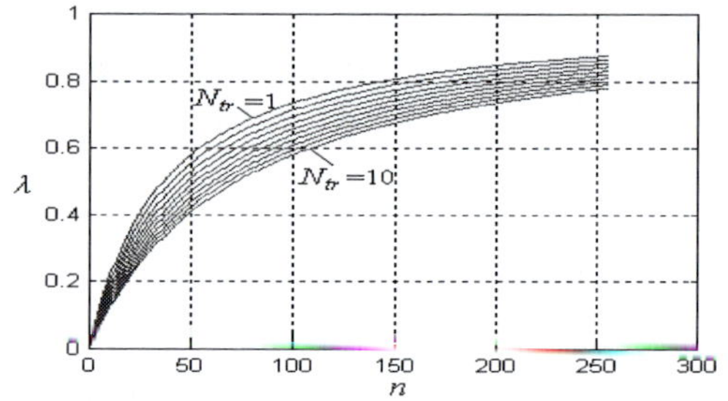

Figure 17. A single data exchange between nodes in Pattern II with acknowledged message used: λ - *n* relationship curves with N_{tr} ∈[1,10], *n*∈[1,256] , $\beta = 31.25Kbps$.

Case2: $\beta = 1Mbps, 2.5Mbps$, $n \in [1,256]$, $N_{tr} \in [10,70]$. λ - n relationship curves are shown in Figure 18.

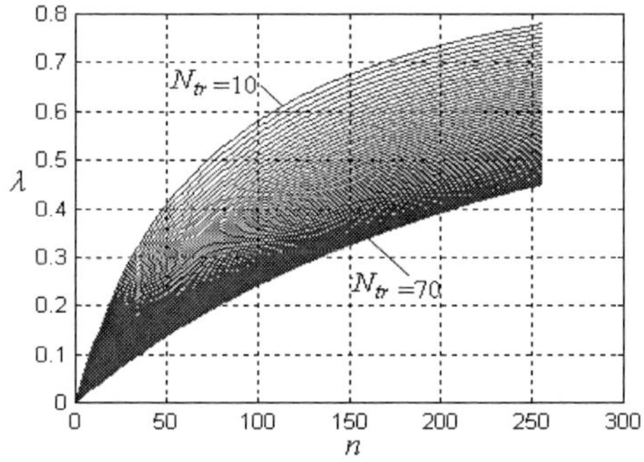

Figure 18. A single data exchange between nodes in Pattern II with acknowledged message used: λ - n relationship curves, $N_{tr} \in [10,70]$, $n \in [1,256]$, $\beta = 1Mbps, 2.5Mbps$.

6.3. Performance Analysis for Data Exchange between Nodes with Maximum Communication Cycles

The assumption is same with that mentioned above.

When Non-Acknowledged Message is Used

$$\lambda = \frac{\sum_{a=1}^{m} n_{ij}}{N_{all}} = \frac{\sum_{a=1}^{m} n_{ij}}{\sum_{a=1}^{m} (n_{ij} + 26 + 4N_{tr})} = \frac{\sum_{a=1}^{m} n_{ij}}{\sum_{a=1}^{m} n_{ij} + 26m + 4mN_{tr}} \tag{18}$$

When Acknowledged Message is Used

$$\lambda = \frac{\sum_{a=1}^{m} n_{ij}}{N_{all}} = \frac{\sum_{a=1}^{m} n_{ij}}{\sum_{a=1}^{m} (n_{ij} + 32 + 4N_{tr})} = \frac{\sum_{a=1}^{m} n_{ij}}{\sum_{a=1}^{m} n_{ij} + 32m + 4mN_{tr}} \tag{19}$$

Case 1: $\beta = 31.25Kbps$, m=1, n∈[1,500], $N_{tr} \in [1,10]$. λ - $\sum_{a=1}^{m} n_{ij}$ relationship curves are shown in Figure19.

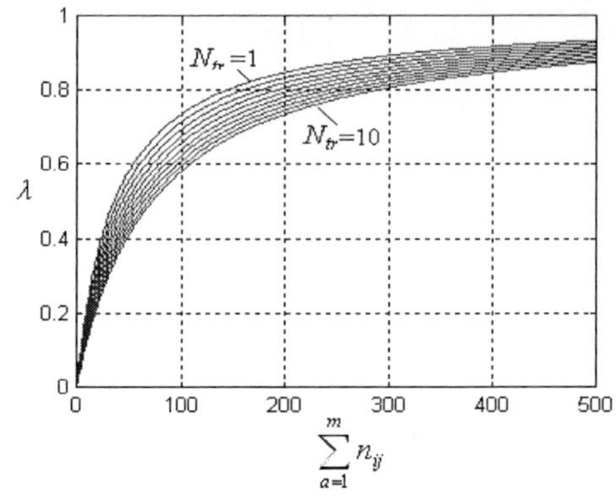

Figure 19. Data exchange between nodes with maximum communication cycles in Pattern II with acknowledged message used: λ - $\sum_{a=1}^{m} n_{ij}$ relationship curves, m=1, N_{tr} ∈[1,10] , n∈[1,500], $\beta = 31.25 Kbps$.

Case 2: $\beta = 1Mbps, 2.5Mbps$, m=1, n∈[1,5000], N_{tr} ∈[10,70]. λ - $\sum_{a=1}^{m} n_{ij}$. The relationship curves are shown in Figure20.

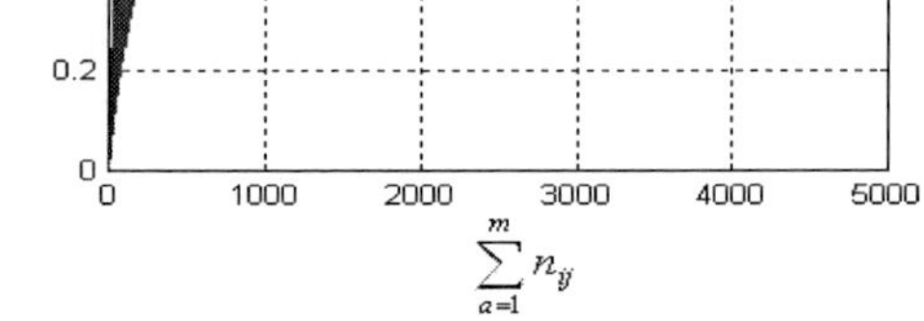

Figure 20. Data exchange between nodes with maximum communication cycles in Pattern II with acknowledged message used: λ - $\sum_{a=1}^{m} n_{ij}$ relationship curves, m=1, N_{tr} ∈[10,70] , n∈[1,5000], $\beta = 1Mbps, 2.5Mbps$.

From the analysis above, we can see that the communication performances are almost the same when non-acknowledged and acknowledged message is applied respectively.

7. Communication Performance Analysis and Comparison for Data Link Layer Transmission Services

7.1. Performance Analysis and Comparison for A Single Data Exchange between Nodes

λ_{var} denotes communication performance in Pattern I ,namely variable exchange-LAS forward. λ_{msg} denotes communication performance in Pattern II , namely WorldFIP periodic message transmission. $\Delta\lambda$ denotes the difference between λ_{msg} and λ_{var}. Namely

$$\Delta\lambda = \lambda_{msg} - \lambda_{\text{var}} = \frac{n}{n+26+4N_{tr}} - \frac{n}{2n+28+4N_{tr}} \tag{18}$$

Case 1: $\beta = 31.25Kbps$, $N_{tr} \in [1,10]$, n∈[1,128]. $\Delta\lambda$ -n relationship curves are shown in Figure 21.

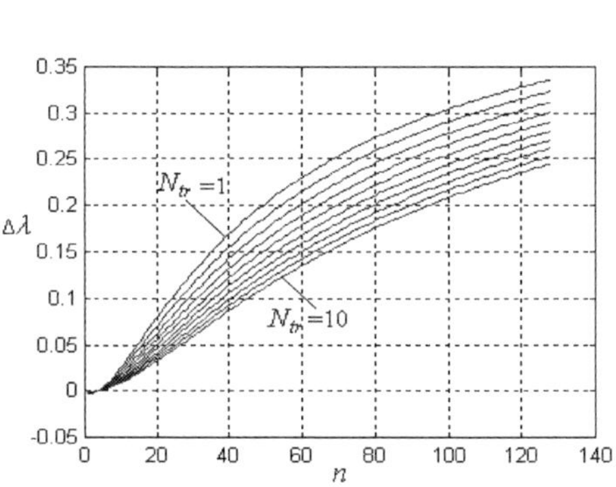

Figure 21. A single data exchange between nodes: $\Delta\lambda$ -*n* relationship curves, $N_{tr} \in [1,10]$, $n \in [1,128]$, $\beta = 31.25Kbps$.

It can be seen that

$\lambda_{\text{var}} > \lambda_{msg}$, when n<4

$\lambda_{msg} > \lambda_{\text{var}}$, when $n \geq 4$

Case 2: $\beta = 1Mbps, 2.5Mbps$, $N_{tr} \in [10,70]$, $n \in [1,128]$. $\Delta\lambda$ -n relationship curves are shown in Figure22.

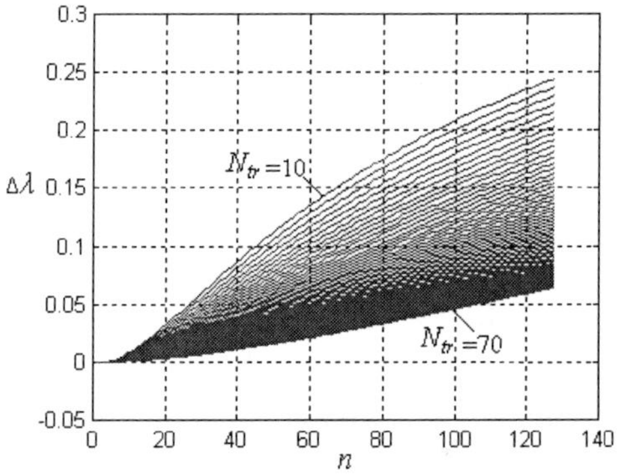

Figure 22. A single data exchange between nodes: $\Delta\lambda$ -n relationship curves, $N_{tr} \in [10,70]$, $n \in [1,128]$, $\beta = 1Mbps, 2.5Mbps$.

It can be seen that the relationship between λ_{var} and λ_{msg} varies with n can be described as

$$\begin{cases} \lambda_{\mathrm{var}} > \lambda_{msg}, \mathrm{n} < 4 \\ \lambda_{\mathrm{var}} = \lambda_{msg}, \mathrm{n} = 4 \\ \lambda_{\mathrm{var}} < \lambda_{msg}, \mathrm{n} > 4 \end{cases} \tag{19}$$

7.2. Performance Analysis and Comparison for Data Exchange between Nodes with Maximum Communication Cycles

$$\Delta\lambda = \lambda_{msg} - \lambda_{\mathrm{var}} = \frac{\sum_{a=1}^{m} n_{ij}}{\sum_{a=1}^{m} n_{ij} + 32m + 4mN_{tr}} - \frac{\sum_{a=1}^{m} n_{ij}}{2 \times \sum_{a=1}^{m} n_{ij} + 28m + 4mN_{tr}} \tag{20}$$

The performance comparison in Pattern Ⅰ and Ⅱ for data exchange between nodes are described in Figure23 and Figure24 when different network speeds applied.

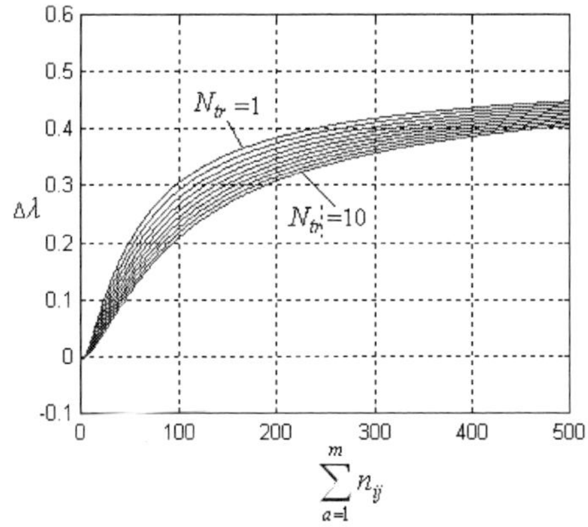

Figure 23. Data exchange between nodes with maximum communication cycles: $\Delta\lambda$ - $\sum_{a=1}^{m} n_{ij}$ relationship curves, N_{tr} ∈[1,10], n∈[1,500], $\beta = 31.25Kbps$.

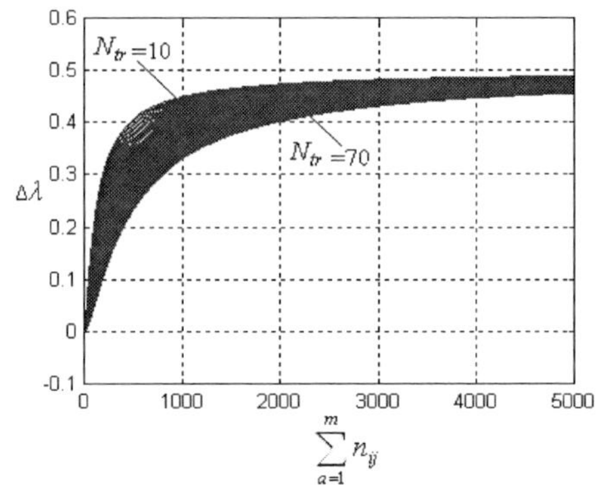

Figure 24. Data exchange between nodes with maximum communication cycles: $\Delta\lambda$ - $\sum_{a=1}^{m} n_{ij}$ relationship curves, N_{tr} ∈[10,70], n∈[1,5000], $\beta = 1Mbps, 2.5Mbps$.

In the case of maximum communication cycles, it can be seen that bus communication efficiency in Pattern II is higher than Pattern I when $\sum_{a=1}^{m} n_{ij}$ >4. Bus communication efficiency increased significantly when $\sum_{a=1}^{m} n_{ij}$ increases. That is

$$\begin{cases} \lambda_{\text{var}} > \lambda_{msg}, \sum_{a=1}^{m} n_{ij} < 4 \\ \lambda_{\text{var}} = \lambda_{msg}, \sum_{a=1}^{m} n_{ij} = 4 \\ \lambda_{\text{var}} < \lambda_{msg}, \sum_{a=1}^{m} n_{ij} > 4 \end{cases} \tag{21}$$

8. Practical Applications

The proposed results in this chapter can find its important uses to help design and improve distributed process control system based on WorldFIP network. Here we present two cases with such use to demonstrate the practical applications of the research.

Application 1: On Design of Logic Control System Based on WorldFIP Network

WorldFIP technology has found its wide uses in digital logic control. A digital logic system for motor control is shown in Figure 25.

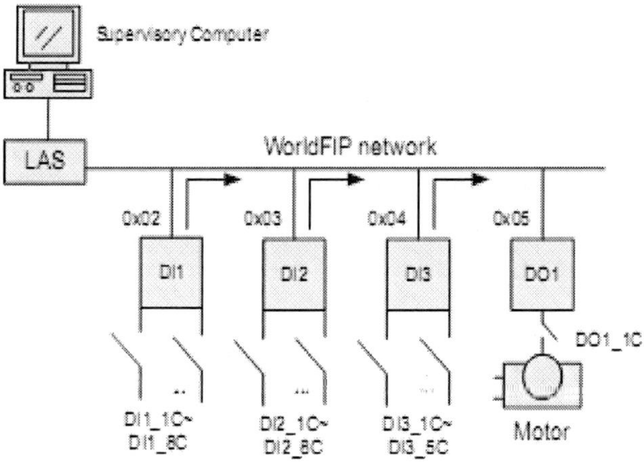

Figure 25. a digital logic system for motor control with WorldFIP network.

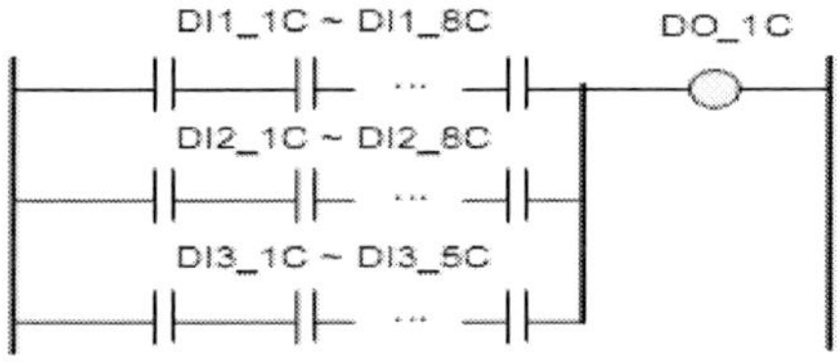

Figure 26. Control logic for the motor control system.

WorldFIP network is applied to serve as data exchange and communication channels by interconnecting bus scheduler LAS, digital input node devices DI1, DI2, DI3 and digital output node device DO1. Node DI1 and DI2 have eight digital inputs from relays in field, which are DI1_1C ~ DI1_8C and DI2_1C ~ DI2_8C respectively. DI3 has five denoted as DI3_1C ~ DI3_5C. The motor is controlled by node DO1 with digital output DO1_1C. The control logic for the system, as shown in Figure20, is run in DO1. According to WorldFIP specification, the four field nodes are assigned the addresses as 0x02~0x05 respectively, as shown in Figure26. Communication controller FULLFIP2 is used in LAS and MICROFIP used in each of the field nodes.

According to the control logic, node DO1 requires data indicating the field relays inputs from nodes DI1~DI3 periodically. Then we can get:

1. The user data exchanged between DI1 and DO1 is eight bits (one byte) with each bit indicating the ON/OFF status of field relay inputs DI1_1C ~ DI1_8C. The data format is shown as Figure 27;

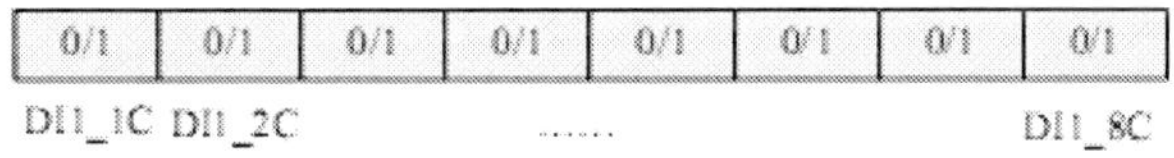

Figure 27. Format of data transmitted from DI1 to DO1 with size of 1 byte.

2. The user data exchanged between DI2 and DO1 is also eight bits (one byte);

3. The user data exchanged between DI3 and DO1 is five bits and packaged as one byte, which is the minimum size of user data. The data format is shown as Figure 28;

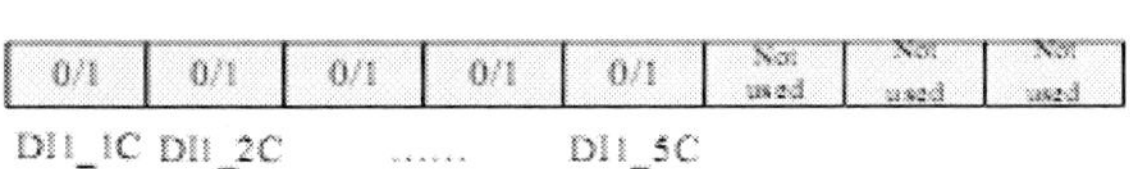

Figure 28. Format of data transmitted from DI3 to DO1 with size of 1 byte.

The data exchange and communication stated above make a macrocycle in scheduling and repeated periodically. The periodic traffic accounts for most of the time in a macrocycle. From Section 3.3, we know that the sum of number of bytes in user data during *m* communication cycles can be represented as $\sum_{a=1}^{m} n_{ij}$. In this application case, output node DO1 requires data from input nodes DI1~DI3 to make a logic operation, in which 3 communication cycles are needed to realized that task. Therefore *m*=3. n_{ij}, which denotes user data transmitted from node DI1, DI2 and DI3 to DO1, can denotes $n_{(DI1,DO1)}$, $n_{(DI2,DO1)}$ and $n_{(DI3,DO1)}$ respectively with *i* represented as DI1~DI3 and *j* represented as DO1.

From above analysis, it can be seen that the user data in periodic traffic in a macrocycle over the network are three bytes in total, That is

$$\begin{aligned}\sum_{a=1}^{m} n_{ij} &= \sum_{a=1}^{3} n_{ij} = n_{(DI1,DO1)} + n_{(DI2,DO1)} + n_{(DI3,DO1)} \\ &= 1+1+1=3\end{aligned} \tag{22}$$

According to Figure 23,24 and Equation (21), i.e.

$$\begin{cases} \lambda_{\text{var}} > \lambda_{msg}, \sum_{a=1}^{m} n_{ij} < 4 \\ \lambda_{\text{var}} = \lambda_{msg}, \sum_{a=1}^{m} n_{ij} = 4 \\ \lambda_{\text{var}} < \lambda_{msg}, \sum_{a=1}^{m} n_{ij} > 4 \end{cases}$$

it is known that bus communication efficiency in Pattern I (denoted as λ_{var}) is higher than Pattern II (denoted as λ_{msg}) when any of the available bus speeds, which are $\beta = 31.25Kbps, 1Mbps$ and 2.5*Mbps*, is chosen since $\sum_{a=1}^{m} n_{ij}$ =3<4 in this application case. That means macrocycle can be reduced to a shorter time-span if Pattern I is chosen instead of Pattern II. Consequently, the real-time performance of the control system can be improved. Therefore, we choose Pattern I for this case to implement data exchange and communication over the network.

Here, we consider using MICROFIP for field nodes in both micro-controlled and stand-alone operating mode to make the application more practical and useful. The implementation processes are described as follows:

1)Configuring produced variables in DI1~DI3, which serve as data sources, to store the input data from field relays. That is,

- Configuring produced variable *0x*0602 in DI1, which is applicable to both micro-controlled and standalone operating mode of MICROFIP;
- Configuring produced variable *0x*0603 in DI2;
- Configuring produced variable 0x0603 in DI3;

2)Configuring consumed variables *0x*0602, *0x*0603 and 0x0604 in LAS, corresponding to the produced variables configured in field nodes, to receive the data sent from those inputting field nodes by means of variable exchange;

3)Configuring produced variables *0x*0505 in LAS to forward data to DO1;

4)Configuring consumed variables *0x*0505 in DO1, which serves as the data destination, to receive data forwarded by LAS.

The process for data exchange is illustrated in Figure 29, where 1,2 and 3 indicates the data exchange sequence in the process.

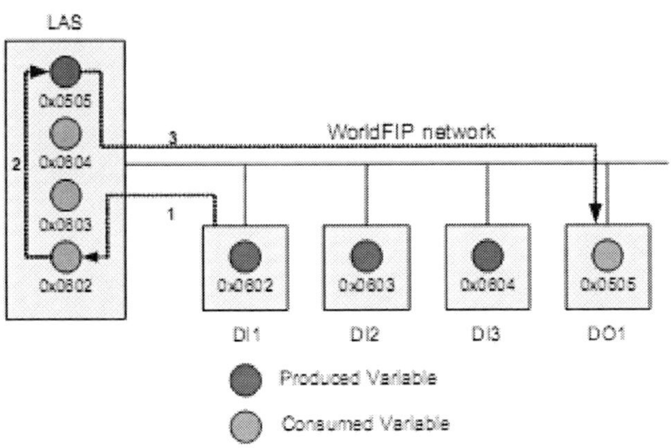

Figure 29. Process for data exchange in Pattern I .1. Variable exchange between inputting nodes and LAS. 2. Data transfer within LAS. 3. Variable exchange between LAS and outputting node.

Application 2: On Design of Process Control System Based on WorldFIP Network

Similarly, the research results can also be used in design of process control system based on WorldFIP network, where most process data generated by control loops are transmitted cyclically with periodic communications. In that case, the user data in periodic traffic in a macrocycle are usually much more than that in Application 1. According to Figure 15~18 , Equation (19) and (21), i.e.

$$\begin{cases} \lambda_{\text{var}} > \lambda_{msg}, \text{n} < 4 \\ \lambda_{\text{var}} = \lambda_{msg}, \text{n} = 4 \\ \lambda_{\text{var}} < \lambda_{msg}, \text{n} > 4 \end{cases}$$

and

$$\begin{cases} \lambda_{\text{var}} > \lambda_{msg}, \sum_{a=1}^{m} n_{ij} < 4 \\ \lambda_{\text{var}} = \lambda_{msg}, \sum_{a=1}^{m} n_{ij} = 4 \\ \lambda_{\text{var}} < \lambda_{msg}, \sum_{a=1}^{m} n_{ij} > 4 \end{cases}$$

Generally, the following condition is met when process control system based on WorldFIP network, instead of digital or logic control system, is concerned.

$$\text{n} >> 4 \text{ or } \sum_{a=1}^{m} n_{ij} >> 4$$

As a result, Pattern II is more favourite to help achieve higher real-time performance in related process control system, according to our research results. Especially, the improvement in communication efficiency is remarkable when the user data traffic in a macrocycle is less than 2000 bytes. The effect became less remarkable when the traffic is more than that figure.

Besides, the research results are also helpful in improving efficiency of existing system by deciding some user-controllable parameters under the circumstance that the communication pattern has been set.

Considering the following case:

Assume that N field intelligent nodes are included in an existing process control system based on WorldFIP network with communication Pattern I , and the pattern need to be reserved for further use. Actually, the user data exchanged among peer nodes are process data in form of float numbers with size of two bytes. Therefore, the efficiency of traffic over the network can be simplified as the case of a single data exchange if we set the size of user data in data frames to be less than four bytes universally. According to Figure 15,16 and Equation (19), it is know that any available bus speed can be adopted in concerned system with improved network communication efficiency. That is, size of user data n in concerned frames used for network communication must be deliberately designed to conform to the requirement

$$n < 4$$

if use of Pattern I is mandatory on some specific occasions. That can help meet the pattern reservation requirements and improve efficiency without any de-functioning of the existing control system.

CONCLUSIONS

In this chapter, we studied two Data Link Layer transmission services in WorldFIP network, and present analysis and comparison of the bus communication performance in both services in terms of some important parameters, such as the numbers of bit in user data and network speed. Some important conclusions, which are qualitative or quantitative, are presented as follows:

1)In both patterns, value of n or $\sum_{a=1}^{m} n_{ij}$, which indicates the number of bytes in user data, has significant effects on communication performance of

WorldFIP network when it is relatively small (n<500 or $\sum_{a=1}^{m} n_{ij}$ <500). Such effects decreased when n increases.

2)In both patterns, bus communication efficiency λ is in direct proportion to bus speed β to great extent while robustness of λ is in inverse proportion to N_{tr} and β.

3)In both patterns, bus communication efficiency λ is in inverse proportion to turn-around time. Both network reliability and efficiency should be considered simultaneously and a balance should be made when turn-around time is chosen. Network reliability can be achieved by taking longer turn-around time while efficiency can be improved with its shorter value.

4)In the case of a single or multi data exchange, bus communication efficiency in Pattern Ⅱ is higher than Pattern I when the total bytes of user data n>4. Bus communication efficiency increases significantly with n increasing.

Opportunities for future work include the analysis and comparison of bus communication efficiency in the case that more than one node works as data receiver over the network when the proposed Pattern I applied. In that case, at least two nodes can receive the data sent by the source node by means of variable exchange simultaneously, and it would be interesting to know whether it is more efficient to use Pattern I in data transmission. Some quantitative analyses could also be carried out. Other topics under investigation include extensions of this work to the design and development of some software, which can be used to help engineers and researchers analyze and optimize protocols and systems in the future.

References

[1] *WorldFIP Protocol*, Version 2, 1998.

[2] Guo Zhenxue, Features and Applications of WorldFIP fieldbus, *Automation and Instrumentation*,(4):53-55, 2005.

[3] L.Alameida, E. Tovar, Schedulability analysis of real-time traffic in WorldFIP: an integrated approach, *IEEE Trans on Industry Electronics,* 49(5):1165-1174, 2002.

[4] Wang Zhi, Song Ye-Qiong, Yu Hai-Bin, Sun Youxian. Worst-case response time of aperiodc message in WorldFIP and its improvement in real-time capability. *ISA Transactions*, v 43, n 4, 623-637, 2004.

[5] Chen Jiming, Wang Zhi. Performance compare with aperiodic messages schedule of WorldFIP and FF, *Chinese of Scientific Instrument*, 386-390, 26(4), 2005.

[6] Chen Jiming, Wang Zhi, Sun Youxian. A basic study on algorithm of real-time schedule table for fieldbus, *Proceedings of the World Congress on Intelligent Control and Automation (WCICA),* v 3, 1760-1763, 2002.

[7] Wang Tianran, Zhou Yue. Analysis and Heuristic Scheduling for Real-time Communication in FF System, *Chinese Journal of Scientific Instrument,* 21(1):1-6, 2003

[8] Chen Jiming, Wang Zhi. Study on schedule problem of aperiodic message traffic in foundation fieldbus, *Joural of Zhejiang University*, 37(3):273-278, 2003.

[9] Geng Liang. A kind of implementation model based on generalized FBD for distributed intelligent control network, Chinese Control and Decision Conference, *CCDC 2008*, 411-414, 2008.

[10] Geng Liang. A kind of function block application model for distributed intelligent control network based on WorldFIP, Chinese Control and Decision Conference, 2008, *CCDC 2008*, 1400-1404, 2008.

[11] Geng Liang, Guotian Yang. A kind of communication simulation system for worldFIP field intelligent control network, *Proceedings of 2009 International Asia Conference on Informatics in Control, Automation, and Robotics,* CAR 2009, 385-389, 2009.

[12] Y. Pang, SH Yang, Nishitani, Hirokazu. Analysis of control interval for foundation fieldbus-based control systems, *ISA Transactions*, v 45, n 3, 447-458, July 2006.

[13] Zhou Yue, Wu Qi, Yang Shaowen. Model and analysis of WorldFIP MAC sub-layer based on DSPN, *Journal of Shenyang Jianzhu University (Natural Science),* v 23, n 3, 518-521, May 2007.

[14] Eduardo André Mossin, Rodrigo Palucci Pantoni, Dennis Brandão. A fieldbus simulator for training purposes. *ISA Transactions*, v 48, n 1, 132-141, January 2009.

[15] Zhai, Weixiang, Bai, Yan, Gao, Feng. Development of intelligent WorldFIP master, *Electric Power Automation Equipment*, v 29, n 2, 121-124+152, 2009.

[16] Shi John Z, Gu Fengshou, Goulding Peter, Ball Andrew. Integration of multiple platforms for real-time remote model-based condition monitoring, *Computers in Industry*, v 58, n 6, 531-538, 2007.

[17] Benzi, Francesco. Communication architectures for electrical drives, *IEEE Transactions on Industrial Informatics*, v 1, n 1, 47-53, February 2005.

[18] www.worldfip.org.

[19] ALSTOM. *FULLFIP2 User Reference Manual* (ALS 50262 d-en),Paris, France, 2000.

[20] ALSTOM. *MICROFIP User Reference Manual* (ALS 50280 d-en), Paris, France, 2001.

[21] Aibing Zhang. Development of Interface Card for WorldFIP fieldbus, *Msc. Dissertation, North China Electric Power University*, Beijing, China, 2003.

[22] Geng Liang, Research and Development of Strategy Configuration Software Package for Distributed Intelligent Sytem Based on IEC61131-3, *Ph.D. Dissertation, North China Electric Power University*, Beijing, China, 2005.

[23] www.worldfip.org.

[24] Alstom. *MICROFIP Manual Reference*,2001.

In: Network Protocols
Editor: Geng Liang
ISBN 978-1-61470-821-6

Chapter 4

NETWORK PROTOCOL SIMULATION FOR A FIELDBUS NETWORK: DESIGN AND IMPLEMENTATION

***Geng Liang*[1] *and Wen Li*[2]**
[1]School of Control and Computer Engineering, North China Electric Power University, Beijing, China
[2]Beijing GUODIANZHISHEN Control Technology Co. Ltd, Beijing, China

ABSTRACT

Simulation of communication system in controlnetwork plays important role in modern industrial productionand can be used in various application. Based on developmentof WorldFIP field intelligent control network, a kind ofcommunication simulation system was designed andimplemented. Simulation principle and implementationmethods for data communication in the network werepresented. Design and implementation for simulation ofnetwork scheduler, intelligent nodes and WorldFIP networkcommunication based on OOP and multi-thread methods werepresented in detail. Visual and multi-layered HMI for thesimulation system was designed. Techniques in OOP were fullyused in design with VC.NET as principle programminglanguage. Complete simulation of WorldFIP communicationnetwork and field intelligent nodes was implemented.Operational practice showed the simulation system was stablein operation, good in flexibility and portability, which showedgood practicability.

1. INTRODUCTION

Communication system simulation plays important roles in modern science research and industry and can be used in fault diagnosis in communication system, improvement of communication schedule algorithms and efficiency in communication, teaching and training. In recent years, fieldbus technology, distributed intelligent network are used widely in process control. WorldFIP is one of the international norms for fieldbus and is process-control oriented. WorldFIP fieldbus is unique with its dual-busarchitecture, which is very meaningful in ensuring communication reliability in process control application, and widely used in distributed intelligent control network. Based on development of field intelligent control network based on WorldFIP, a kind of communication simulation system was designed and implemented. Simulation principle and implementation methods for data communication in the control network were introduced. Design and implementation in simulation of network scheduler and intelligent nodes based on OOP and multithread methods were presented in detail. VC.NET was used as programming language. Techniques in OOP were used in programming. Complete simulation of WorldFIP communication network and field intelligent nodes was implemented. Operational practice showed the simulation system is stable in operation, good in flexibility and portability, which showed good practicability.

2. SIMULATION PRINCIPLE AND SCHEME DESIGN FOR DATA COMMUNICATION IN WORLDFIP FIELD INTELLIGENT CONTROL NETWORK

WorldFIP protocol is a model and platform to implement network communication and data transmission. Physical layer, data linkage layer and application layer in ISO/OSI 7-layer reference model are adopted in reference model for WorldFIP fieldbus communication.Composition of WorldFIP communication protocol is shown in Figure 1.

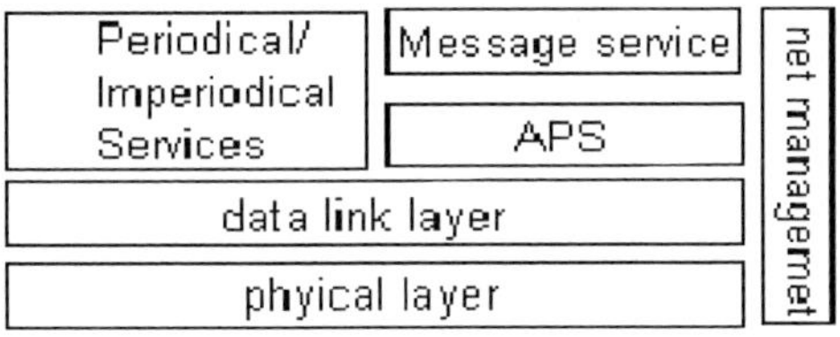

Figure 1. Composition of WorldFIP communication protocol.

WorldFIP communication is master-slave typed. The whole network is composed of bus schedulers which serves as master and field intelligent nodes which are subordinate. Value exchange between periodical and non-periodical variables and messages exchange are scheduled with bus chedulers. Two types of data exchange are used in network: data exchanges based on variable exchanges, which are usually used to transmit real-time and periodical data, and message exchange based on physically addressing. Detailed information can be referred to related reference. The following types of frames are used to exchange data over WorldFIP network.

The following is based on variables exchange:

ID_DAT: sent by bus scheduler and used to initialize avariable exchange process;

RP_DAT: sent by a field intelligent node and used to respond to ID_DAT to realize the data transmission based on variable exchange.

The following is based on message transmission:

ID_MSG: sent by bus scheduler and used to initialize a message transmission process;

RP_MSG: sent by a field intelligent node and used to respond to ID_MSG to realize the message transmission.

RP_MSG_ACK: sent by bus scheduler and used to acknowledge the data sent by field intelligent node; RP_FIN: sent by a field intelligent node and used to respond to RP_MSG_ACK to finalize a message transmission process. In the proposed model, RP_MSG_ACK is used to assure the reliable data transmission. Format of WorldFIP message frame is shown in Figure2.

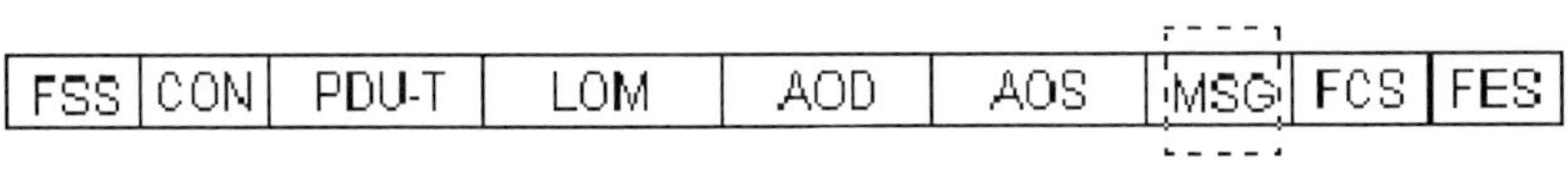

Figure 2. Format of WorldFIP message frame. FSS: frame starting series; CON: control. PDU_T: type of protocol data unit; LOM: length of message; AOD: address of destination; AOS: address of source; MSG: user's message; FCS: frame check series: FES: frame ending series.

In above frame format, all fields except "MSG" field are specified by WorldFIP protocol and have nothing to do with user layer in WorldFIP protocol. Therefore, "MSG" are theonly field users can control use freely. Although physical layer, data link layer and application layer in WorldFIP communication reference model are standard, it is noticeable that there is no concept of user layer in the reference model. Norm for user layer are not specified yet. No universal norm is specified for user's data wrapped by application layer. A kind of user layer model in WorldFIP communication protocol is proposed according to "MSG" field in Figure5 with process control as its application object. For those field intelligent nodes using WorldFIP FULLFIP2 chips in communication, the maximum length of message is 256 bytes; for those using MICROFIP chips, the maximum length of message is 128 bytes. In the proposed user layer model, user's data are divided into several subfields illustrated by Figure6, which relates closely to the data storage segmentation model in field intelligent nodes.

ID code	input index	data (float type)
1 byte	2 bytes	4 bytes

Figure 3. User layer model in WorldFIP communication protocol.

ID code: the field is set for system extension in future. Currently, ID code bears only 1 value that means "link operation" corresponding to the data transmission between FBs in different field intelligent nodes; Input_index: index for the input terminal in input segment of lower-reach FB in remote linkage between FBs in different field intelligent nodes. Data (float type): data wrapped in message. Control strategies specified by users through configuration are executed in field intelligent nodes. Data and instructions are downloaded from users' PC to field nodes over network link scheduler. A "passive" schedule algorithm is used, which is different from "active" schedule algorithm in local nodes. In this mode, only compel data (CD) are transmitted between bus scheduler and element intelligent nodes. The compel data can be defined as a constant instruction execution in element nodes is scheduled by bus scheduler. Current instruction pointed by instruction pointer is to be executed only after receipt of compel data from bus scheduler. Field element nodes wait until the next compel data are received after finishing executing current instruction. The data, which are not constant, transmitted between different field intelligent nodes are those needed by remote FBs in FBA. FBs are executed repeatedly. Each repetition is a macro cycle. Any instruction executions within field intelligent nodes are under full-time schedule in each macro cycle. The "passive" schedule algorithm based on compel data are described as followed: Bus scheduler sends compel data to field element intelligent nodes over network in periodical variable exchange form at certain time-tick specified by schedule table. Instructions are executed in the element nodes after the compel data are received. Detailed implementation is described as followed.

(1)production variables corresponding to each element node are established in bus scheduler before startup of the whole control system. For example, 0x0501 is a consuming variable in element node N1, 0x0502 is a consuming variable in element node N2. Then 2 production variables 0x0501 and 0x0502 corresponding to the 2 consuming variables are established in bus scheduler;

(2)CD are written into the production variables in bus scheduler;

(3)scheduling item dealing with variable exchange , which are {0x0501,ID_DAT}and {0x0502,ID_DAT} in this example, are added to bus schedule table. Thus, variable exchange can be implemented conforming to the time-tick specified by the schedule table over WorldFIP network, illustrating in Figure4. After the CD is received as a consuming variable by element node, current instruction pointed by a pointer in FB instruction segment are executed. The pointer is moved backwards to next instruction after the execution of current instruction.

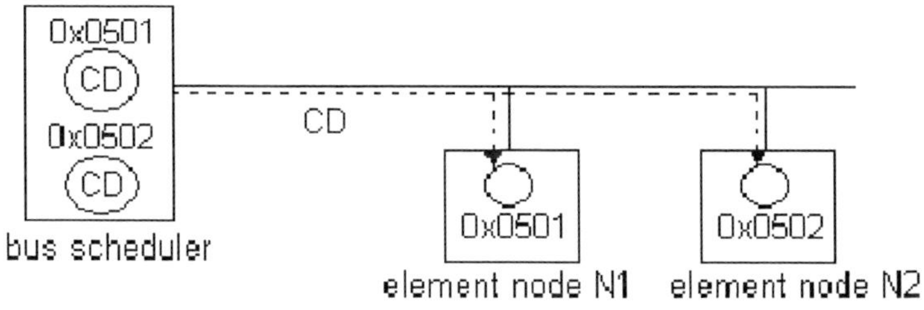

Figure 4. "Passive Schedule" based on compel data.

When MicroFIP chips are used in field intelligent nodes, data exchange can not be implemented between field intelligent nodes and can only be implemented by forwarding of bus scheduler, which make the communication less efficient. In the proposed model, periodical message exchanges between nodes are chosen to solve the problem. The data to be transmitted are wrapped in a message frame based on the above mentioned "data model in user layer ", which ensures direct data exchange between element nodes and real-time in communication. Application example: one of the outputs in function block A in node 1 (with consumption variable 0x0501, production variable 0x0601) is connected with one of the inputs in function block B in node 2(with consumption variable 0x0502, production variable 0x0602). The data transmission with periodical variables and periodical messages exchange is executed as follows:

(1)Periodical variables and periodical messages exchange is executed over network: compel data (CD) in production variable 0x0501 in scheduler is sent to consumption variable in node 1. Compel data is received by node 1 and the current instruction in node 1 is executed. The data is packed and ready to be sent if the current instruction is a "remote transmission" instruction;

(2)Frame (D_MSG , 0x0601) is sent by bus scheduler to initiate message transmission.

(3)Frame (D_MSG, 0x0601) is responded by node 1 for 0x0601 is a production variable in node 1: the packed data is sent to network in form of frame （RP_MSG, 2, 1）,in which 2 is for destination address and 1 is for source address.

(4)Frame （RP_MSG, 2, 1） is received by node 2 and data is retrieved from the frame and put into the address specified by the data in the frame. Above process execution is scheduled. The related schedule item {0x0601, ID_MSG } should be added into the bus schedule table.

3. Design and Implementation of the Simulation System

The following problems are to be solved in the design of the simulation system:

(1)network nods exists simultaneously. A proper method should be chosen to simulate the condition.

(2)No real physical devices, such as bus scheduler and node devices, exist in simulation environment. These objects should be simulated by software properly.

(3)Data and information transmitted over network are visible to all devices in a real system. The condition and property should be simulated by software with a suitable method.

Base on the above analysis, the following simulation scheme are designed and implemented to solve the problems.

(1)Multi-thread technology is used to solve problem No.1;

(2)several multi-threads are used to simulate network nodes and a special thread is used to simulate the bus scheduler.

(4)Message mechanism between different threads are used to solve the problem No.3.

Design is implemented with VC.NET. A sub-class derived from base class CWinThread is defined to simulate data and instruction storage in network nodes.

class CDeviceThread : public CwinThread

```
{
......
    BYTE m_device_addr; //4 arrays  :
    CArray<COMMAND_FOR_DEVICE,COMMAND_FO R_DEVICE> m_command_array; // to
simulate instruction storage
    CArray<float,float> m_inputparam_array; // to simulate input data storage
    CArray<float,float> m_outputparam_array;// to simulate output data storage
    CArray<BYTE,BYTE> m_containedparam_array;// to simulate contained data storage
    3 mappings are defined to indicate the addresses for instruction and data in network nodes.
    CMap<BYTE,BYTE,WORD,WORD> m_map_sectionNoToInputparamStartIndex;//to simulate
    mapping between segment number and the starting index for input parameters in the segment.
    CMap<BYTE,BYTE,WORD,WORD> m_map_sectionNoToOutputparamStartIndex;// to simulate
    mapping between segment number and the starting index for output parameters in the segment.
    CMap<BYTE,BYTE,WORD,WORD> m_map_sectionNoToContainedparamStartByteNums; // to
    simulate mapping between segment number and the starting index for contained parameters in the
    segment.
    //defining the index for the current instruction
    WORD m_current_command_index;
    BYTE m_current_section;
    BYTE m_section_array_upperbound; //defining production variables and consumption variables:
    CMap<WORD,WORD,BYTE,BYTE>                    m_map_ProduceVarIDToValue;
    CMap<WORD,WORD,BYTE,BYTE> m_map_ConsumeVarIDToValue;
    A device thread array, in which bus scheduler is included, is defined to simulate the information
    broadcasting over network:
    CArray<CWinThread*,CWinThread*>* m_ptr_DeviceThreadPtrArray;
    Several structures and variables are defined to simulate the buffers in nodes, in which the messages to
    be sent are stored (e.g. to simulate the BUFFER in MIRCROFIP chip )
    MSG_PACKAGE m_msg_package;
    WORD m_ConsumeVarID_receive_RP_DAT;
public:
    void Execute_Command(WORD var_id);
```

```
.......
A group of message responding function are defined in CdeviceThread to simulate the response to various
frame over network by different nodes:
protected:
LRESULT OnWM_ID_DAT(WPARAM
wparam,LPARAM lparam);
LRESULT OnWM_ID_MSG(WPARAM
wparam,LPARAM lparam);//response to frame
ID_MSG
LRESULT OnWM_RP_DAT(WPARAM
wparam,LPARAM lparam);// response to frame
RP_DAT
LRESULT OnWM_RP_MSG(WPARAM
wparam,LPARAM lparam);// response to frame
RP_MSG
.......
}
Class CpciThread derived from CDeviceThread is defined to simulate bus scheduler:
class CPciThread : public CDeviceThread
{
......
bool m_bRunning;
DWORD m_current_scheduleTime_us;
CArray<PTR_LISTS,PTR_LISTS>*
m_p_PtrListArray;
CArray<PTR_INSTRUCTIONS,PTR_INSTRUCTIONS
>* m_p_PtrInstructionsArray;
// Operations
public:
void wait_to(DWORD time_offset);
void wait(BYTE session_type);
void Execute_session(BYTE
session_type,WORD var_id);
void schedule();
LRESULT OnWM_PCI_START(WPARAM
wparam,LPARAM lparam);
.....
};
```

As multi-thread technology is used in the simulation, resource allocation between different threads is a necessary. In this design, critical section is used to solve the problem.

4. Design of HMI in the Simulation System

The principal HMI includes three parts: network topology sub-window, communication record subwindow and device information sub-window.

4.1. Network Topology Display

Bus topology and the operational status of the simulated field devices are showed in network topology sub-window as illustrated in Figure5. bus interface devices is located in the upper-left part of the window. Symbols for all field devices are organized in form of bus units. Up to 254 symbols for devices can be shown in a bus unit and up to 10 buses can be shown in the window. VFD name for each device is shown below the symbol. symbols for field devices are managed by device threads. When simulation is started, symbols for field devices are colored differently according to type of the current instruction executed by field devices including function block instruction, link instruction and segment ending instruction, which is manipulated by the device threads and can give user clear and visual effects of system operation.

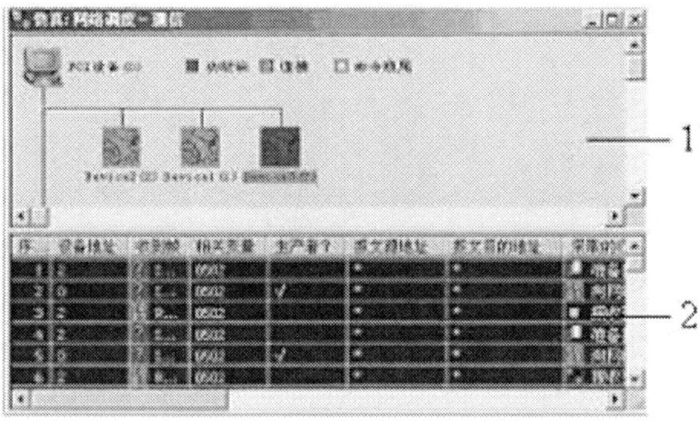

Figure 5. Network topology child window and communication record child window. 1.child window for network topology display. 2.child window for communication recording display

4.2. Network Communication Recording and Display

Information about network data communication are shown in the sub-window, including:

1)Device address: indicating the device which received the data frame;
2)Frames received by nodes: including types of ID_DAT、RP_DAT、ID_MSG、RP_MSG;
3)related variables: variables contained in the frames received by nodes;
4)source address for received messages
5)destination address for received messages
6)opration: operation node devices take after receiving different types of frame;

In simulation, content of each above mentioned field in frames received by nodes are shown in the subwindow. Visual illustration is used when "frame"and "operation" are shown in the sub-window.

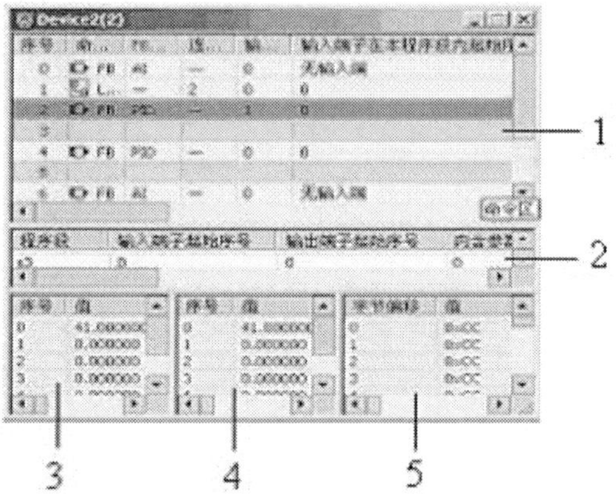

Figure 6. Network communication recording and devices information child window. 1.instruction area (dynamic display). 2.segment index. 3.input data area. 4.output data area. 5.parameters area.

4.3. Devices Information Display

Devices information sub-window corresponding to a devices shows when symbol for the device in device

topology sub-window is double-clicked as Figure6. The whole window includes following parts:

1)instruction area: showing the data in the instruction area of the specified device , including the following fields:
   instruction type: function block instruction or link instruction;
   function block type: such as PID;
   address for the destination devices: If the instruction is a link type, the field indicates the address for the destination devices which is linked by a link instruction.
   starting index for the output data in current segment;
   starting index for the input data in current segment;

2)input data area
3)output data area

In simulation, the instruction currently executed is high lighted with red color to improve the visualization effects.

4.4. Simulation Tools

Simulation tools are designed for users to operate simulation, such as start, pause and stop etc. the tools are integrated in a simulation toolbars as shown in Figure7.

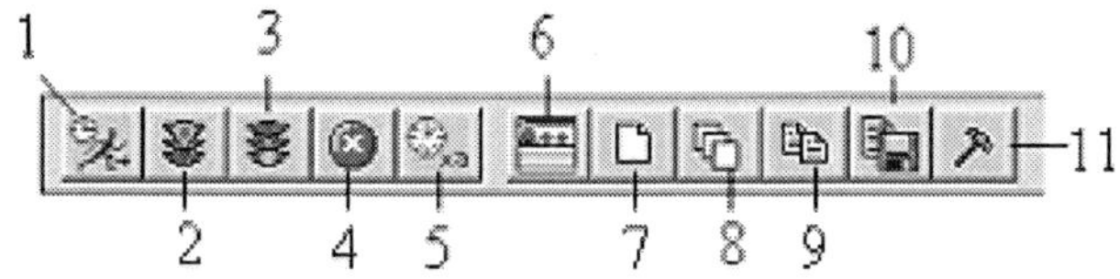

Figure 7. simulation tools. 1. start simulation. 2. pause simulation. 3. resume simulation. 4. stop simulation. 5. configration of simulation step. 6. toggle simulation window. 7. clear communication records. 8. select all communication records. 9. copy communication records. 10. save communication records. 11. simulation options.

CONCLUSION

System simulation and visualization OOP technology are combined and a kind of communication simulation system orienting the WorldFIP intelligent control network is designed and implemented by taking full advantage of OOP based on Windows operating system and VC.NET platform. Design and implementation for simulation based on OOP and multi-thread programming are presented. Simulation of data storage in nodes and information exchange over network are implemented completely. Visual and multi-layered HMI for the simulation system is designed. The developed simulation system has been used in the optimization of schedule algorithm for WorldFIP field intelligent control network and training of personnel. Practice showed that the system is stable and reliable in operation, good in flexibility and portability. HMI is highly user-friendly.

REFERENCES

[1] LIANG Geng, BAI Yan, LI Wen, The Simulation Research of FCS Upper-level Supervision and Control System for Ball Miller Control in Power Plant, *Acta Simulata Systematica Sinica*, 16(4):720- 723,2004.

[2] BAI Yan; LIANG Geng (communication author), Design And Implementation Of Control Strategy Configuration Software For Worldfip Fieldbus Control System, *Proceedings of the CSEE*, 24(2):150-156,2005.

[3] Liang Geng, Bai Yan, Li Wen, Development of Scheme Configuration Software for WorldFIP FCS Based on Object Model, *Chinese Journal of Scientific Instrument,* 26(12):1293-1297 ,2005.

[4] Diedrich, Christian, Function block applications in control systems based on IEC 61804, *ISA Transactions*, vol.43, no.1, 123-131, 2004.

[5] Neumann, Habil P, "Free configurable function block application software in distributed control systems", *IEEE International Symposium on Industrial Electronics,* Vol.1, No.1, 293-298,1996.

[6] Tang Mingbao, *Xuejiaquan,Design of Fieldbus Control Simulation System,Programmable controller and Factory Automation(PLC and FA),(*11),44-46,2007.

[7] Yuan Mingzhe, *Design of Fieldbus Control Simulation System*, 2004, (2): 49-53.

[8] Yo Funaki1 Virtual test function for control application, *ISA EXPRO/* 1999 , 11-15.

[9] Nan Ye , Sairam Valluri , Mitch Barker , Po2Yang Yu1 Integration of advanced process control and full2scale dynamic simulation , *ISA EXPRO/* 1999 : 5-7.

[10] Deltef Bauerle and Wolfgang Popp1 Simulation of communication system in industrial area , *Proceedings of the Fieldbus Conference FeT'99*,1999: 23-24.

[11] Liu Hui. Communication simulation system and its application, *Communication World,* (16),42-43,2002.

[12] Shi Zhaoxiang, Research On Simulation Platform Of Communication Systems, *Computer Simulation*,30(3),43-45,2000

In: Network Protocols
Editor: Geng Liang
ISBN 978-1-61470-821-6

Chapter 5

CONTROL CONFIGURATION PLATFORM FOR FIELD INTELLIGENT CONTROL NETWORK: RESEARCH AND DESIGN

Geng Liang
School of Control and Computer Engineering, North China Electric Power University, Beijing, China

ABSTRACT

A Control Strategy Configuration Platform for field Intelligent control network is introduced and expounded in this chapter. The structure and composition of the configuration platform are expounded systematically and the configuration modes of the platform are discussed. The design and implementation methods for the objects model of the platform are given in detail. Design principle and compiling mode of compiler based on object-oriented approach (OOA) are expounded. Design of the configuration platform is standardized and the user interface is friendly. Users can program the control strategy in IEC61131-3 standard programming language efficiently and construct various algorithm and strategy orienting field intelligent control network with different scale flexibly to realize automation and intelligence for process control.

1. INTRODUCTION

WorldFIP is one of the international fieldbus standard and is a process control-oriented data bus. Real-time and random data can be transferred over WorldFIP fieldbus. WorldFIP fieldbus is a kind of real-time, predicable and future oriented bus which can connected with Internet.. The unique dual-bus redundancy structure provides powerful assurance of operational reliability. The field intelligent control network based on WorldFIP technology including WorldFIP bus network, intelligent instruments based on WorldFIP protocol and gateway connecting upper-level computers or Ethernet with field bus network. Control strategy configuration platform (abbreviated as CSCP for convenience) orienting field intelligent control network is the interface between the control network and users. The organization and implementation of field intelligent instruments and communication network, design and implementation of control strategy for the network are the core task of CSCP. Users can program algorithm for intelligent control network in GUI way effectively, construct and implement various control strategy orienting field control. The platform holds very important position in the whole system and is a indispensable part of it.[1-6]

2. ARCHITECTURE OF CSCP

Development of control strategy configuration platform (CSCP) is a complicated and systematic work. CSCP can be divided into 4 parts in design and implementation according to the function to be realized by CSCP in macro-scale:

(1) general framework of CSCP
(2) physical configuration subset
(3) logic configuration subset
(4) OPC client

The connection and organization of components of the platform, such as organization of user's interface and access of project files etc., are managed by general framework; the main content in physical configuration subset is configuration for field network in which "soft" configuration process dealing with control network such as selection of intelligent field instruments and control strategy function blocks is included; plan and design of control strategy used in operation of control network is the main content of logic configuration subset including selection, linkage, parameters setting, communication setting, system variable configuration etc. of function blocks in field intelligent instruments. Logic configuration is process of programming control strategy and is the core of the functions of CSCP; OPC client is responsible for the communication with OPC server which links to field control network interface to implement the download of configuration to the field instruments, serving as bridge between CSCP and field instruments.[8-9] The general framework of CSCP is shown in Figure1.

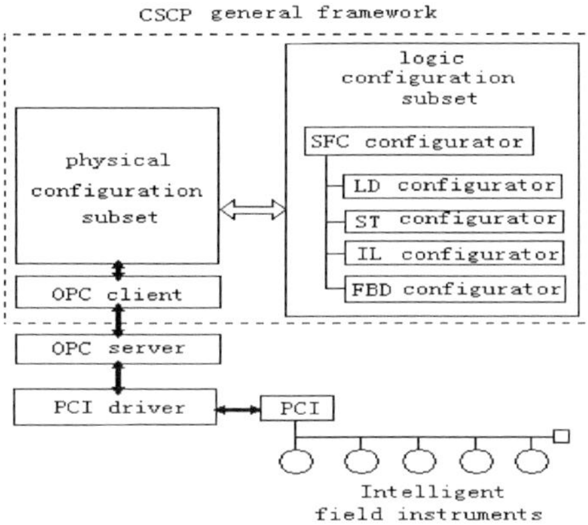

Figure 1. General Framework of CSCP and the Connection with Field Intelligent Control Network.

Logic configuration is the main part in the architecture. Different control sub-strategies are implemented by programming languages such as FBD,LD,IL,ST while SFC plays the role of organizer and acts in a upper level to coordinate the function programmed by other languages. Design and implementation of logic configuration subset mainly deals with configuration tools of 5 programming languages specified by IEC61131-3.

3. Configuration Mode of Logic Configuration Subset in CSCP

2 standard configuration modes of logic configuration subset in CSCP are realized: text mode and graphical mode.

Various algorithms are designed into a sequence of readable instructions or sentences conforming to certain format in text mode, which is very flexible and transparent and provides powerful programming means in implementation of control algorithm. IL and ST provide configuration means in text mode. Various algorithms are designed into a serial of graphical symbols in graphic mode. Users can select various control function blocks and link them together according to control logic. Users can also set parameters of various function blocks in this mode. It is very effective way for user to make configuration in this mode. FBD,LD and SFC provide configuration means in graphic mode.

4. Object Models in Logic Configuration Subset of CSCP

Main parts of object models in logic configuration subset of CSCP are graphic editor and algorithm compiler module.

5 different configuration tools are included in CSCP and have different object models respectively. 2 modeling methods are used in graphic configuration platform, i.e. function-oriented and object-oriented (OO) methods. OO is the most advanced modeling method in software design, in which the software system is treated as set of a serial of discrete objects. Data and operation are included in these objects. OO is general-purposed, clear in structure, flexible and reliable, easy to maintain and suitable for design of multi-function software. CSCP is designed based on OO modeling method. Different object classes are constructed according to different programming language elements used by different configuration tools to represent their different forms and achieve different function. Function Block Chart (FBD) configuration tool in logic configuration set is taken as an instance here to expound on the object models.

4.1. Object Models Constructed in FBD Configuration Tool

Object models in FBD configuration tool are constructed based on the language elements specified by IEC61131-3. Function block (FB) is the fundamental language element in FBD, in which user's configuration data and algorithm stored. The visualization of function block object can not be realized only with these data. Some important data is needed to meet the requirement of data storage and object visualization.

FB can be divided into 3 categories according to the function implemented by FB and way of representation:

- IEC standard FB: associated with various operation specified by IEC61131-3.[7] Graphic representation and inner implementation are all conformed to the specification
- Derived FB (DFB): defined by users. A complicated algorithm programmed with different languages can be encapsulated in a FB. DFB is associated with user-defined control algorithm. The implementation and representation of DFB are clearly specified by IEC61131-3.
- Control algorithm FB: associated with commonly used algorithm in process control such as PID etc. No concrete implementation and representation are specified.

The main differences between 3 types of FB are graphical representation way and associated algorithm. 3 types of FB differ only in associated algorithm if standard graphical representation is used for all of them. A union set including IEC standard algorithms and control algorithms can be acquired by expanding category definition. 3 types FB can be differentiated by choosing standard FB or derived FB and choosing standard algorithm or control algorithm from the union set, by which the design procedure is simplified. The following definition is used in the generation of the union set for FB algorithms in design of FBD configuration tool.

```
typedef enum FB_TYPE{
fb_derived,//whether or not a derived FB
fb_add,fb_sub,fb_mul,fb_div,fb_mod,fb_expt,fb_move,
fb_abs,fb_sqrt,fb_ln,fb_log,fb_exp,fb_sin,fb_cos,fb_tan,fb_asin,fb_acos,fb_atan,
fb_and,fb_or,fb_not,fb_xor,fb_shl,fb_shr,fb_rol,fb_ror,
fb_gt,fb_ge,fb_eq,fb_le,fb_lt,fb_ne,fb_sel,fb_max,fb_min,fb_limit,fb_mux,        fb_converter,
fb_sr,fb_rs,fb_sema,fb_r_trig,fb_f_trig, fb_tof,fb_ton,fb_tp, fb_ctu,fb_ctd,fb_ctud , //above are IEC standard
algorithms
fb_pid,fb_integral,fb_linear,fb_ramp,fb_input_selector,fb_signal_characterizer,fb_splitter,fb_timer//above   are
control algorithms
}
```

A class CFunction_Block is defined to realize the function of 3 types of FB:

```
class CFunction_Block
{
public:
    int input_num;// number of input
    int output_num;// number of output
    CRect outer_rect;//outer rectangle for FB
    CString caption;//name for FB
    int seq_no;// sequential Number for FB
    FB_TYPE m_fbtype;//type of FB
     bool m_bMultiInput;
     bool m_bSelected;
    ......//other properties and operations
    };
```

Derived FBs and standard FBs can be divided by assignment of the property "fb_derived" with different values with above FB object model.; IEC standard algorithms and control algorithms can be divided by assignment of the property "m_fbtype" with different values with above FB object model.

4.2. Compiler Module

4.2.1. Design Principle

The whole control strategy constructed by users with graphical editor in CSCP is compiled by compiler module and converted into data and code recognizable by field intelligent instruments to implement pre-configured control strategy.

Finite automaton theory and modality language are used in the procedure of data structure construction in compiler.[10] All connected symbols are scanned in sequence from a input terminal until a output terminal is reached, which makes a finite automaton procedure. The whole configuration chart can be processed by scanning all input terminals to output terminals in sequence, which makes a group of finite automatons. A finite automaton model in compilation procedure can be constructed easily for any control sub-strategy.

4.2.2. Compilation Mode

Control strategy configuration by users can be compiled into connections and relations between different FBs. The interpretation and execution are done by field intelligent instruments. Connection of different algorithms and data are implemented in upper-level computers running CSCP .Algorithms are implemented by field instruments by means of interpretation. It is very flexible in form and easy to transplant with this kind of compilation mode.

Compilation mode used in CSCP follows the following principle: 1) logic field instruments in physical configuration works as the organization unit 2) logic configuration mode "multi program segment" is adopted 3) clustering operation for the users-configured FBs owned by different field instruments is used by means of mapping table in the process of compilation to organize them into different logic field instruments. The compilation mode used in CSCP is shown in Figure2. Four types of data set are constructed in the logic field instruments configured in physical configuration, which are instrument instruction data, input data for instrument FBs, output data for instrument FBs, and contained-parameters for instrument FBs as shown in Fig2 as ①, ②, ③, ④.

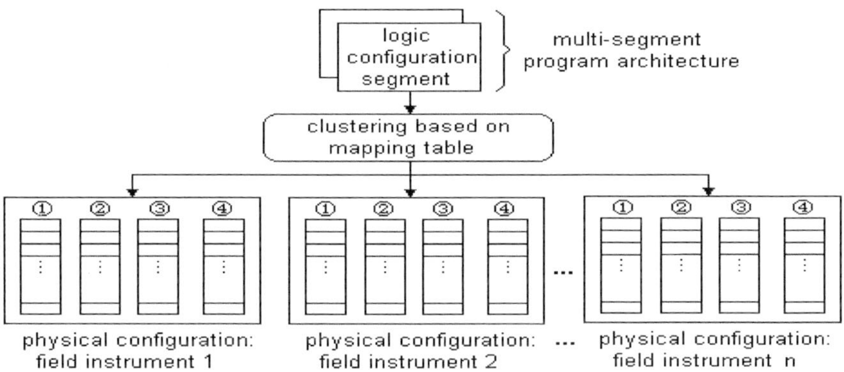

Figure 2. Compilation Mode of CSCP.

Implementation of instrument instruction data set in c++ language is given as following as an instance.

```
typedef struct FBINFO_FOR_DEVICE
{
    BYTE type_flag;// instruction type
    BYTE fb_type;// FB type;
    WORD in_param_start_index;
    WORD out_param_start_index;
    WORD contained_param_offset_bytes;
};
```

```
typedef struct    LINKINFO_FOR_DEVICE
{
    BYTE type_flag;
    WORD out_param_index;
    BYTE link_device_addr;
    WORD in_param_index;
};
typedef union COMMAND_FOR_DEVICE
{
FBINFO_FOR_DEVICE fbinfo_for_device;
LINKINFO_FOR_DEVICE    linkinfo_for_device;
};
```

The implementation of clustering operation is based on mapping table to achieve mapping relation between physical address in physical configuration and various data set in logic configuration, which converts logic configuration unit based on program segments into physical configuration unit based on "instrument". Implementation of mapping table is given as following in VC++ language.

1)Mapping table of physical address of field instrument to instruction array:
CMap<BYTE,BYTE,CArray<COMMAND_FOR_DEVICE,COMMAND_FOR_DEVICE>*,CArray<COMMAND_FOR_DEVICE,COMMAND_FOR_DEVICE>*> m_map_AddrToCommandArrayPtr;

2)Mapping table of physical address of field instrument to input data array
CMap<BYTE,BYTE,WORD*,WORD*>
map_AddrToInputParamNumtr;

3)Mapping table of physical address of field instrument to output data array
CMap<BYTE,BYTE,WORD*,WORD*>
m_map_AddrToOutputParamNumtr

4)Mapping table of physical address of field instrument to contained parameters: CMap<BYTE,BYTE,void*,void*>
m_map_AddrToCONTAINEDPARAMArrayPtr;

Logic configuration mode characterized by multi-segment in design of CSCP improves the flexibility and efficiency of users' programming of control strategy.

5. HUMAN MACHINE INTERFACE OF THE DESIGNED PLATFORM

The platform is designed with Windows 2000 and Visual C++ 6.0. The platform can implement the following functions specified by IEC61131-3:

1)Function Block Diagram (FBD) programming
2)Ladder Diagram (LD) programming
3)Structured Text (ST) programming
4)Instruction List (IL) programming
5)Sequence Function Chart (SFC) programming

The respective HMI for user programming is shown in Figure3-Figure 7.

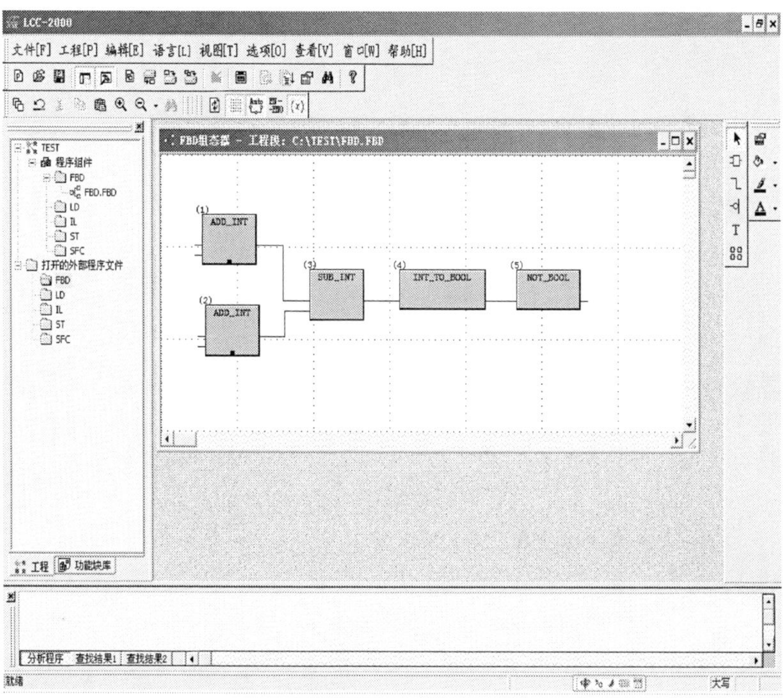

Figure 3. HMI for FBD programming.

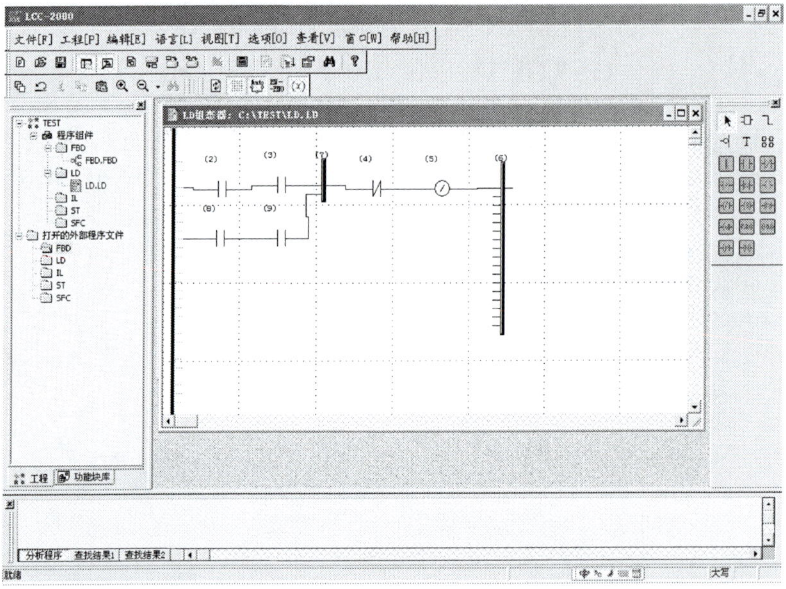

Figure 4. HMI for LD programming.

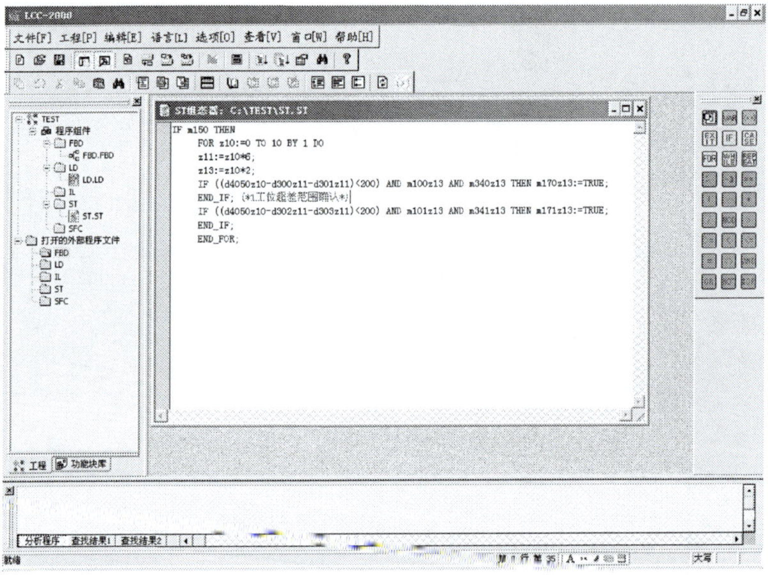

Figure 5. HMI for ST programming.

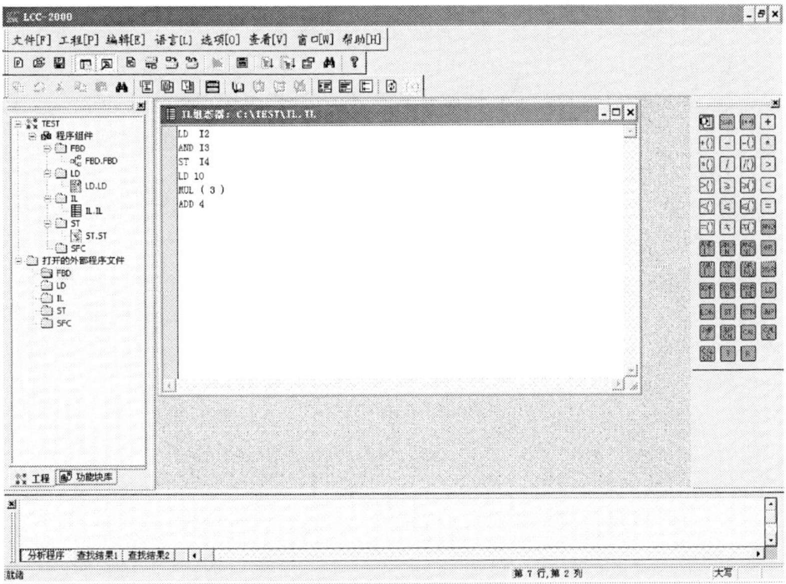

Figure 6. HMI for IL programming.

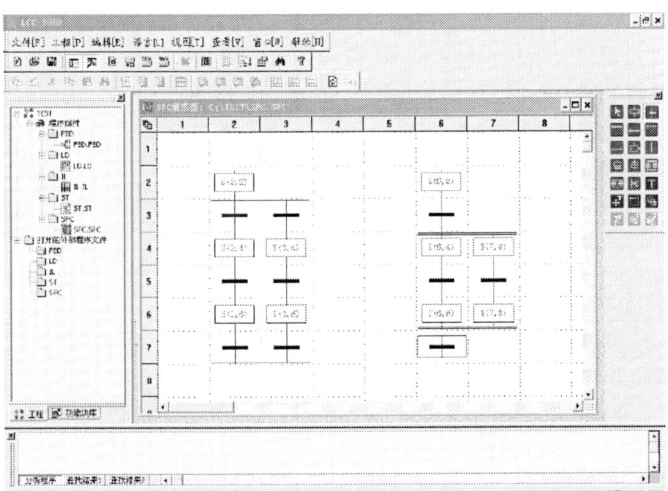

Figure 7. HMI for SFC programming.

Conclusion

Research and design of CSCP for field intelligent control network based on OOA are expounded above. Design environment is Windows 2000 and VC++. Designed CSCP conforms to standard. Human-machine interface (HMI) of it is highly friendly to provide users with quick and convenient means in configuration of intelligent control network. Users can program the control strategy in IEC61131-3 standard programming language efficiently and construct various algorithms and strategies orienting field intelligent control network with different scales to realize automation and intelligence for process control flexibly.

Reference

[1] Shi Xueling, WorldFTP Fieldbus Technology, *Industrial Control Computer*, No 2,2001.

[2] Li Wen, Design for the Converter of Analog to Fieldbus Based on WORLDFIP, *Instrumentation Technology*, No 1, 2005.

[3] Zhang Aibing, The Driver Development of an Interface Card Based on WorldFIP, *Industrial Control Computer*, No 2,2003.

[4] Zhang Aibing, Fieldbus Interface Card Based on WorldFIP, *Process Automation Instrumentation*, No 2,2004.

[5] Zhang Qizhi, The Development of Smart Pressure Transducer Based on WorldFIP Fieldbus Technology, *Sensor World*, No 3,2003.

[6] LI Hui yu , The application of WorldFIP bus in the intelligent modulized substation automatic systems, *Telecommunications For Electric Power System,* No 1,2002..

[7] Peng yu, The Status and Development of IEC61131-3, *World Instruments and Automation*, No 2,2002.

[8] Xue Fuzhen, Simulation Software of Control System Diagram Configuration Base on Elements, *Journal of System Simulation*, No 7, 2002.

[9] Liu Sixun, He Jiaxiang, Design and Implementaion of Control Algorithm Graphical Configuration Software, *Chinese Journal of Scientific Instrument*, No 2,1997.

[10] Lu Lingjie, Design of the configuration software based on direct graph spreading technology, *Journal of Daqing Petroleum Institute*, No 3, 2000.

In: Network Protocols
Editor: Geng Liang
ISBN 978-1-61470-821-6

Chapter 6

APPLICATION LAYER IN NETWORK PROTOCOL FOR DISTRIBUTED INTELLIGENT NETWORK: OBJECT DESCRIPTION METHODOLOGY WITH ITS IMPROVEMENT

Geng Liang[1] and Wen Li[2]
[1]School of Control and Computer Engineering, North China Electric Power University, Beijing, China
[2]Beijing GUODIANZHISHEN Control Technology Co. Ltd, Beijing, China

ABSTRACT

Object description (OD) and object dictionary construct the kernel parts of application layer of network protocol for distributed intelligent network with fieldbus as its paradigm. At present, objects dictionary and object descriptions used in fieldbus intelligent instruments are based on variable-sized storage and constant property values, which constrains the flexibility and portability in data access and modularization and encapsulation in system design. In this chapter, a kind of universal data structure for object description in OD was presented. Universal management of object description with different types could be realized with the proposed structure. Based on principle and methodology of Object-Oriented Design (OOD), an improved model for object description was proposed. In the improved model, constant value used in object code field of object description is replaced by function pointer pointing to object instance handler for data process of object instances belonging to the same class. Universal function structure is used for all class object instance handlers for different classes but instances belonging to different classes are manipulated differently with their own handlers. The improved model for OD and object description was proven effective and efficient by the practice of development and design of intelligent instruments in distributed control network.

1. INTRODUCTION

Object Description is widely used to specify the formats and meanings of various data in network application of fieldbus technologies, such as Foundation Fieldbus (FF), Profibus and CAN. It is integrated into Objects Dictionary (OD), which is an important part of Field Intelligent Devices (FID) and used to manage various objects in devices deployed over distributed control network. OD is a tool to secure and implement the openness, inter-operability and inter-changeability of fieldbus control systems. Essentially, OD can be viewed as grouped objects in pre-defined order, including objects on communication, function blocks, links and alarms. Each object in OD can be accessed with a primary index plus a sub-index and mapped into data types and values in memory [1-6].

Presently, widely used ODs are designed based on non-equal memory storage and constant property description. To some extent, it constrains flexibility and portability in data access, hampering the modularization and encapsulation in designs of control system based on fieldbus. Many researches have focused on application of object description and OD in distributed control system. Paper [7] presented a method instantiating function blocks based on OD in FF; paper [8] proposed implementation of inter-operability for FF based on OD; paper [9] analyzed the principles in implementation of list of "link" objects; paper [10-12] proposed an approach to implement Device Description (DD) by means of XML. In this chapter, we studied an improved universal data structure for object description in OD. Universal management of object description with different types could be realized with the proposed structure. Based on principle and methodology of Object-Oriented Design (OOD), an improved model for object description was also proposed. Clear boundaries can be built between modules to ensure substantial modularization of system design with the proposed methodologies, which facilitates the modularization in system design.

2. General Description of Object Dictionary

Object dictionary contains the description of the parameters as well as a pointer to the local instance of the parameter.

All parameters of a FB that should be visible from the network must have an entry in the OD

Every object description contains:

- an index,
- an object code, (is the identifier of the object and indicates which class this object belongs to)
- further object attributes, (object specific)
- system specific reference to the real object
- a name (if needed)
- an extension (if needed) (application specific) (contains length information for the extension and optionally further object attributes. The value 0 for the length means: no further object attributes)

Object is addressed by the index and identified by the object description. The data used in user layer is partly represented as a index in OD. The data related to OD is parsed by Fieldbus Message Specification (FMS) layer in application layer.

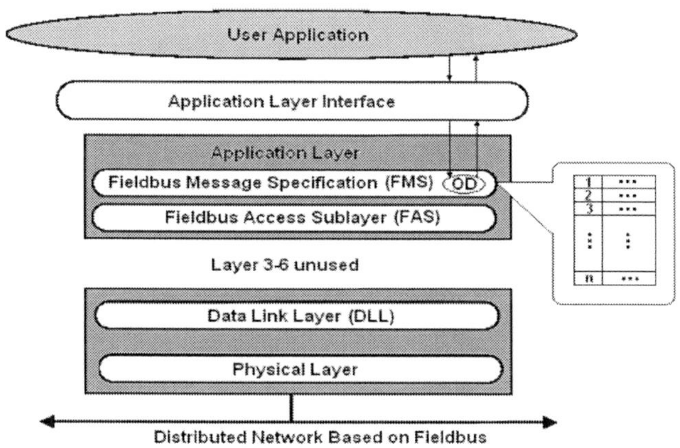

Figure 1. location of OD in communication stack.

The location of OD in communication stack and its use by client and server over network is shown in Figure 1 and Figure 2.

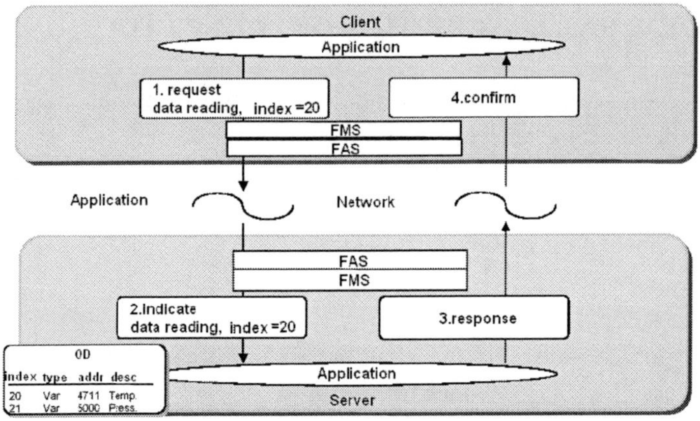

Figure 2. use of OD by client and server over network.

3. Data Formats of OD and Objects Description

Structure of OD used in industrial fieldbus can be summarized into several components as follows:

1)Data Types: ST-OD
2)S-OD Static Objects: S-OD
3)Dynamic Objects: D-OD

To improve the efficiency in objects access, arrays are used to implement the static parts of OD and chained lists, with which objects can be dynamically created or deleted to make the management of objects convenient, are used for dynamic parts. The entire OD can be viewed as a collection of indexes to objects stored in Network Management Information Library (NMIL). Accesses to visual objects over network are conducted via OD. The corresponding items, with information such as data type, access authority and physical address for the storage of the objects included, can be found with the logic index provided by access requester. Objects can be directly read or written with their physical address in memory.

4. Structures of OD for FF, CAN and Profibus

As far as the whole OD is concerned, the first item is the description of the whole OD, indicating the starting index and numbers of ST-OD, S-OD, DV-OD and The index for ST-OD is specified according to the standard, comprising objects description of data types and such as data structure, bit string, integral and float. Standard types of data are defined within index No.1 to 63. Data structures are defined from index No.64.

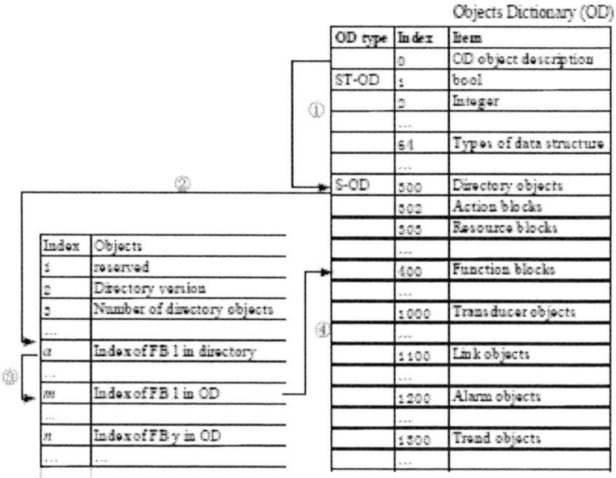

Figure 1. Structures of OD in FF field intelligent devices.

S-OD objects refers to those that cannot be created dynamically in the process of function block application. Simple variables, arrays, records, domains and events are all included and assigned a string-typed name The starting index of S-OD is greater than 256. The first item of S-OD is the object description for directory of function block objects. The detailed object description for each one in S-OD and DV-OD is placed in order with the starting index specified by manufacturers. D-OD is designed for the application objects generated during Application Process (AP), including variable lists and programs. OD and directory objects are used together in FF intelligent devices, as shown in Figure1. Structures of OD in Profibus are shown in Figure 2.

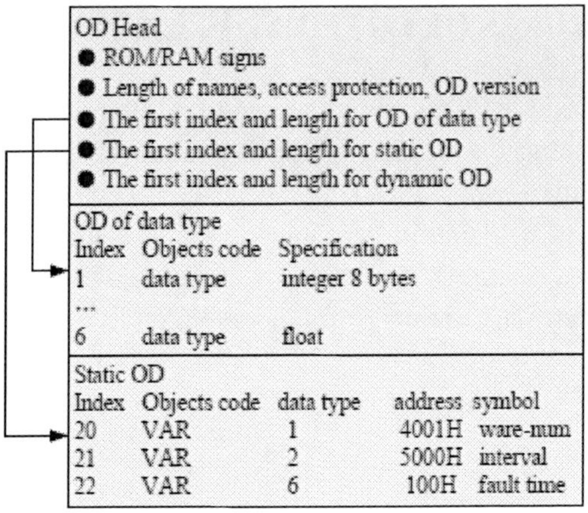

Figure 2. Structures of OD in Profibus field intelligent devices.

5. STRUCTURES OF OBJECT DESCRIPTION

Object descriptions are the fundamental elements in OD. Object descriptions for each object comprise the components: 1) Index 2) Object Code 3) Object data type 4) Object name (optional) 5) 16-bit address for inner use 6) Access authority 7) User-defined parts. Categories objects belong to are indicated by their object codes, including simple variable(VAR), arrays(ARRAY), records(RECORD) and variable lists (VAR_LIST) etc.. ARRAY is a collection of variables with the same data types while RECORD is that with different data types, which is corresponding to a data structure; VAR_LIST is collection of variables mentioned above with its object description including an index list for variables with types of VAR, ARRAY and RECORD. Data types of different objects, such as VAR and ARRAY, can be used to access instance data correctly. Data type of a RECORD-typed variable is not used in that case. The length and other properties of the extended parts are included in User-defined parts. It indicates that no other properties of the object is included by setting the "length" to 0.

A typical OD and object descriptions within are shown as Figure2. When addressing object description for a specific function block, the first index and length of static OD is found within OD Head with length-fixed addressing. Then, the detailed object descriptions corresponding to related variables can be found in the static OD by traversing. The starting part of S-OD in FF is directory object description pointing to directory object, in which the index and number of all the objects involved in an AP are included. The object descriptions of function blocks can be found by their names or indexes and the data can be found subsequently according to the information about address.

6. IMPROVING METHODOLOGIES FOR OD AND OBJECT DESCRIPTION BASED ON OBJECT-ORIENTED DESIGN

It is observed that there are two drawbacks in the structure of OD stated above as follows:

(1) Variable-length storage is used in OD for various objects. That is, the data structures described with their object descriptions are different. It is also the case as far as the memory used is concerned, e.g. the object descriptions with and without extended information. The extended information parts are quite different in terms of length and meaning since object descriptions for extended information have closely related to the specific information of their own. Consequently, it hampers the universal management of various objects. At most of the time, direct physical address has to be used to access concerned object description, which restricts flexibility and portability in data access.

(2) In each object description, constants are used to describe the two properties 1) object code 2) data type. However, there are many object codes and data types in object descriptions. Plenty of "switch" and "case" statements have to be used in the same program module, such as the main function, to analyze the real meaning of these properties. Therefore, the means to manage object descriptions in OD is never universal and simple enough, which obstructs the modularization and encapsulation of program and influences the flexibility in system's improvement, update and maintenance.

6.1. Improved OD Model Based on Universal Structure for Object Description

Aiming at the existing drawback 1) in currently used OD as stated above, we propose a universal structure for management of object descriptions, as shown in Figure 3.

Properties	Object Code	Data Type	Address	Name
Length	2 b	1 b	2 b	20 c

b: byte c: character

Figure 3. the proposed universal structure for management of object description.

Where, the meaning of each property involved is same with that of currently used OD. With the proposed universal structure, each object in OD can be managed in a universal way.

For example,

- As for the object descriptions in ST-OD, their object codes can be TYPE with data type, address and name setting to null at the same time;
- As for object descriptions for ARRAY in S-OD, their object codes can be ARRAY and data type can takes that of elements within with address and name setting to null;
- As for object descriptions for RECORD in S-OD, their object codes can be RECORD and address can takes the starting addresses of object instances with data type setting to null

Each object in OD can be represented with this structure. Thereby, OD is simplified as an array of objects with the proposed structure. Each element in OD can be addressed with subscript, which is equal to the currently used index in OD, and manipulated as array element, facilitating convenient implementation of various algorithm and programming.

6.2. Improved Model for Object Description Based on Class Pointers

Aiming at the existing drawback 2) in currently used OD as stated above, we propose an improved model for object description in OD by referring the concept and thought of Object-Oriented Design (OOD), where the constant object codes are replaced with handler function pointers. In the currently used OD model, indicates the categories the objects belong to are indicated by object codes and instances indicated by addresses. According to OOD, data can be divided into classes and objects. Classes represent the common properties while objects represent the individual properties. Different handling procedures are assigned to different objects. The same functions can be used to handle object instance belonging to the same classes. If the constant object codes are used to indicate the categories the objects belong to, the handling function modules identifying the code are required necessarily. Namely, cross-references occur among modules, which hampers the independence of modules and restricts the modularization of system software. Furthermore, that also impacts on flexibility of system in revision, update and integration.

Here we propose a solution to the problem mentioned above. That is using the pointers pointing to the handlers of classes, which the objects belong to, to replace the object code by filling the property "object code" with the pointer parameter of class handler, as shown in Figure 4.

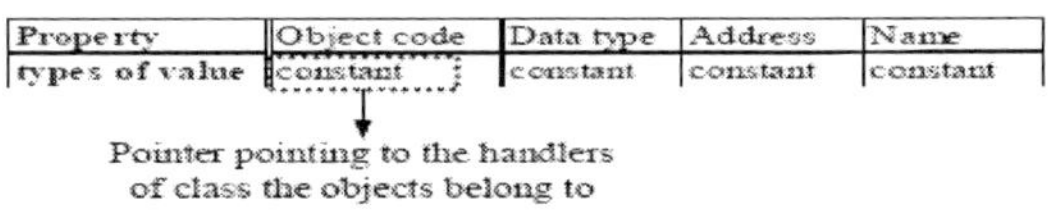

Figure 4. the improved model for object description based on pointers of class handlers.

The universal model can be applied to object descriptions in every section in OD, including ST-OD, S-OD and D-OD. Handlers of "data type" in ST-OD can handle basic types and structured data, such as integer, float and manufacturer-defined data structure; Handlers of "data type" in S-OD and D-OD can handle simple variables, arrays, records and programs. Input parameters for these handlers are the same. When the object codes are accessed by system, the handlers' pointers are access instead. Therefore, the procedure can jump into the corresponding handlers unconditionally, which realize the separation of instance reading modules and instance handling modules and build a clear boundary between modules. Objects belonging to the same categories are handled with the same handlers but different instance data. Developers need not care the design of data reading modules in revising or updating instance handlers. Reading and analysis of objects data are implemented completely in a separated module. Thus, independence of module design is realized.

The running process is described as follows:

(1) ① The index and length of the first item in static OD in the head of OD are found by means of fixed-length addressing, and then the head of S-OD is located;
(2) The object description of a certain function block can be found within the OD with the index provided by users; otherwise, the target

function block can be located by means of traversing within the whole OD with its name;

(3) The pointer of class handler is obtained by reading the first field in the object description, and data in the second and third field together with some parameters provide by users are taken as the input parameters of the class handler. Then, current procedure jumps into the class handler to deal with operations such as data reading and analyzing;

(4) If a basic data type needs to be analyzed in the class handler, the parameter "data type" input into the class handler is used to locate the index of the object description corresponding to the "data type". Then, the procedure can jump into the handler corresponding to the specified "data type" to deal with various operation.

All the class handlers in OD in the improved model adopt the same definition of function structure in C++ language as follows:

*void (*classhandler)(BYTE data_type, void*p_data, int subindex, BYTE opr_instruction, void*p_out);*

Where,

-- *data_type*: Indicating the data type of the object dealt with. This parameter is valid if the object is VAR, ARRAY. It is invalid if the object is record (RECORD) or variable list (VAR_LIST);

-- *p_data*: Indicating the pointer of class instance. This parameter can be obtained from the field "Address" in the object description dealt with;

-- *subindex*: Indicating the sub-index of a member in the object dealt with, and provided by user. It is no use if the object is a simple variable (VAR). Instead, it carries meaning when the object is an ARRAY, RECORD or VAR_LIST;

-- *opr_instruction*: Indicating the operational instruction for the object, such as reading and writing;

-- *p_out*: Indicating the pointer to buffer for data output. It is provided by users.

In practical use, a pointer variable needs to be defined at first and then used to manipulate the corresponding class handler. For example,

```
typedef void (*classhandler)(BYTE data_type, void*p_data, int subindex, BYTE opr_instruction, void*p_out);
classhandler datatype_classhandler;
datatype_classhandler (5,0x5000,0,0,&data);
```

CONCLUSIONS

Aiming at the two drawbacks in OD and object description in intelligent field devices based on fieldbus, we propose a universal structure and an improved model for object descriptions within OD based on Object-Oriented Design. Practice shows that the improvement effects that the durations of development, commissioning, maintenance and update are shortened remarkably with a little memory use increasing, demonstrating the improved model is better in adaptability, flexibility and encapsulation in modularization of system design if compared with the old one.

REFERENCES

[1] Foundation TM Specifications Function Block Application Process Part1 FF2890 FS114. *Fieldbus Foundation* , 1999.

[2] Foundation TM Specifications Function Block Application Process Part2 FF2891 FS114. *Fieldbus Foundation* , 1999.

[3] Foundation TM Specifications Fieldbus Message Specification FF2870 FS115. *Fieldbus Foundation* , 2001.

[4] Foundation TM Specifications System Architecture , FF2581FS111. *Fieldbus Foundation* , 2000.

[5] N.P.Mahlik. *Fieldbus Technology*, Springer-Verlag, Berlin, 2003.

[6] X.H. Yang. Fieldbus *Technology with Application* , Tsinghua University Press, Beijing, 1999.

[7] GX Chen, DQ Feng, J Chu. Principle and Realization of Instantiation of Foundation Fieldbus Function Block , *Process Automation Instrumentation*, 27(5): 1-4, 2006.

[8] ZJ Yang, Y Lin. Technical Means of Interoperable Foundation Fieldbus, *CONTROL and AUTOMATION*, 14(3):4-7,1998.

[9] CJ Liu, DQ Feng.HSE Analysis on the establishment of the link between objects in function block application process of foundation fieldbus based on high speed Ethernet, *Industrial Instrumentation and Automation,* (1):3-6,2005.

[10] Zhongfeng Wang; Haibin Yu. The research of XML-based extensible device description for FF fieldbus system; Industrial Electronics Society, 2004. *IECON 2004. 30th Annual Conference of IEEE*, Volume 3, 2-6 Nov. 2004 Page(s):2600 - 2603 Vol. 3

[11] J Liu, DQ Feng. The Device Description Technology Based XML, *Industrial Control Computer*, 16（11）:32-34,2003.

[12] K Zhao, YB Pang. Research on Interoperability of Fieldbus Equipment Based on XML, *Process Automation Instrumentation*,26（4）:10-13,2005.

In: Network Protocols
Editor: Geng Liang

ISBN 978-1-61470-821-6

Chapter 7

CONTROL PERFORMANCE IMPROVEMENT IN FIELDBUS AND ETHERNET BASED NCS: FOCUSING ON NETWORK AND COMMUNICATION DESIGN

***Geng Liang*[1]*, Wen Li*[2] *and Hong Wang*[3]**

[1]School of Control and Computer Engineering, North China Electric Power University, Beijing, China

[2]Beijing GUODIANZHISHEN Control Technology Co. Ltd, Beijing, China

[3]Control System Center, the University of Manchester, UK

ABSTRACT

Practical design and implementation of a network-based cascade control system with a real laboratory pilot plant involved using two different control approaches based on FF fieldbus and Ethernet respectively are presented in this chapter. In the proposed network control platform, FF fieldbus subsystem is combined with an industrial Ethernet based subsystem. Two different kinds of function block scheme fulfilling the cascade PID control by fieldbus intelligent instruments are presented, analyzed and compared. With the improved function block configuration scheme proposed in this chapter, shorter control cycle and thereby more efficient control can be achieved. As for the industrial Ethernet based subsystem, we also propose a new solution based on function block

MBCS provided by DFI302 combining fieldbus subsystem and PLC world closely in a simple but more flexible way. Effects on control by transmission time delay in fieldbus and Ethernet based subsystem are analyzed. No mismatch and asynchrony between taking real actions of control moves and generation of feedback exists in Fieldbus-based control scheme thanks to its cyclic FB scheduling. Degradation of steady state response can be mainly attributed to asynchrony of control moves and feedback under circumstance of continuous control as far as the Ethernet based control system is concerned. As one of the improvement measures for control effects in industrial Ethernet based networked control system, we propose a synchronization control methodology based on IEC61499 to control the execution of each function block in PLC controller with Events and some specific action control logics. Meanwhile, we propose an output estimation algorithm based on neural network to compensate for the transmission delay in feedback. In order to reduce network transmission delay itself by improving hardware and network architecture , we present three engineering-practical methods in detail. Control effects under the proposed methodologies are also given. Experimental and on-site practice show the effectiveness of the proposed methodologies in a networked control involving fieldbus and industrial Ethernet technologies.

NOMENCLATURE

ASIC	Application Specific Integrated Circuit
ERTEC	Enhanced Real-Time Ethernet Controller
EWS	Engineer Workstation
FB	Function Block
FF	Foundation Fieldbus
FFCS	Foundation Fieldbus Control System
HMI	Human Machine Interface
LAS	Link Activities Scheduler
MBCS	ModBus Control System
NCS	Networked control system
NNE	Neural Network Estimator
OPC	OLE for Process Control
OWS	Operator Workstation
PLC	Programmable Logic Controller
UDFB-CM	User Defined Function Block for Control Moves
UDFB-DA	User Defined Function Block for Data Acquisition

1. INTRODUCTION

The use of automatic electronic devices in the process control industry is nothing new. Since 1970s, automatic devices have been used first in process control, and then in distributed control system (DCS) or programmable logic controllers (PLC). The spread of microcontrollers' technology in the 90's enabled the development of smart field devices and field based measurement and control network,with requisites of real time systems. Figure 1 shows the basic architecture of a fieldbus network, composed of field devices, the fieldbus communication channel, the controller unit(s) and specialized engineering host stations.

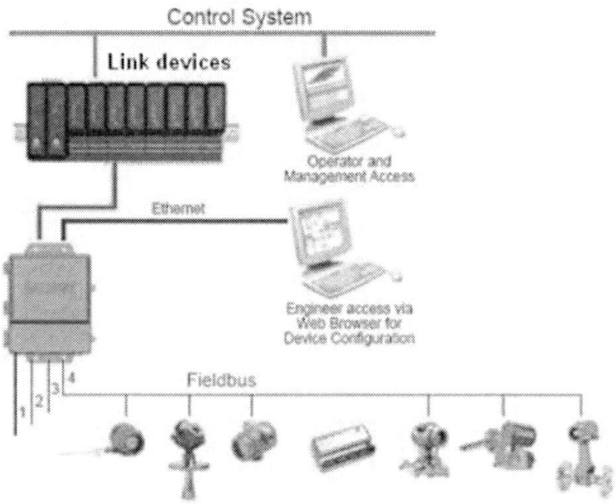

Figure 1. Basic fieldbus network architecture.

The great interest in this network model led several manufactures to implement their own communication protocols, to enable communication among their devices, and during the last two decades, some criteria were defined in order to standardize the communication model, and enable communication among different models of devices, developed by different manufacturers. There are several standard and widespread fieldbus protocols available in the market, such as CAN (Control Area Network), Interbus, DeviceNet, Hart, Modbus, AS-I (AS-Interface), Profibus and FOUNDATION Fieldbus. This article refers to the FOUNDATION Fieldbus (FF) protocol, one of the fieldbuses designed for typical industrial process control applications.

The combination of two or more protocols on integrated hybrid systems, as well as the use of such systems on process or equipment with fast dynamic responses, motivates the scientific community to evaluate the performance of networked control systems (NCS). Such studies result in advances and optimization of transmission media technologies, communication methods, new smart transmitters capabilities (sensors, controllers and actuators), as well as advanced industrial control strategies. Although being standardized, there are complex concepts and architectures behind these systems. At the same time, the development of communication network and technology has brought many remarkable changes to traditional control fashion in modern industries. IEC802.3 Ethernet and field based intelligent controls, which are combining communication and control technology closely, are playing an active role in modern industrial automation with greatly improved functions and performance but much reduced cost, offering more flexible and practical approaches to solve problems whose solutions were only be considered in theoretical ways in cybernetics before.

Fieldbus is the foundation of field-based intelligent control with its highly reliable, deterministic real-time performance in communication between field instruments such as transmitters and actuators. Self-diagnosis, easy maintenance and reduction in cost and commissioning time are also its remarkable advantages. Among the fieldbus technologies, Foundation Fieldbus (FF) is one of the most popular fieldbus widely used in industrial process control Two prominent features of FF lie in its Function Block (FB) scheme and cyclic scheduling strategy, enabling closed loop control and self-diagnosis be realized within field level and laying the foundation of entirely distributed control based on field.

As for IEC802.3 Ethernet, high speed in communication, good compatibility and large covered area are its main advantages. It is a quite suitable communication fashion for higher levels in industrial automation architecture. Ethernet was developed in the 1970s primarily for use as a local area network (LAN) technology for office environments. In 1985, Ethernet was established as a true international standard. Just recently, two developments in Ethernet technology emerged and these are Fast Ethernet and Gigabit Ethernet. Both reduce the realized throughput to less than 10, or 100 times that of 10 Mbit Ethernet. At present, some of the protocols being implemented over Ethernet include DECnet, Novell IPX, MAP, TOP, the OSI stack, AppleTalk, and TCP/IP. The same Ethernet IT uses to connect PCs to the enterprise and ultimately the Internet is emerging as another choice for fieldbus network. Ethernet, already wired into most manufacturing plants for information networking, is now used to connect controllers with remote I/O modules as a fieldbus.The lower cost of network cable, interface cards, network analysis tools and network management software are the major component of control system. The Ethernet based control system requires servers, networks, hubs, switches and other network connected devices. These are not multi drop network but are cascade star networks with distributed switches which is remotely queried and controlled. Figure 2 showed the architecture of Ethernet based control.

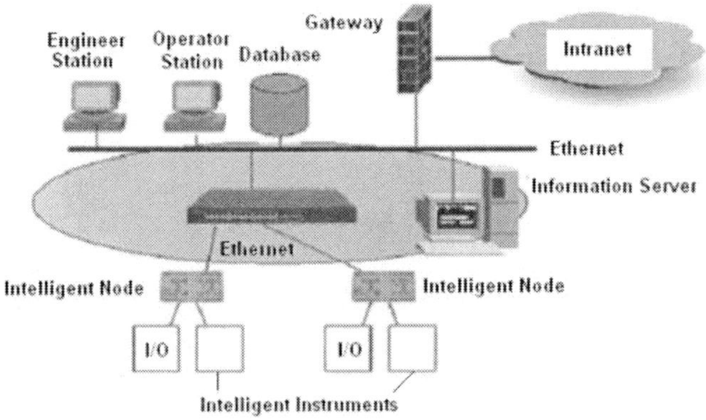

Figure 2. Architecture of Ethernet based control.

Networked control system (NCS) is mainly based on it, in which closed loop controls are implemented in upper-level controller while data acquisition and device actuation are distributed in field. Communicates between the two levels are mainly over IEC802.3 Ethernet. However, non-determinism and time delay in communication transmission often cause degradation in control effects. Many researchers have explored and investigated improvement methods in perspective of control science, such as studies on maximum allowable transmission for control and various controller' parameters tuning algorithms, etc. A. Fadaei proposed a new fuzzy PID control tuning methodologies based on IEC802.3 Ethernet networked PLC system.

In this chapter, two different designs and implementations for a traditional cascade control system based on FF and IEC802.3 Ethernet respectively were presented. Differences between them were analyzed. Advantages of system implementation by fieldbus were presented. Degradation in control effect of the networked control system caused by network transmission time delay was investigated. Improvement measures for control performance by reducing or compensating network transmission time delay in terms of network configuration and control algorithms were proposed. Experimental and on-site practice shows the proposed methodologies are effective in preventing performance degeneration in networked control system Based on FF Fieldbus and IEC802.3 Ethernet.

This chapter is organized as follows: In section 2, we introduced the general principles of control system implementation in FF fieldbus and IEC802.3 Ethernet fashion respectively. In section 3, we present two experimental control systems based on FF and IEC802.3 Ethernet. Detailed analysis on the performance degeneration caused by transmission delay and methodologies for improvement are presented in section 4. Some conclusions, which are useful in design of networked control system, are given in the last part of the chapter.

2. Foundation Fieldbus Protocol

FOUNDATION Fieldbus indicates the protocol specified by the Fieldbus Foundation. It is a digital, serial, bidirectional, and distributed protocol, which interconnects field devices such as sensors, actuators and controllers. Basically, this protocol can be classified as a LAN (Local Area Network) for instruments used in process and industrial automation, with the ability to distribute the control application through a network.

This protocol is based on the ISO/OSI (International Organization for Standardization/Open System Interconnection) sevenlayer reference model. Although being based on the ISO/OSI model, the FF does not use the network layer, the transport layer, the section layer, nor the presentation layer, because it is restricted to local applications. The entire network structure of the FF concentrates on the physical layer, the data link layer (DLL) and the application layer. Besides these three implemented layers, the protocol defines an additional layer called User Application Layer.

The FF Physical Layer, named H1, uses a shielded twisted pair cable as a communication medium. The H1 specifies a 31.25 kBit/s baud rate with Manchester bit codification over a bus powered channel. The network topology configuration is flexible: it is typically configured with a trunk and several spurs, attending certain physical and electrical limitations regarding maximum length and number of transmitters.

The DLL carries the transmission control of all messages on the fieldbus and its protocol grants to the FF network temporal determinism. The communication is based on a masterslave model with a central communication scheduler (master), named Link Active Scheduler or LAS. This node performs the medium access control (MAC).

Two types of DLL layer are standardized: Basic and Link Master. A Basic DLL transmitter does not have LAS capabilities, it operates passively as a communication slave. A Link Master DLL transmitter, on the other hand, can execute LAS functions and thus, if the active LAS node fails, become the LAS node.

The FF Data Link Layer supports two transmission policies: one addressed to scheduled cyclic data, and another to sporadic (unscheduled) background data. These two communication policies share the physical bus, but they are respectively segmented in cyclic time slots or periods. In the scheduled communication period, most process variables generated by periodic processes are transmitted cyclically according to a static global schedule table loaded on the LAS node. This cyclic transmission mode has higher priority over acyclic transmission modes.

A periodic process can be defined as a process initiated at predetermined points in time, also called a time-triggered process. The period for this class of process is typically some milliseconds, and it is mandatory to consider that the generated data must be delivered before the next data is available. This type of periodic data is usually related to measurement and control variables.

Sporadic or unscheduled communication is used to transmit non periodic, or aperiodic, data generated by sporadic processes not directly related to the control loop cycles, but to configuration actions and data supervision efforts. The unscheduled transmissions are dispatched under a token pass scheme. A token that circulates among all active nodes on the bus is used in FF protocol. Once a transmitter receives the token, it is granted the right to send pending aperiodic messages with a minimum priority for a specific time period.

Non periodic (or event-triggered) processes are initiated as soon as specific events are noted. The event-triggered processes are unpredictable and usually related to alarm notifications, configuration data and user commands as cited before. Although acyclic traffic is less frequent than the cyclic one, the acyclic data should also be delivered prior to a certain time deadline, according to the system requirements. For a description of theMACoperation on both cyclic and acyclic phases, refer to.

The FF User Layer is directly related to the process automation tasks themselves, and it is based on distributed control or monitoring strategies of Function Blocks. Function Blocks (FBs) are User Layer elements that encapsulate basic automation functions and consequently make the configuration of a distributed industrial application modular and simplified Distributed among the transmitters, the FBs have their inputs and outputs linked to other blocks in order to perform distributed closed control loop schemes. When blocks from different transmitters are linked together, a remote link is configured and mapped to a cyclic message. Considering that all cyclic messages should be released in a predetermined instant defined on a schedule table, and that they carry data generated by the FBs, it is adequate to synchronize the execution of the FB set on the system with the referred cyclic transmissions schedule table. This solution leads to the concept of joint scheduling.

The Foundation Fieldbus standardized a set of ten basic function blocks, a complementary set of eleven advanced control blocks, and a special flexible function block intended to be fully configurable, i.e., internal logic and parameter, by the user. The standard and advanced block sets provide mathematical and engineering calculations necessary to configure typical industrial control loop strategies, while the flexible function block can be applied to custom or advanced controls or to complex interlocking logics based on ladder nets. It is important to state, however, that the standard is open at this point, permitting the integration of "user-defined"' custom function blocks in order to enhance the capabilities of FF control system, and make the integration of novel control techniques possible.

3. Principles of Control System Implementation

3.1. Control System Implemented in Fieldbus Fashion

When fieldbus-based control fashion is applied, the whole system can be divided into 2 levels basically, which are field level and upper supervisory level. Various intelligent instruments, such as transmitters, valve positioners and actuators, deployed and interconnected with each other by FF in field level. Industrial control computers can serve as the upper supervisory level to monitor operation in field, display data from field and download some modified parameters such as setting point to field level. Some specific configuration software for programming control strategies implemented with FF instruments in field locally is installed in the supervisory computer called

Engineer Workstation (EWS) while HMI software for users' supervision and control are installed in computer called Operator Workstation (OWS). A gateway, connected with supervisory level by Ethernet while with field level by fieldbus, is used to connect the field and supervisory levels.

Function Block (FB) scheme is the foundation of control implementation. Function Blocks (FBs) are User Layer elements that encapsulate basic automation functions and consequently make the configuration of a distributed industrial application modular and simplified [5]. Distributed among the transmitters, the FBs have their inputs and outputs linked to other blocks in order to perform distributed closed control loop schemes. The Foundation Fieldbus standardized a set of basic function blocks [6], a complementary set of eleven advanced control blocks [7], and a special flexible function block intended to be fully configurable, i.e., internal logic and parameter, by the user [8]. The standard and advanced block sets provide mathematical and engineering calculations necessary to configure typical industrial control loop strategies, while the flexible function block can be applied to custom or advanced controls or to complex interlocking logics based on ladder nets. FBs are distributed among the field intelligent instruments. Users can construct complete control strategies by selecting some specific FBs, setting parameters and connecting them through configuration platform provided in supervisory level.

When function blocks from different transmitters or actuators are linked together, a remote link is configured and mapped to a cyclic message. Considering that all cyclic messages should be released in a predetermined instant defined on a schedule table, and that they carry data generated by the FBs, it is adequate to synchronize the execution of the FB set on the system with the referred cyclic transmissions schedule table [9]. All field devices can be scheduled to execute the function blocks in a pre-determined sequence and publish the results at a pre-determined time. Function blocks, located in the other field devices, may use the results too. These function blocks will be executed only after the required inputs are scheduled to be available. To address the case, where a device providing an input becomes unavailable, the user can configure the number of consecutive communications that may be lost before the input status of the receiving device is set to the bad state and consequently the actual mode of the block using this input switches to manual [10,11].

A typical control system implementation with fieldbus is shown in Figure 3.

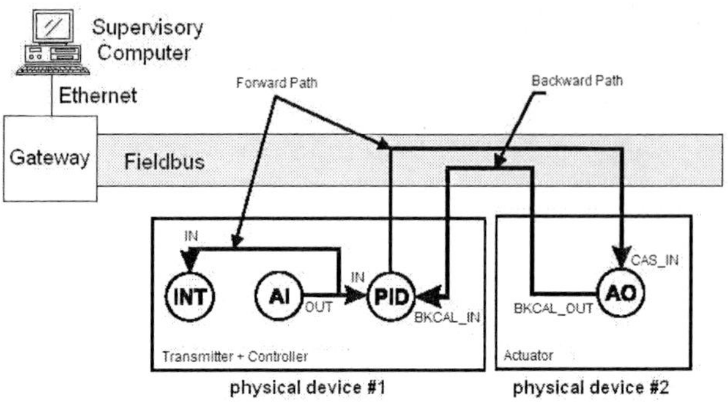

Figure 3. A typical control system implementation with fieldbus.

The procedures of implementing control system with Foundation Fieldbus can be typically summarized into the following steps, which are carried out with some specific configuration software:

(1) Hardware configuration
- Adding a "new fieldbus";
- Adding and defining a "new bridge", which usually serves as a Link Activities Scheduler (LAS) for the whole fieldbus, under the added "new fieldbus";
- Adding and defining various "instruments" including transmitters and actuators, which are connected to the bridge and with each other by fieldbus, under the added "new bridge" according to the composition and function of the Foundation Fieldbus control system.
- The bridge assigns a unique tag to each instrument and communicates with them as a master on the network using the assigned tags for identification.

(2) Control strategies configuration
- Adding and defining appropriate FF "Function blocks" under each added "instrument" according to the design of control strategies. It should be noted that most Function Blocks are common while some few are instrument specific. Function blocks may be defined in different modes such as manual, single loop (PID and PD), automatic mode, cascade control, over-ride mode etc. according to control applications.

- Connecting the defined Function Blocks, which are located in different instruments, according to control logic after setting parameters for the Function blocks
- Downloading the control strategies configuration to the bridge and field instruments.

3.2. Control System Implemented in Industrial Ethernet Fashion

When industrial Ethernet based networked control fashion is applied, the whole system can be divided into 3 levels, which are field level, control level and supervisory level. Some intelligent field instruments or remote digital I/O modules serves as field level, only providing services such as data acquisition and control move actuation. Typically, a PLC executing communication with field level and closed loop control within serves as control level. The upper supervisory level is the same with fieldbus based control fashion. A gateway, connected with control level by Ethernet while field level by fieldbus, is used to connect the field and control levels. Supervisory level and control level are connected by industrial Ethernet by means of a hub. Various control strategies, which are configured in EWS by users, can be implemented within PLC.

The procedures of implementing control system with this fashion are approximately the same with that of fieldbus based control system, which includes hardware and software configuration.

(1) Hardware configuration: Configuring the PLC modules physically and various parameters by means of configuration software installed in EWS for correct recognition of PLC modules by PLC's main processor and communication purpose.
(2) Control strategies and HMI configuration: Including PLC programming and HMI designs by means of configuration software installed in EWS and HMI software installed in OWS respectively.

4. Control System Architecture and Configuration

The control strategy of the pilot control system is chosen as typical cascade control. The testbed is as shown in Figure 4 involving 2 cascaded tanks. The first tank serves as the controlled plant, which is commonly used to represent many practical industrial processes. The water level in the first tank can be controlled. The water flow into both tanks can be controlled as well with water flow into the first tank as the control action while that into the second tank simulating disturbance. To keep water level in the tank stable is the main control objective of the cascade control system. In this system, an outer water-level loop is applied with a level transmitter LD302 and a primary PID control to keep level stable. An inner flow loop is applied with a flow transmitter, also in form of LD302, and a secondary PID control to keep the feeding water flow stable. The block diagram of the cascade control is shown in Figure 5.

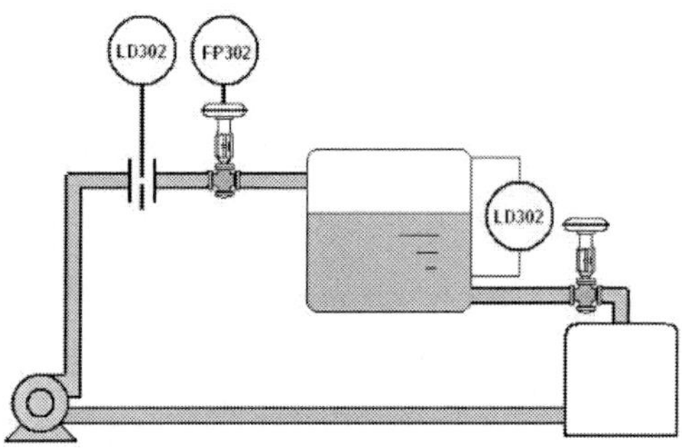

Figure 4. The testbed for a typical cascade control system.

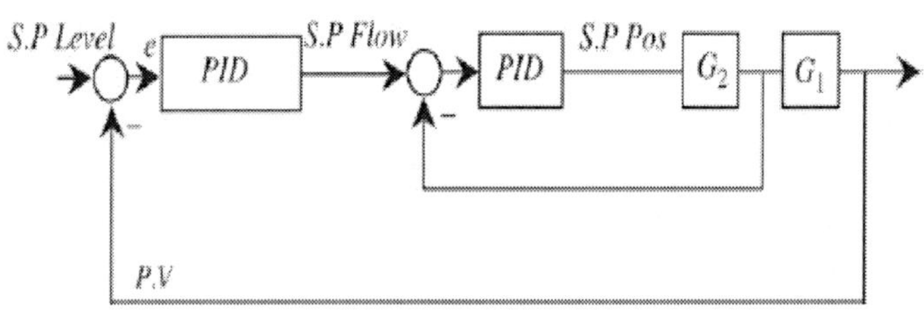

Figure 5. Block diagram for the cascade control system.

Based on the principles of control system implementation given above, here we presented a hybrid control system architecture involving FF subsystem and industrial Ethernet based networked subsystem at the same time, which provides a desired experimental plant for test and analysis of them. The system is shown as Figure 6.

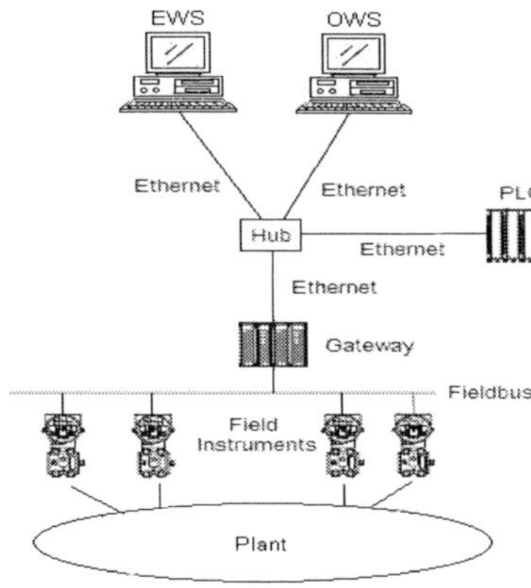

Figure 6. The proposed hybrid control system architecture involving FF subsystem and industrial Ethernet based networked subsystem.

FF subsystem was composed of upper supervisory computers, gateway module DFI302 from Smar Co. Ltd. and field intelligent instruments which were connected with each other by FF H1 fieldbus. Intelligent field instruments from Smar Co. Ltd. including flow/level transmitter LD302 and fieldbus-to-pressure converter FP302 were applied to the plant mentioned above. Industrial Ethernet based networked subsystem was composed of supervisory computers, Siemens S7-300 series PLC, gateway, field intelligent instruments and FF H1 fieldbus. The gateway served as a common intersection in topology by connecting FF intelligent instruments with supervisory computers and PLC. Industrial Ethernet was used as a common transmission network as well shared by PLC and FF Control System (FFCS). Upper supervisory computers include EWS and OWS. FFCS control strategy configuration software Syscon from Smar Co. Ltd. and Siemens PLC configuration and programming software STEP7 are installed in EWS. HMI software such as WinCC or other brands is installed in OWS for process supervision. An Ethernet hub was applied in connecting supervisory computers, PLC and gateway module.

5. Fieldbus-Based Control System Implementation

The procedures of implementing FFCS including hardware and software configuration have been summarized before. Two level transmitters LD302 detecting water level and flow respectively and a fieldbus-to-pressure converter FP302, which converts fieldbus digital signal to pneumatic pressure to actuate the valve, are used as the fundamental elements. Fields instruments are connected to the upper-level supervisory OWS and EWS by means of fieldbus-to-Ethernet gateway DFI302, as presented above.

All control strategies are implemented and executed entirely within field instruments by means of Function Block. The principal part of the implementation lies in the control strategy implementation with Function Block by configuration software Syscon installed in EWS. Two different kinds of function block scheme can be configured to fulfill the cascade PID control by fieldbus intelligent instruments, as shown in Figure7 and Figure8.

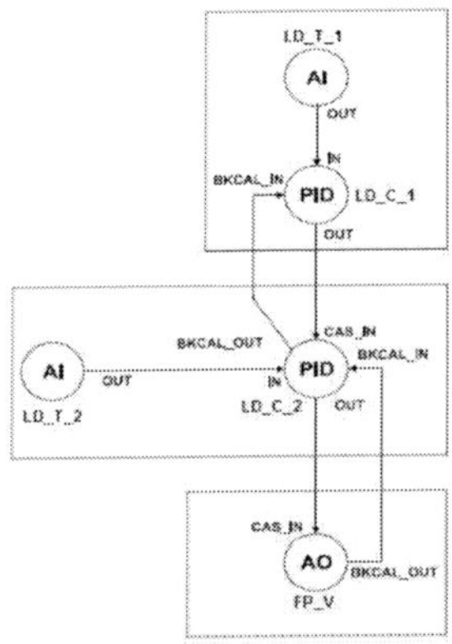

Figure 7. Function blocks configuration scheme I for cascade PID control.

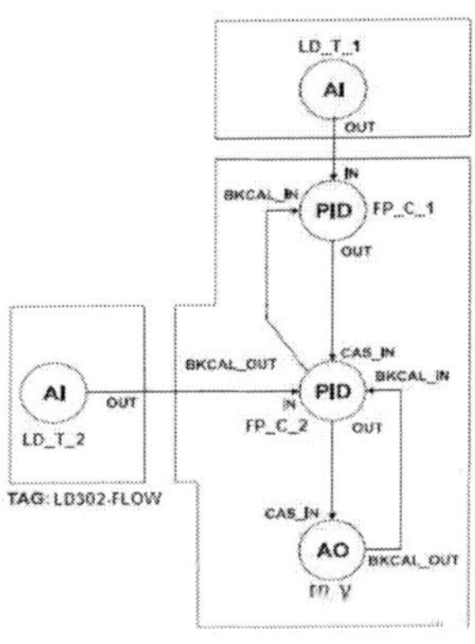

Figure 8. Function blocks configuration scheme II for cascade PID control.

From the figures, it can be seen that the all connections and parameters of function blocks involved keep the same while the distribution of the function blocks within the field instruments are quite different. In both figures, rectangular blocks represent different instruments with some function blocks included. No communication via fieldbus network takes place when connected function blocks are within the same instruments, namely no network induced transmission delay happens for data exchange between these function blocks, and vice versa. For the former case, only some processor time, which is quite small and often ignored in calculation, is taken to achieve the data exchange inside the host instruments. In Figure 6, 1 analogue input function block AI and 1 PID controlling function block are allocated to water level transmitter LD302-LEVEL, 1 AI and 1 PID allocated to flow transmitter LD302-FLOW, 1 analogue output function block AO allocated to FP302. Connections of function blocks within different instruments amount to 4 in number. In Figure 8, the function blocks distribution is quite different with 2 AI function blocks allocated to two LD302 transmitters respectively while both PID function blocks and AO allocated to FP302. Connections of function blocks within different instruments are only 2 in number. Therefore, configuration scheme shown in Figure 7, which make fieldbus network transmission time less and consequently the control cycle shorter, are more efficient in control and preferable.

Some parameters in control such as proportion and integral values in PID, and setting point value can be obtained and modified in EWS with Syscon or OWS with WinCC. Various process parameters can be monitored in form of graphic or text display by WinCC HMI set up in OWS. Fieldbus OPC server provided by the fieldbus system manufacturer, it is Smar OPC server in this case, is essential in the implementation of data communication between the field and upper supervisory level by communicating with DFI302. All technique specific procedures and details on data acquisition and download are wrapped in OPC server and only uniform data access interfaces are provided to user. Smar OPC server is installed in EWS, and OWS at the same time to provide support for communication with OPC client, which is used by supervisory softwares such as Syscon and WinCC to exchange data with OPC server in form of reading and writing. Data transmission process between field and supervisory levels are shown in Figure 9. it is to be noted OPC server software along with the fieldbus hardware, which is in the dotted block in the figure, is also provided by Smar Co. Ltd.

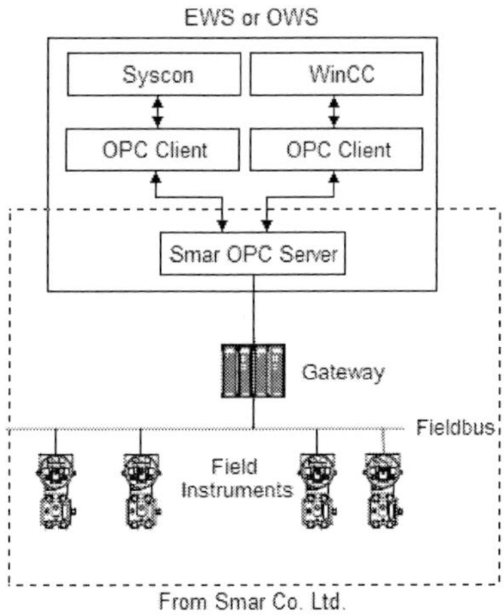

Figure 9. Data transmission process between field and supervisory levels.

After the fieldbus system is correctly configured and the validity of the connections between OWS/EWS, DFI302 and field instruments are confirmed, the level set-point is set to 50% to check the process response in this control fashion. The obtained response result is shown in Figure 10.

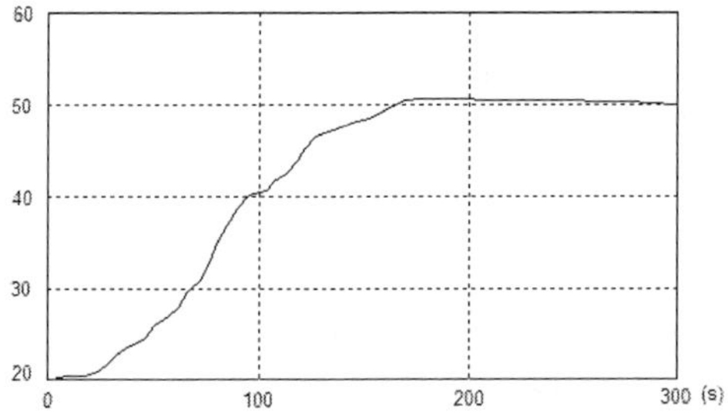

Figure 10. Step response for level set-point disturbance with fieldbus control subsystem and function blocks configuration.

6. Industrial Ethernet Based Networked Control System

In the Ethernet based control system, it is the Siemens S7-300 series PLC that plays the main role with all control strategies implemented and executed within it. Fieldbus intelligent instruments only serve as remote digital I/O modules for data acquisition and control move actuation. The communication between the PLC and DFI302 is via Ethernet Modbus link.

In this fashion, cascade PID control strategy is implemented in the Siemens S7-300 series PLC. Field data acquisitions, such as water level and flow here, are executed by field intelligent instruments in fieldbus subsystem and control moves generated by PLC are sent back to FP302 for actuation. The essentially important part in this control fashion implementation is to achieve data exchange between PLC and field intelligent instruments serving as I/O modules. Some researchers proposed a method by exporting WinCC OPC tags into S7 protocol suite to provide I/O data interface for PLC control program. Here we propose a new solution based on Function Block MBCS provided by DFI302, which combines fieldbus subsystem and PLC world closely in a simpler but more flexible way.

MBCS block generates a communication strategy between a Modbus master and a Fieldbus Foundation slave. In the present case, the slave is the Smar's linking device DFI302 that has slave behavior for the Modbus network. It allows Modbus variables to be associated with Fieldbus variables and data between these two "worlds" to be exchanged through DFI302. Every time a MODBUS parameter is changed it is necessary to set the ON_APPLY parameter of the MBCF block to "Apply". Otherwise these alterations will not be effective. The architecture of the control system involving PLC, DFI302 and MBCS function block is shown in Figure 11. Control strategies are located in PLC. Acquired field data by LD302 is sent to PLC and control move is sent by PLC to FP302 for actuation with function block MBCS as the data exchange interface.

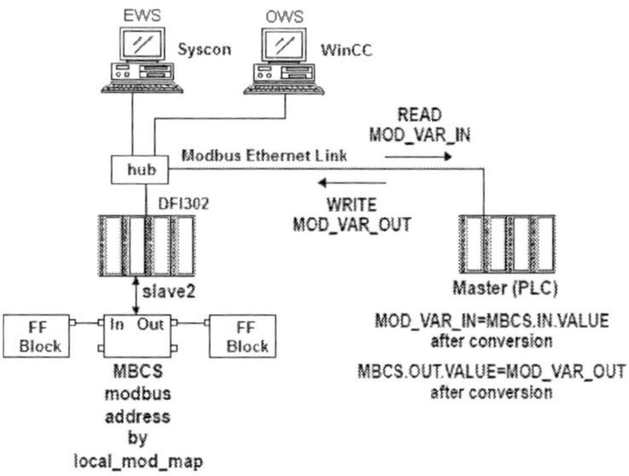

Figure 11. Architecture of the control system involving PLC, DFI302 and MBCS function block.

The MBCS block has 4 digital inputs, 4 analog inputs, 4 digital outputs and 4 analog outputs that may be connected to other FIELDBUS function blocks or to the MODBUS world.

- IN1, IN2, IN3 and IN4 are analogue inputs
- IN_D1, IN_D2, IN_D3 and IN_D4 are digital inputs
- OUT1, OUT2, OUT3 and OUT4 are analogue outputs
- OUT_D1, OUT_D2, OUT_D3 and OUT_D4 are digital outputs

Digital outputs and Digital inputs are of the DS-66 data type [12]. Thus they contain both a Status and a value (both unsigned 8). The analogue outputs and inputs are of the DS-65 data type, containing status and value as well [12]. The schematic of function block MBCS is shown in Figure12.

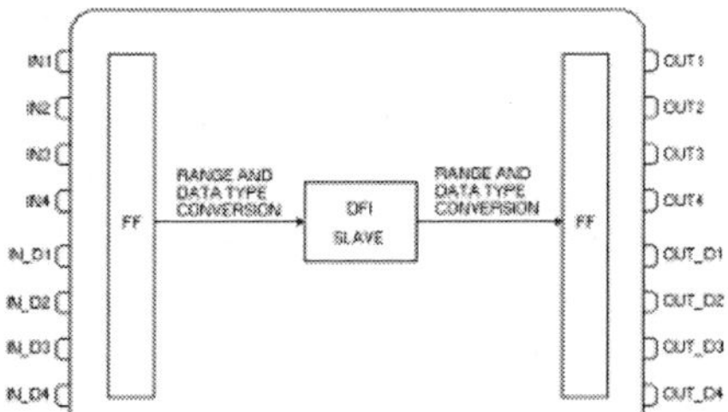

Figure 12. Schematic of function block MBCS in DFI302.

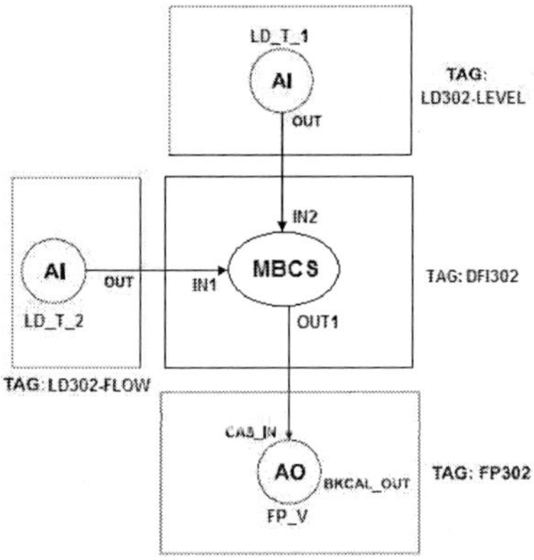

Figure 13. Control strategies configuration for Fieldbus subsystem based on MBCS provided by DFI302.

Some extra strategies need to be configured for Fieldbus subsystem with Syscon in order to exchange I/O data with PLC by means of function block MBCS and Modbus Ethernet. The control strategies configuration for Fieldbus subsystem based on MBCS provided by DFI302 is shown in Figure 13.

The level set-point is set to 50% to check the process response under this control fashion. The obtained response result is shown in Figure 14.

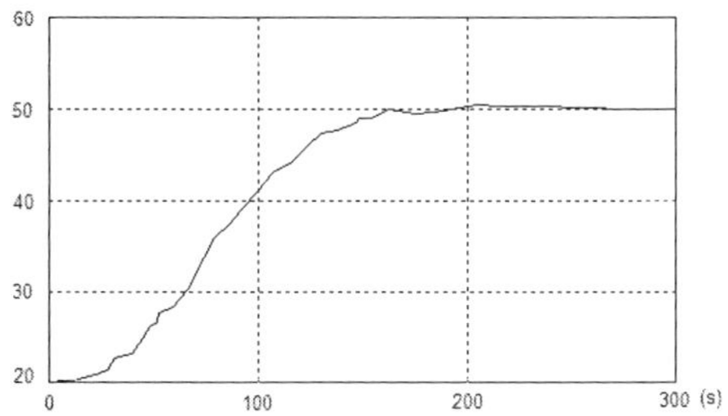

Figure 14. Step response for level set-point disturbance with control system involving PLC, DFI302 and MBCS function block.

7. Analysis of Effects on Control by Transmission Time Delay

As a matter of fact, data transmission time delay consists of two different parts: ①transmission time delay caused by microprocessors' data processing within computers or field instruments ②transmission time delay caused by data transmission over communication links. Generally, the former is often ignored for that the microprocessors' processing speed is much faster than ever before and much less when compared with the latter. Therefore, transmission time delay caused by communication links is the principal element.

7.1. Fieldbus Based Control System

From the control system implementation scheme based on field intelligent instruments, with distributed function blocks execution and bus scheduling as the main mechanism (see Figure 7 and Figure 8), it can be seen that each function block within control strategy is executed serially and deterministically in chronological order by scheduling since bus network media is unshared by any node at any time. This kind of mechanism makes sure that downstream function blocks will be executed only after the required data from upstream function blocks, no matter over network or inside instruments, are transmitted to them successfully. If not, the status values of function block inputs will indicate an error, which will trig an appropriate handling process by the function blocks. When distributed control strategies are scheduled, control moves sent to actuators are scheduled at the end of this cycle. Function block AI, by which outputs of plants are acquired, is scheduled at the beginning of the next cycle. As thus, control moves taking action is always prior to feedback from plant, which ensures the correct timing sequence in control.

Therefore, no mismatch and asynchrony between control moves taking real actions and feedback being generated exists in Fieldbus-based control scheme thanks to its cyclic FB scheduling, by which the control moves and feedbacks are in deterministic sequence. Only some minor transmission time delay, which is deterministic and can be predicted based on the fieldbus communication speed and numbers of FB to be scheduled, takes place over fieldbus between two consecutive control moves.

7.2. Ethernet Based Networked Control System

In this fashion, transmission delay is mainly caused by Ethernet. It occurs on 2 paths including downward path on which data are downloaded to the field and upward path on which data are uploaded to the controller. The two paths correspond to control channels and feedback channels respectively as shown in Figure15. Data transmission delay in control channels and feedback channels are represented as $e^{-t_c s}$ and $e^{-t_f s}$. Non-determinancy, which lies in that of transmission time itself and sequence in control causing mismatch and asynchrony between control moves and feedback and consequently degrade the control effect, is the main features of transmission over Ethernet.

Some researchers investigated the degradation of control effects caused by Ethernet transmission time delay and pointed out that Increasing transmission delay reduces the rising time and degrades the steady state response for typical PID cascade control [4]. The conclusion was based on the assumption that control moves are generated continuously despite of the delayed control moves actuation and feedback. Degradation of steady state response can be mainly attributed to asynchrony of control moves and feedback under circumstance of continuous control.

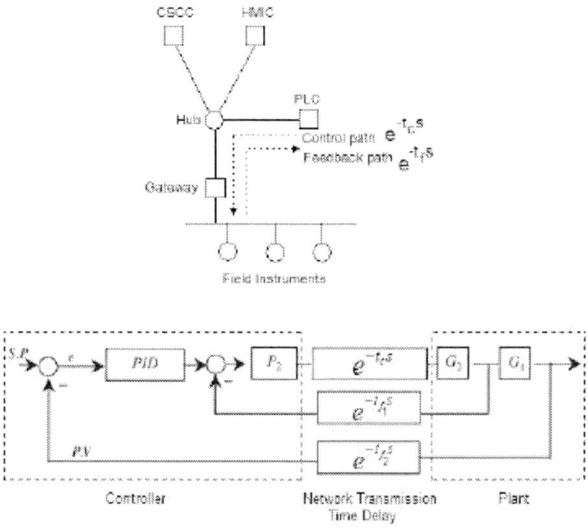

Figure 15. Transmission time delay in control channel and feedback channels.

8. Improvement Measures for Control Effects in Industrial Ethernet Based Networked Control System

To improve control effects degraded with network transmission time delay in industrial Ethernet based case, 2 problems should be considered and solved. Firstly, the asynchrony between control moves and feedback caused by transmission delay should be reduced as much as possible. Secondly, network transmission delay itself should be reduced by means of hardware or network architecture improvements. Alternatively, some compensation methodologies in perspective of control theories can be applied in order to counteract the effect by the transmission delay.

8.1. Reducing Asynchrony between Control Moves and Feedback Caused by Transmission Delay

As mentioned before, asynchrony between control moves and feedback mainly existed in NCS fashion. Therefore, the solutions proposed in this section are used for Ethernet based NCS fashion.

Synchronization control is necessary to reduce asynchrony between control moves and feedback caused by transmission delay. IEC61499, an international standard for fully distributed process control based on IEC61131, provides a synchronization control mechanism for NCS fashion [13]. Since it is based on event-triggered mode, some specific events can be correctly set for PID blocks in PLC to control the synchronization between control moves out of PID blocks and feedbacks into PID blocks. PLC programming compatible with IEC61499 is supported with some of the Siemens products. Here we propose a methodology to realize the synchronization control based on IEC61499.

Events need to be configured to control the synchronization between feedback data acquisition and control move actuation. To control the sequence between data acquisition and control algorithm execution, event signals in PID block need to be configured. The configured event in PID block will not be triggered until the feedback from the plant over Ethernet is fully available at the inputs of PID blocks by means of data acquisition block. The event is triggered by the data acquisition block upstream to PID block. Therefore, PLD control algorithm will not be executed and no new outputs are generated if the event is not triggered. As for feedback, the acquisition of data from field will not be executed only if the generated control moves by PID blocks are sent to field. To achieve this, an event signal is dispatched to data acquisition block by control moves output block to control the sequence. Data acquisition block and control moves output block are user defined blocks which are very flexible and can be programmed with 5 standard languages specified in IEC61131-3. The schematic of the proposed methodology is shown in Figure16.

In configuration, the proposed scheme consists of a User Defined Function Block for Data Acquisition (UDFB-DA), a PID block compliant with IEC61499 and a User Defined Function Block for Control Moves (UDFB-CM). Two global time variables T_{fb} and T_{cma}, which represents the time tick when data from field is sampled and the control move is surely actuated in field respectively, need to be created to store the two time ticks. A scheme dealing with control moves download and a readback is used to decide the time when the control move is surely actuated in field. The flow chart of the scheme is shown in Figure 17.

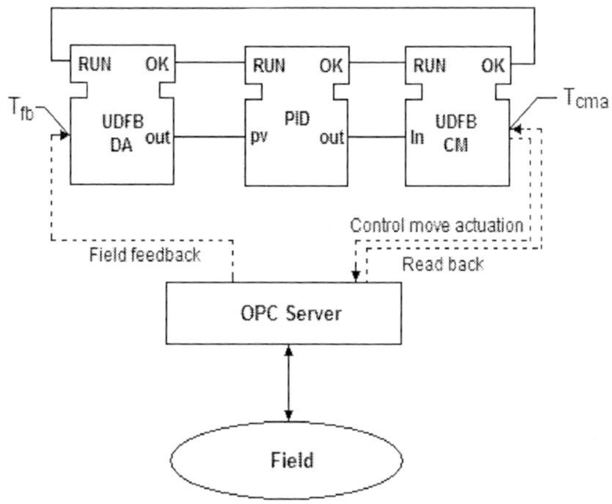

Figure 16. Schematic of the proposed methodology based on IEC61499.

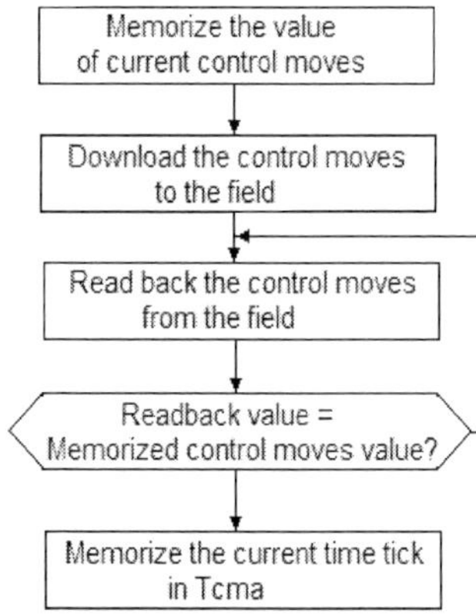

Figure 17. Flow chart of the proposed scheme based on IEC61499.

The main function of block UDFB-DA is to control the sequence of feedback acquisition and control move actuation to make it deterministic that control move actuation is prior to feedback acquisition in each execution of control strategy by means of global time variables T_{fb} and T_{cma}. The execution control logics of UDFB-DA are shown in Figure 18.

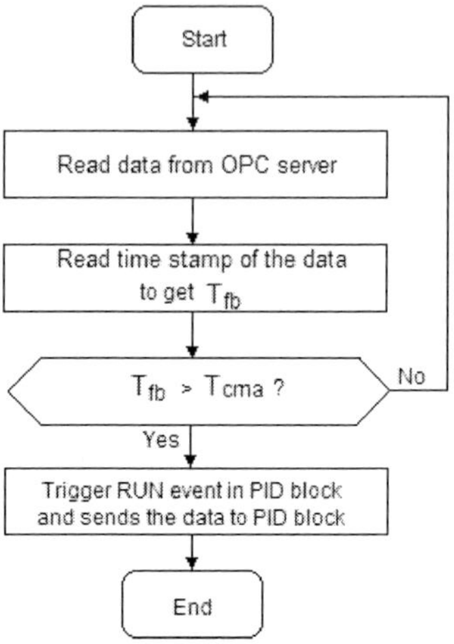

Figure 18. Execution control logics of UDFB-DA.

The execution control logics of PID are shown in Figure 19.

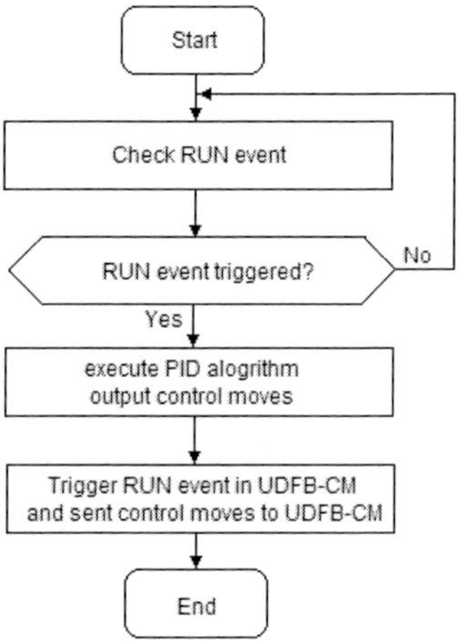

Figure 19. Execution control logics of PID.

The main functions of block UDFB-CM is to download the control move generated by PID block to field and record the time tick when the download and actuation is finished. Readback check is used to make sure that the control move has been downloaded to the field successfully. The execution control logics of UDFB-CM are shown in Figure 20.

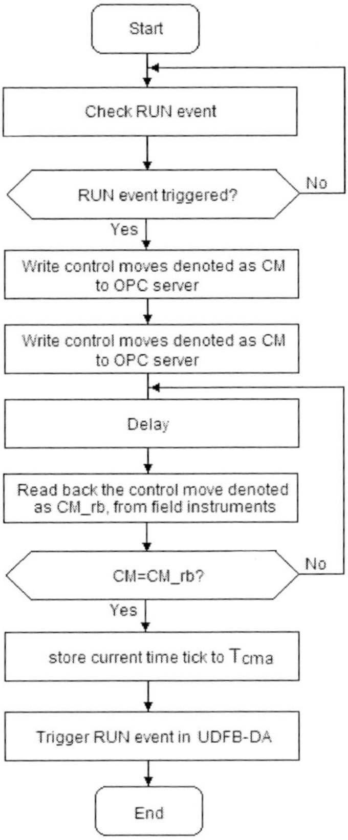

Figure 20. Execution control logics of UDFB-CM.

The level set-point is set to 50% to check the process response under this improved control fashion. The obtained response result is shown in Figure 21.

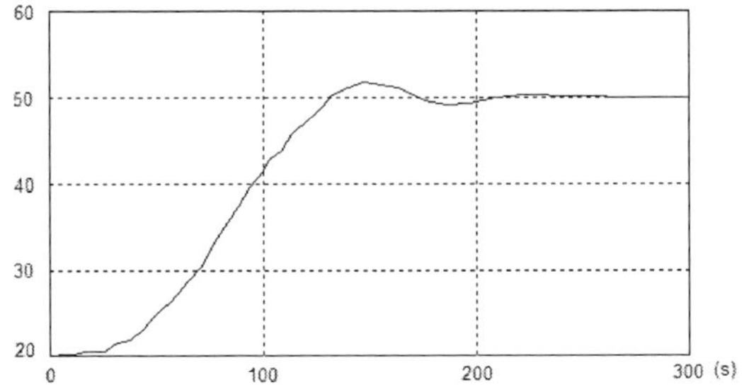

Figure 21. Step response for level set-point disturbance with the Ethernet based control system and PLC using the proposed control scheme based on IEC61499.

Some extra design and programming are necessary for those with which IEC61499 standard is not supported.

8.2. Using Output Estimation to Compensate for the Transmission Delay in Feedback

Transmission delay in feedback path will cause the feedback data from the plant field not updated within some time-span. It can be observed by upper supervisory workstation (OWS or EWS) by means of "time-stamp" property of data acquired by OPC server. Since the maximum time delay caused by the industrial Ethernet can not be predicted while regulation must be continued to keep system stable, it is necessary to get estimation of the output of plants to take the role of the real output which is not available at current time tick. There are many ways to achieve the estimation. Here we proposed an output estimation scheme based on neural network since any non-linear mapping can be realized by means of it. Neural network are used to predict the output of plant. In this case, predicted output by neural network instead of the real one is used as inputs of block UDFB-DA to be sent to PID to generate control moves.

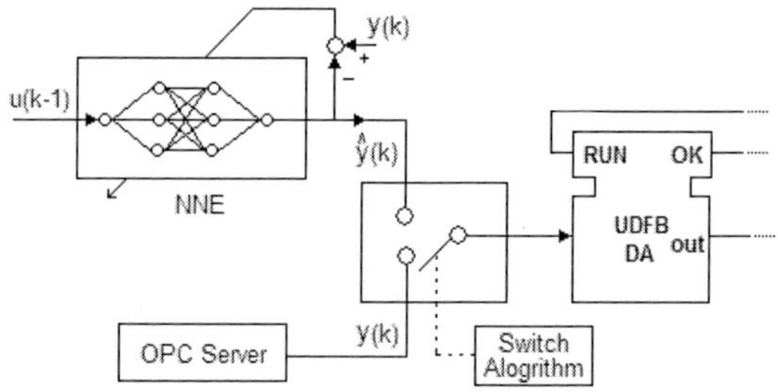

Figure 22. Schematic of output estimation with neural network.

Schematic of output estimation with neural network was shown in Figure 22. In this scheme, a neural network estimator (NNE), with 1 input layer, 2 hidden layers and 1 output layer, is used to estimate the output of plant in the case that the up-to-date output of plant can not be obtained from OPC server within certain time limit T_{opc_max}. Control move $u(k-1)$ serves as input of NNE. $\hat{y}(k)$ is the estimated output of plant by NNE. Gradient descending algorithm is used to training NNE. The running of NNE is parallel to data acquisition by OPC server. At the same time, a switch is used. If field data from OPC server is up-to-date, which can be judged from "time-stamp" property of data acquired by OPC server, the output of plant by OPC server is switched to block UDFB-DA for further use. Otherwise, the estimated output by NNE is switched to block UDFB-DA. The switching algorithm is shown in Figure 23.

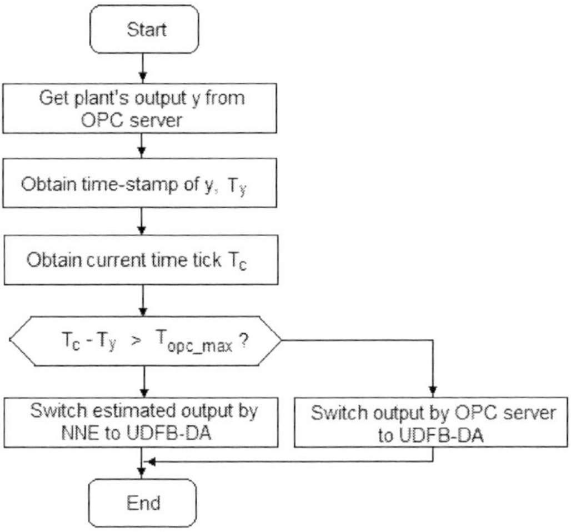

Figure 23. Flow chart of switching algorithm.

8.3. Reducing Network Transmission Delay Itself

8.3.1. By Improving Hardware and Network Architecture

Because the network communication over industrial Ethernet is CSMA/CD based, the time uncertainty of data communication between different nodes increases greatly with network traffic load, which is proportional to the number of nodes connected to the same network segments, to cause network transmission delay to different extent. Here we propose 3 principal ways to reducing network transmission delay itself by improving hardware and network architecture. Firstly, raising the whole network communication speed, especially the communication speed of PLC, DFI302 and hubs, by improving related hardware; secondly, leaving more bandwidth to communication between PLC and DFI302, which is more time critical, by properly dividing the whole network into different segments with routers to block broadcasting storm and other data communication unrelated to that between PLC and DFI302 from contention of bandwidth; thirdly, try to reduce the time in store-and-forward by related network components , such as routers.

1. Increasing Network Communication Speed

Since the communication between PLC and DFI302 that exchanges I/O data with field instruments, is time critical, raising Ethernet network communication speed along the path between PLC and DFI302 quite contributes to reducing the network transmission delay. Three key components along this communication path, including PLC, hub and DFI302, are dealt with. Communication speed for each component must be raised simultaneously to achieve the overall communication speed increment. Any ignorance among the three will cause a bottleneck effect in communication speed increment. As for PLC and hub, faster Ethernet interface such as 100M instead of 10M should be selected to serve. Ethernet interfaces above100M is not available in DFI302 itself currently and a 10/100 Mbps Ethernet Switch-DF61 must be used to achieve the speed enhancement for DFI302. After connecting 10 Mbps port of DF61 with 10 Mbps port of DF51 using DF54 cable, the 100 Mbps port of DF61 is ready to be connected to a 100M hub. The connection schematic is shown in Figure24. Since it is a peer-to-peer connection between DF61 and DFI302 and no bandwidth contention exists along the path between them, the bottleneck effect is much less remarkable.

In addition, a switch is more preferred to hub to raise network communication speed for its more efficient and faster data transmission speed.

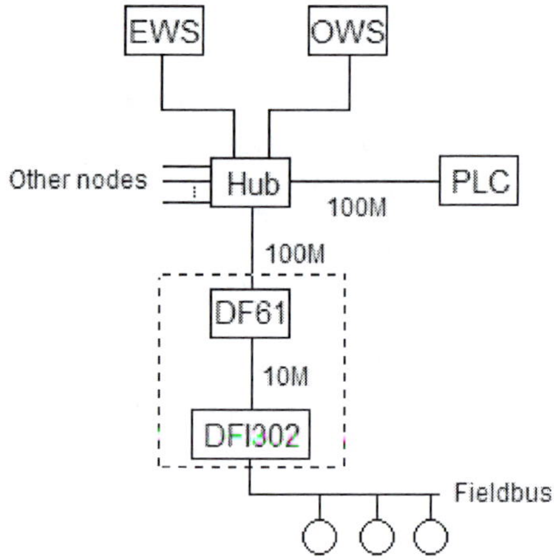

Figure 24. Schematic of network connection for enhancing the entire network speed.

2. Dividing Ethernet Network into Different Segments Based on Time Critical Requirement Rating to Leave More Bandwidth to Time Critical Communication

Network bandwidth contention increases with the number of nodes connected when all the nodes are allocated in the same network segment. Available bandwidth for time critical communication, such as that between PLC and DFI302 here, is in reverse proportion to the number of nodes connected within the segment. However, priorities of communication among nodes are quite different within. Data transmission between PLC and DFI302 is quite time critical for its control function while that between OWS,EWS and PLC are not since only setting point data and some supervision-based data need to be exchanged. Therefore, communication between nodes should be grouped and rated based on their time critical requirements. And then divide the whole network into several different segments using router to allocate the nodes involved in different communication priorities into those segments. Traffic load within segment is lowered greatly and efficiently since bandwidth contention from nodes outside local segment is blocked. Besides, broadcasting data flow within the same segment, known as "broadcasting storm", is also effectively blocked and screened.

As far as the control system investigated in this chapter is concerned, communication between nodes can be classified into 2 groups based on their time critical requirements. One group is the non-time-critical communication including that between OWS, EWS, PLC and other computers. The other is the time-critical communication, namely data transmission between PLC and DFI302. The two groups are divided into 2 different network segments with different subnet mask and gateway configuration, by means of a router. Nodes in each segment are interconnected by means of a hub. The corresponding schematics of network structure and subsections according to the scheme proposed above are shown in Figure25. The corresponding network configuration for each segment and node is shown in Table 1.

Table 1. Network configuration for segments and nodes

	Segment1		Segment2	
Mask	255.255.255.0		255.255.255.0	
Gateway	168.195.200.254		168.195.201.254	
Nodes IP	PLC	168.192.200.1	OWS	168.192.201.1
	DFI302	168.192.200.2	EWS	168.192.201.2

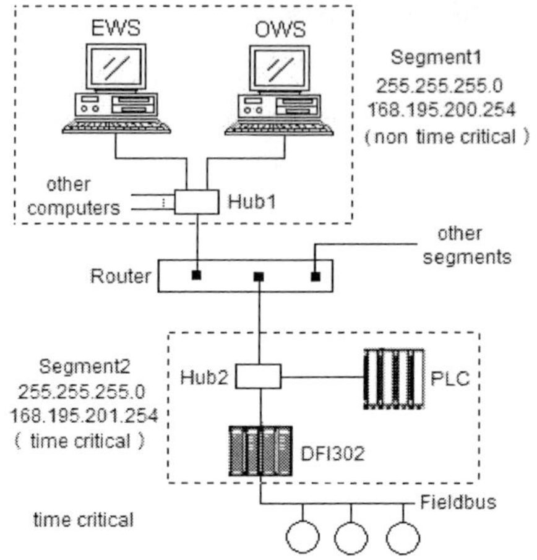

Figure 25 Schematics of network structure and subsections.

Obviously, it can be seen from Figure24 that broadcast storms from other segments are blocked outside the segment 168.192.201.*, in which PLC and DFI302 reside, by the router and no bandwidth contention from any node in segment 168.192.200.* or other segments comes up. Full bandwidth in segment 168.192.201.* is available to the communication between PLC and DFI302, which ensures the stable and reliable data exchange between them in turn.

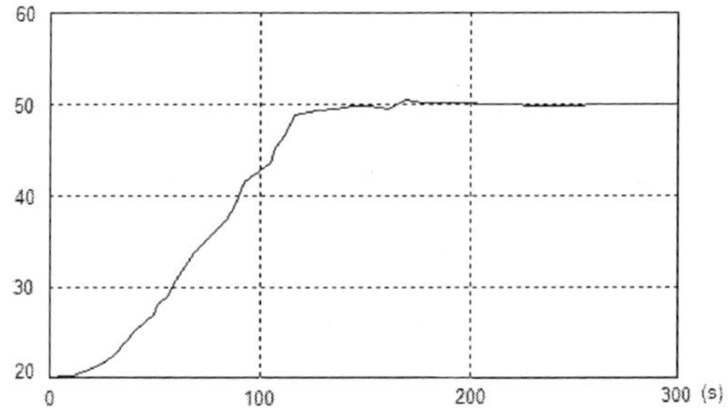

Figure 26. Step response for level set-point disturbance with Ethernet based control system using the proposed methodologies of improving network architecture.

The level set-point is set to 50% to check the process response under this improved control fashion. The obtained response result is shown in Figure 26. It can be seen that control effect in NCS fashion with improved network structure is better than that without any improvement in network structure with the same PID parameters since shorter control cycle can be achieved.

3. Reducing Transmission Delay from Store-and-Forward by Related Network Components

With no sense of priority, an industrial telegram, which may be critical for operating some machine, might be delayed, sitting in some switch's store-and-forward buffer waiting for an IT telegram to pass through. The store and forward buffers in Ethernet switches are the source of the problem for industrial telegrams. First, as the telegram passes through the switch, it gets stored in a buffer until the entire message is received; only then it is forwarded out of the switch. Second, if the industrial message arrives at the switch at the same time the switch is processing an IT telegram, it must wait until the entire IT telegram passes through the switch before it can move on. Because a frame with a higher priority is always given precedence, automation frames are delayed if the queue buffers are filled with frames that have the same or higher priority. And, automation frames can be delayed for an unpredictable amount of time. There may also be congestion at the switch's output port: When the output port is filled with frames, high-priority frames have to wait until the port is available again. Some companies and organizations, such as Harting, have proposed some effective solutions to the problems. The solutions are to, first of all, pass all automation telegrams straight through the switch, bypassing the store-and-forward mechanism. Secondly, if an industrial telegram arrives at a switch while an IT telegram is being processed, that processing stops immediately and the industrial telegram is given clearance to pass through. After it has cleared the switch, the IT telegram is re-transmitted through the switch. This is called a "cut through" method. Experiments haves shown that the delay for the time critical industrial messages is over 2,000 microseconds with standard "store and forward" switching, but when the Fast Track Switching with the proposed solutions is turned on the maximum delay is only about 50 microseconds. Siemens has designed its ERTEC (Enhanced Real-Time Ethernet Controller) Profinet chips to deal with the situation. These industrial Ethernet ASICs are high-performance Ethernet controllers (based on 32-bit ARM 946 processors) that have integrated real-time switches especially developed for industrial use. The chips prioritize the isochronous real-time motion control telegrams and make sure they get to their destination in a timely fashion. Besides, Phoenix Contact has also announced a Profinet enhancement to speed up industrial frames.

8.3.2. By Some Compensating Methodologies in Perspective of Control Theory

In recent years, many researchers have focused on solution to the network transmission delay in Ethernet-based control system by means of control theoretical methods and many algorithms, such as fuzzy PID control strategy[4], augmented deterministic discrete-time model control[14], optimal stochastic control methodology [15], robust control methodology [16] and end-user control adaptation methodology [17], were proposed, to compensate for or counteract the degradation in control effect caused by the Ethernet transmission delay. These control methodologies cover a large variety of systems and protocols. To design an NCS with a certain networked control methodology, a designer has to clearly understand an application whether it is feasible, acceptable, and reliable enough to be controlled by the methodology under a selected network protocol. There are also additional factors of concern including the price for the network protocol, and the size and distance of the application. The premises and conditions under which these methodologies were used were summarized by Yodyium Tipsuwan and Mo-Yuen Chow [18].

CONCLUSION

- As for design and implementation of fieldbus system, configuration scheme on allocating function block to different field instruments can notably affect the control performance and worth paying attention to. With the improved function block allocation and configuration scheme proposed in this chapter, shortercontrol cycle and thereby more efficient control can be achieved.
- As for the design of industrial Ethernet based system, function block MBCS provided by DFI302 combining fieldbus subsystem and PLC world closely provide a simpler but more flexible way to implement a hybrid system.

- No essentially uncertain data transmission delay was involved and thereby no degradation caused by it in control when control strategies were implemented with fieldbus control system with by means of function blocks and fully distribution in control was achieved, which demonstrated the apparent advantage over general networked control system.No mismatch and asynchrony between control moves taking real actions and feedback being generated exists in Fieldbus-based control scheme thanks to its cyclic FB scheduling. Degradation of steady state response can be mainly attributed to asynchrony of control moves and feedback under circumstance of continuous control as far as the Ethernet based control system is concerned.

- Methodologies based on IEC61499 proposed in this chapter can be utilized to control the execution sequence of each function block in PLC controller with events and some specific action control logic.The proposed output estimation algorithm based on neural network can also compensate for the transmission delay in feedback effectively.
- It is a effective and efficient way to reduce network transmission delay itself by improving hardware and network architecture.3 methods, which are raising network communication speed, dividing Ethernet network into different segments based on time critical requirement rating and reducing transmission delay from store-and-forward by related network components, are proposed to achieve this aim. When the network segmenting solution proposed in this chapter is applied, the control system can operates well without the proposed sequence control scheme. When the most adverse network structure is applied, namely without any improvement in network components and structure, the proposed sequence control scheme is quite preferred.

Consequently, as proposed and proved in this chapter, many problems existing in networked control, in which communication and control technologies involved at the same time, can be solved to great extent by means of network related methodologies, which provides alternative or most possibly comprehensive solutions.

References

[1] Ma C, Chen S, Liu W. Maximum allowable delay bound of networked control systems with multi-step delay. *Simulation Modelling Practice and Theory* 2007;15:513–20.

[2] Imera OC, Y¨ukselb S, Basar T. Optimal control of LTI systems over unreliable communication links. *Automatica* 2006;42:1429–39.

[3] Hua LS, Baia T, Shib P, Wu Z. Sampled-data control of networked linear control systems. *Automatica* 2007;43:903–11.

[4] A. Fadaei, K. Salahshoor1. Design and implementation of a new fuzzy PID controller for networked control systems, *ISA Transactions* 2008:47:351–361.

[5] Chen J, Wang Z, Sun Y. How to improve control system performance using FF function blocks. In: *IEEE international conference on control application.* 2002.

[6] Fieldbus Foundation. FF-890-1.3: *Foundation specification function block application process, part 1.* Austin, USA. 1999.

[7] Fieldbus Foundation. *Foundation specification function block application process Part 3*: FF-892 FS1.4. Austin, USA. 1999.

[8] Fieldbus Foundation. *Foundation specification function block application process Part 5*: FF-894 DPS0.95. Austin, USA. 1999.

[9] Eduardo André Mossin, Rodrigo Palucci Pantoni, Dennis Brandão. A fieldbus simulator for training purposes, *ISA Transactions* 2009; 48: 132-141.

[10] Ferreiro Garcia R, Vidal Paz J, Pardo Martinez XC, Coego Botana J. Fieldbus: Preliminary design approach to optimal network management. In: *IEEE international workshop on factory communication systems.* 1997.

[11] Fieldbus Foundation. FF-890-1.3: *Foundation specification function block application process, part 1.* Austin, USA. 1999.

[12] Smar Co. Function blocks instruction manual. 2003.

[13] Valeriy Vyatkin. *Information infrastructure of intelligent machines based on the IEC61499 architecture.*

[14] Halevi, Y., and Ray, A. (1988). Integrated communication and control systems: Part I—analysis. *Journal of Dynamic Systems, Measurement and Control,* 110, 367–373.

[15] Nilsson, J., 1998. *Real-time control systems with delays. Ph.D. dissertation,* Lund Institute of Technology.

[16] G.oktas, F., 2000. *Distributed control of systems over communication networks. Ph.D. dissertation,* University of Pennsylvania.

[17] Tipsuwan, Y., and Chow, M.-Y., 2001. Network-based controller adaptation based on QoS negotiation and deterioration. *The 27th annual conference of the IEEE industrial electronics society (IECON 01),* Vol. 3 (pp. 1794–1799). Denver, CO.

[18] Yodyium ; Chow, Mo-Yuen Source: *Control Engineering Practice*, v 11, n 10, p 1099-1111, October 2003.

In: Network Protocols
Editor: Geng Liang
ISBN 978-1-61470-821-6

Chapter 8

WEB SERVICES IN COMPREHENSIVE INFORMATION INTEGRATION AND PROCESS SUPERVISION AND CONTROL: DESIGN AND APPLICATION

***Geng Liang*[1]*, Wen Li*[2] *and Dazhong Li*[3]**

[1]School of Control and Computer Engineering, North China Electric Power University, Beijing, China.

[2]Beijing GUODIANZHISHEN Control Technology Co. Ltd, Beijing, China.

[3]Automation Department, North China Electric Power University, Baoding, China

ABSTRACT

Main problems existing in remote supervision and control system (RSCS) in power plants today in China are that various software and hardware platforms exist in the integration of all parts of RSCS. Implementation of data exchange with these traditional methods is not general-purposed, information and data are difficult to transverse firewall installed by enterprises because of the private protocols used in distributed object technology. A RSCS in power plants based on Web Services are presented in this chapter. Architecture, operational pattern and main features of Web Services are expounded. 2 kinds of nodes are included in RSCS in Power Plants Based on Web Services. Data acquisition based on OPC, data encapsulation based on Web Services, publication of Web Services, and design of supervisory and control service system (SCSS) orienting remote clients based on Web Services are included in design of gateway connecting local and remote nodes base on Web Services. Remote clients exchange data with SCSS by browsers. SCSS data exchange between SCSS and Web Services gateway is implemented with services description files and SOAP message. Developed and designed RSCS is applied in the remote supervision and control for water level in drum of boiler in a power plant. Project practice shows that designed RSCS in power plants based on Web Services is stable and reliable in operation with high integrability and openness and is worthy of application and popularization.

1. Introduction

Computer, network and database technology have developed greatly in recent years. Technology and software or hardware platforms from different manufacturers in different periods are introduced and integrated into the platform for information comprehension and utilization. Many subsystems dealing with production, capital construction, material purchase and management are constructed on the comprehensive information platform continuously. However, many problems exist in information comprehensive utilization and management in power plants of China as following:

(1) Manual collection, filing, summarization and management of data information and material are used widely, which makes it a heavy workload for man. Data and material are easy to be lost. Many errors occur in data filing. It is with high cost in management, heavy workload and low efficiency in work.

(2) Available massive information and data in wide range net (WAN) can not be fully used to serve construction and production of local power plants.

(3) It is long in time consumption of information handling and high in management cost.

(4) various software and hardware architecture and application in different categories and levels, such as operating systems, programming languages for user's application, software development models and databases, exist in the integration of new system application. Data with considerable proportion in management

information system (MIS) of power plants are stored in form of non-relational files (VSAM). C++, Java, Visual Basic and other various programming languages are used in the development of user's application in construction of information subsystems and technological innovation for power plants.

Comprehensive information integration systems are required to possess the ability in not only handling information from various subsystems but also coordinating and managing the information exchange between various subsystems to make them inter-operable. To integrate and comprehensively utilize massive information, all applications are required to integrate and exchange data with applications in other heterogeneous platforms. Some special methods, such as file transmission and analysis, message queue and API only suitable for some conditions, are used to implement the tasks. Problems in generalization are raised and information sharing and reusability are limited by those implementation schemes. Therefore, a general-purposed standard for information exchange independent of platforms, component models and programming languages is necessary to solve these problems in information integration and sharing for power plants WAN. A neutral platform can be provided with Web Service based on open standard to integrate various application to achieve the inter-operability in information over WEB and can be used in integration of various application system effectively, easily and universally.

At the same time, large-scaled and open systems using network are the development trend of process supervisory and control system for power plants. Production process, measurement and control devices are increasingly widely distributed in fields. The whole system covers large area and contains massive information. Restriction in area to remote supervision and control system (RSCS) in power plants today is removed with application based on distributed software and network technology, which provides users with more convenient way in supervision and provides conditions for realization of integration of management and control. Main problems existing in RSCS in power plants today in China are: various software and hardware platforms such as operating systems, users' programming languages, software development patterns and database systems and various applications with different sorts and levels, exist in RSCS. Applications developed in time of system constructions and innovations are different in platform and programming languages, such as C++, Java and Visual Basic etc. Implementation of data exchange with Traditional methods, such as file transmission and analysis, message queue, is not general-purposed. Flexibility and re-usage of services provided by servers are restricted with the fast couple architecture. For instance, distributed object technology developed by different manufactures is used in many RSCS in power plants, such as DCOM of Microsoft, RMI of SUN and COBRA of OMG, for which many servers and clients have their own private protocols and data formats and services can only by used by the clients using the same protocols. Therefore, data exchange and information sharing are restricted by specified developers, platforms and languages. Meanwhile, information and data are difficult to transverse firewall installed by enterprises because of the private protocols used in distributed object technology.

2. Architecture, Operational Pattern and Features of Web Services

Web Services are self-contained, self-described and loosely coupled software components. Web Service can be viewed as a comprehension of a serial of standards including XML, SOAP, WSDL and UDDI etc. with which a loosely coupled and distributed computing environment is constructed. All application entities are abstracted as services in Web Services. 3 entities and 3 operation are included in it: ① Service provider ② Service requester ③ Service broke. Architecture of Web Service is shown in Figure1.

Web Services are extension of object component technology in Internet and function sets are encapsulated as single entity and published over network to be used by other application. Web Services can be distributed on any node in network and called each other to implement certain functions. Descriptions of the provided services are registered with a service registry broker server UDDI. Services requesters search service description on local or remote service registry broker server and can use the service by binding after the needed services are found. Services description, request and feedback of result are based on XML documents and can be transferred in HTTP protocol in Web Services. SOAP is used to access Web Services developed by any tool and programming language with HTTP protocol. Web Services are running in the background of Web servers. SOAP request created by client is embedded into a HTTP request and sent to Web server. The SOAP request is processed by Web server and corresponding responds are created and sent to client in HTTP form as well. [1][2].

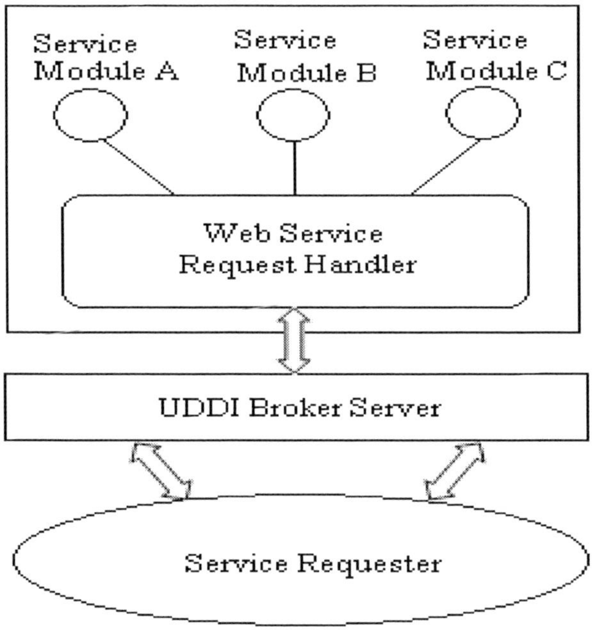

Figure 1. Architecture of Web Services.

Construction of RSCS in power plant in WAN based on Web Services has the following advantages and features:

1)Excellent integrability. Web Services can be integrated into application system over network to implement special functions. Wide-range resources are fully used to construct distributed multi-module supervisory model. Meanwhile, various services and resources are integrated into local power plant node information system. Web protocols used as the specification on component interface description and coordination description, which screens the difference between software platforms such as COBRA, DCOM and EJB to implement inter-operability, to achieve the most excellent integrability in current supervisory and control platforms [3].

2)Good openness. All Web services are described, transferred and exchanged based on universal and open protocols, by which interconnections between heterogeneous servers/clients can be implemented easily. Meanwhile, SOAP messages are transferred by HTTP protocol and can transverse firewall of enterprise without any blocks, which makes it convenient for integration of more resource and information and utilization by users in WAN [4].

3)Good encapsulation. Physical location and concrete implementation are transparent for caller of services. Any change in the implementation of Web Services does not affect callers' use of services, which make it easy for update of resources, services and algorithms in servers or clients.

3. Comprehensive Information Integration of Plants in WAN Using Web Services

3.1. Framework of System

Web Services have remarkable advantages in data communication between different operating systems and users' applications. Therefore, Web Services are introduced into the construction of comprehensive information platform of power plants in WAN.

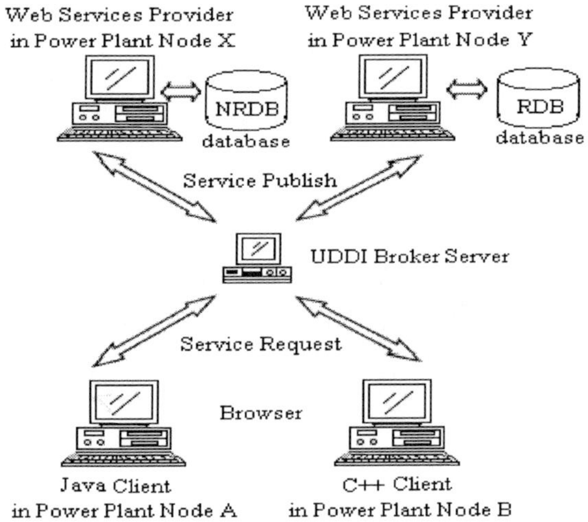

Figure 2. Framework of Comprehensive Information Integration of Power Plants in WAN Based on Web Services.

In the framework of the platform, information resources Web service can be provided by any programming languages developers of each power plant node or resource provider are familiar with. A mapping relation is constructed between current information architecture and standard model of meta data to make SOAP messages are received and responded by current information architecture in universal format [5][6]. WSDL files are used to describe the provided Web service and published on UDDI broker servers in the comprehensive information network. The WSDL can be found by any client application on the UDDI broker servers. Information resources provided by power plant nodes are called by client applications selectively according to the WSDL description documents [7][8].

System integration based on Web Services on application level is used in integration of modules in the whole information platform. Messages and data transfer and exchange among system modules are implemented based on Web Services on different platforms.

3.2. Design and Application

MIS in power plants is a comprehensive management platform including multi subsystems such as capital construction, material management and operation management. Comprehensive information platform based on Web Services can be constructed for multi power plants in WAN. The platform is above MIS level and implements integration of resources management methods, services and information sharing, which improves usage of information and provide guide for optimization for power production in WAN.

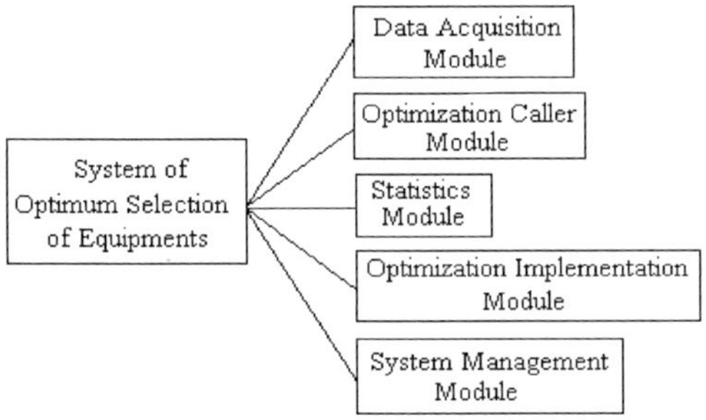

Figure 3. System Composition of Optimum Selection of Equipments in Power Plants.

Various information services modules are to be created firstly in the construction of information platform of power plants in WAN based on architecture of Web Services such as:

1)Services module of unit performance analysis and optimization: units' efficiency is computed based on sampled data and performance of units is analyzed. Operation guide under current load, optimum operational mode and main parameters guide are provided based on computing of sampled data.

2)Service module of cost computation and analysis on plant level: including cost analysis, information query and index computation services;

3)Services module of material purchase and management optimization on plant level: optimizing material purchase and management for the whole plant.

Above service modules works as services providers. Services information is registered with and published on UDDI broker servers in WAN based on corresponding specification. When related subsystems are constructed with users of local node plant, information on services of specified category can be found on UUDI and a service request is created from subsystems. Power plant systems in WAN can be divided into 2 levels, i.e. client and server, based on level of service calling. Clients and servers are not strictly separated for any 2 nodes power plants in WAN in the application. Clients are generally the local power plant and shares information in WAN by calling various service modules provided by servers.

Comprehensive information integration for power plants in WAN is expounded as following with optimum selection of equipments in power plants as a case.

Service providers consist of modules in 4 levels in optimum selection of equipments, which are data acquisition module, optimization caller module, statistics module, optimization implementation module and system management module. The composition of the platform is shown in Figure3.

Data acquisition module: to acquire related information on equipments in WAN over network or by users' automatic processing procedure and store it into database of local node.

Optimization caller module: to create and maintain multi broker servers, by which optimum selection service of equipments is provided over communication in WAN.

Statistics module: to generate statistic on various information on equipments based on data stored on database in local or remote nodes and generate spreadsheets for printing and storage.

Optimization implementation module: to get the optimum selection result by judging all of them based on some user-specified judgment rules and make comparison among and summary about various data to generate reports to users;

System management module: to implement functions including user's authentication management, report formats, system parameters configuration etc.

Local node acquires large amount of information and data dealing with equipments with optimization caller module provided by other nodes in WAN. Optimum selection of equipments is implemented with other nodes providing statistics services and optimization implementation services to provide support for managers' decision-making of local node power plant. Relation between any 2 nodes in WAN can be peer to peer relation providing Web Services to each other or client/server relation in which services are provided by the nodes with rich resources while other nodes shares the services. Architecture of optimum selection system of equipments for power plants in WAN is shown in Figure4.

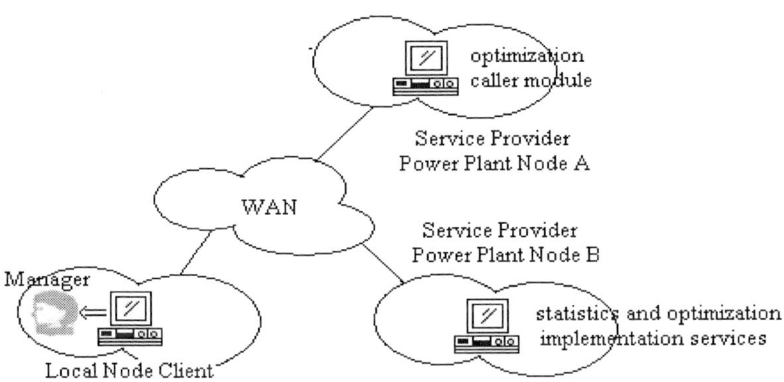

Figure 4. System Architecture of Optimum Selection of Equipments for Power Plants in WAN.

4. Design of RSCS in Plants Using Web Services

4.1. Architecture

Two kinds of nodes are included in RSCS in Power Plants Based on Web Services: local nodes and remote nodes. Data acquisition and execution of control function are implemented in local nodes. Local nodes consist of following levels:

1)Field level: including traditional and intelligent field devices, such as process I/O modules in DCS or fieldbus instruments. Field data acquisition and direct process control are implemented in the level;

2)Process level: including process control units, upper level supervisory and control units and database units and serving as HMI in local nodes, supervising and controlling production process. Various sorts of data from field devices, such as real-time sampling value, trend data and alarm data etc.. OPC severs are provided by device manufactures. Data communication in OPC is based on private OLE/COM technology developed by Microsoft and same with distributed components technology developed by other vendors, which is self-closed and cannot traverse the firewall of enterprises. Therefore, data in OPC servers cannot be accessed outside enterprises' firewall with private components technology. DCOM security authentication, which is very complicated and unstable in operation, is to be executed between OPC clients and OPC servers, which increases the difficulties in system development and application.[5][6]. Gateway level above process level provides solutions to the problems.

3)Gateway level: connecting with nodes in process level downwards with Ethernet and collecting data from process level and forwarding instructions from remote nods to process level; connecting with supervisory and control system upwards. Functions traversing firewall of enterprises and executing supervision and control to field process and not be implemented in process level are implemented in gateway level. Computers in gateway level acquire data from OPC servers as OPC clients, re-organize them based on certain rules and provide them to remote client nodes after encapsulating them in form of Web Services. Instructions or data to field from remote nodes are forwarded by supervisory and control service system to gateway level and forwarded to field devices by gateway using OPC technology.

4)Supervisory and control service system (SCSS) orienting remote clients based on Web Services: connecting with gateway level with Ethernet and collecting data from process level and forwarding instructions from remote nods to process level; traversing firewall and connecting with remote nodes over Internet. Functions such as data publishing and remote instruction receiving can be implemented here. Meanwhile, data and instructions from remote client nodes are sent to supervisory and control service system by traversing firewall in HTTP protocols. [7][8] Supervisory and control service system can be developed with any Web Server development platform, such as ASP.NET.

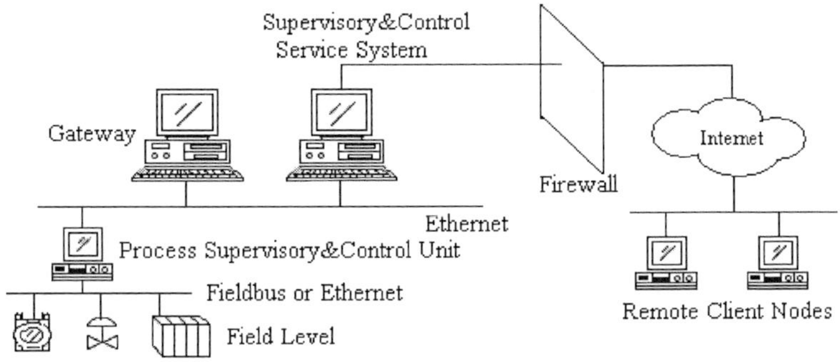

Figure 5. Architecture of RSCS in power plants based on Web Service.

Remote nodes are mainly various HMI such as PC, PDA, laptop computers and mobile phones. Universal HMIs, which are simple and friendly, such as Web browser is provided in remote nodes. Universal HTTP protocol and HTML are used in data exchange between remote nodes and local nodes in process fields. Architecture of RSCS in power plants based on Web Services is shown in Figure5.

4.2. Design of Gateway Connecting Local and Remote Nodes

1) Data Acquisition Based on OPC

Main data accessed by gateway connecting local and remote nodes are instructions from remote nodes and real-time data from field nodes. Functionally, gateway is not only OPC client but also interface for data exchange. OPC servers are provided by OEM with each equipment and access data in physical devices by drivers for field devices and provide them to OPC clients in request of data from OPC clients. Various sorts of data such as data from devices and system, alarm and event data and history data as well can be acquired by OPC server. Acquired data from field is stored in real-time database and some protocol or middleware technologies such as ODBC, ADO are used to access database. Main methods for data access by OPC clients are: ConnServer(), used to connect OPC server; GetItemsValue(string ItemIDs),used to get a group of items' value; WriteItemValue(string ItemID, short Value), used to write data into some item in OPC server.

2) Data Encapsulation Based on Web Services

Data acquired with OPC is needed to be encapsulated as Web Services to be accessed by remote nodes. Interfaces need to be decided by callers before encapsulation of data. Interface is to be defined based on interface definitions in certain programming language environment such as Java. Special tools such as Java2WSDL are used to generate Web services description file with WSDL based on interface definition file. Special tools such as WSDL2Java are used to generate corresponding server codes frame and concrete services implementation codes are added into the frame manually. Considering Web services are the interface to outside, concrete logics are implemented in form of modules. Data encapsulation can be implemented with developing tools such as Visual Studio.net, WebSphere, JBuilder etc. Services description written in WSDL need to be presented for calling by remote clients.

3) Publication of Web Services

Gateway registers provided Web Services with UDDI service broker server UDDI. Services descriptions describe the requests and responds supported by the services. Remote clients find the services, in which data from field is encapsulated, and call the corresponding services using SOAP after binding with them. If the gateway and clients are in the same local area net (LAN) and system extension in the future is not considered, services description files can be directly provided to clients without being registered with UDDI service broker server.

4.3. Design of Supervisory and Control Service System (SCSS)

To lower cost in software and hardware development on client nodes, supervisory and control service system based on Web page service is used to provide universal HMI for remote clients. Remote clients can request data from SCSS provide Web browsers are installed. SCSS acquires service description of various field data provided by gateway and a SOAP message is generated based on service description. The request message is send to Web services request handler in gateway and Web services for various field data are called by Web services request handler. Corresponding SOAP response in returned to SCSS after requested data is acquired. Data is retrieved from SOAP response by Web Services stub in SCSS. Data storage, report generation, charts and curves illustration can be implemented by SCSS. Field data can be accessed by remote clients by accessing SCSS, which serve as the bridge for data exchange between remote client nodes and gateway. Following code illustrate the data acquisition process of water level in drum in RSCS in power plants.

```
Dim soap As MSSOAPLib.SoapClient
Set soap = New MSSOAPLib.SoapClient
soap.mssoapinit(http://102.55.71.253/LevelControl/OPCDATA.wsdl)
soap.GetWaterLevelofDrum("1")
```

mssoapinit is called firstly in the instance and URL of services description files is sent to SoapClient. SoapClient get all methods of Web Services and can call them directly initialization.

In implementation, SCSS and gateway can be located in same node or distributed on different nodes. For system extension in the future, loose couple architecture is used in deployment of gateway and SCSS, in which gateway and SCSS are located in different nodes and connected by Ethernet.

4.4. System Application

Designed and developed RSCS is applied in the remote supervision and control for water level in drum of boiler in a power plant. Architecture of the system is shown in Figure 6.

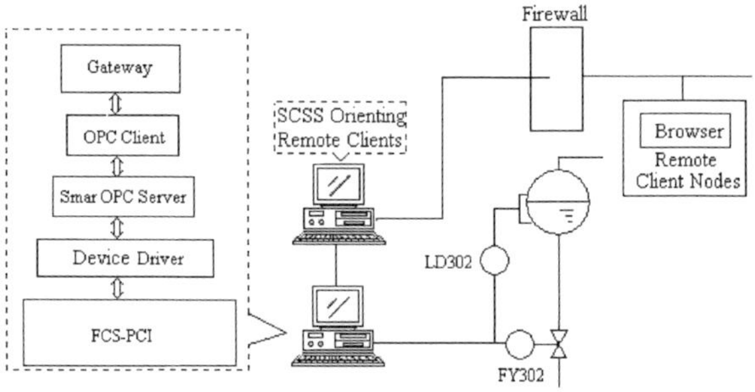

Figure 6. RSCS for water level in drum of boiler based on Web Services.

FF fieldbus intelligent instruments are used in field level. Differential pressure transmitter LD302 is used in measurement of water level in drum. Fieldbus valve positioner FY302 is used in control of water-feeding. PCs are used in supervisory and control level, installed with FF fieldbus control system

OPC server used to access data in field instruments. OPC server and gateway serving as OPC client are installed in the same PC. Gateway accesses data from OPC server and encapsulate them into Web Services. SCSS installed in another PC calls the services provided by gateway. Remote clients can traverse firewall and exchange information with SCSS in form of Web pages. Trend curve of water level in drum generated in SCSS and accessed in form of Web page by remote clients is shown in Figure 7.

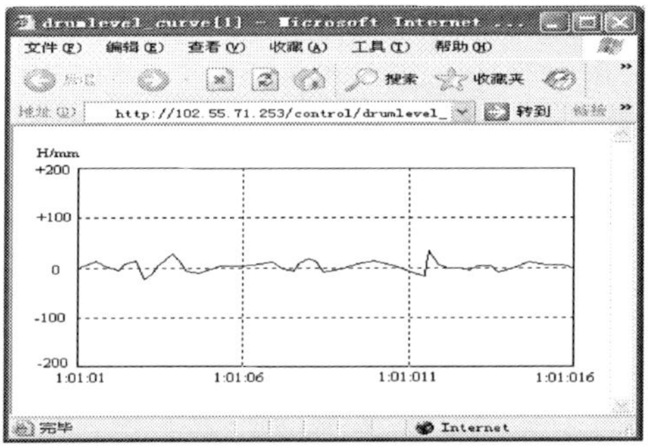

Figure 7. Trend curve of water level in drum accessed in form of Web page by remote clients.

CONCLUSION

A information platform including services with different granularities and supporting multi-level services calling constructed by full use of Web Services in the comprehensive information system for plants in WAN based on Web Services is presented above. Information, resource and services sharing between different nodes in the system are implemented based on the presented platform. Data exchange between different plants and inter-operability between heterogeneous subsystems are implemented successfully, which improves overall performance of the information platform and implements integration of related applied system in each plant in WAN and possesses good openness and scalability. Implementation and application of the platform enhances mutual supplementary of advantages between different plants, avoiding repeated construction of resource effectively, improving usage of resources, saving massive human resources and material resources, and provides more and better services for power enterprises.

It will be a good prospect for the development of Web Services with its increasingly wide use. Web Services will play more important roles in industry management and control in the future. A RSCS platform for power plants including services with different granularities and supporting multi-level services calling constructed based on Web Services is presented in this chapter. Information and data exchange between different nodes in the system and inter-operability between heterogeneous subsystems, which improves overall performance of the RSCS and implements integration of related applied system in power plants, are implemented based on the presented platform. The presented RSCS shows good openness and scalability. Project practice shows that designed RSCS in power plants based on Web Services, with which data exchange between nodes in system can traverse firewall without any blocks, is stable and reliable in operation with high integrability and openness and is worthy of application and popularization.

REFERENCE

[1] YANG Zhihe. Research and Design of Education Resource Sharing Platform Based on Web Services, *Journal Of Shanghai Dianji University*. Vol.10, No.1, 2007.

[2] Zhang Xia. Application of Web Service in Enterprise Application Integration, *Journal of Wut (Information and Management Engineering)*. Vol.27, No.1, 2005.

[3] ZHU Bo. Networked Optimal Cutting stock System Based on Web Service, *Journal of Chongqing University (Natural Science Edition)*. Vol.28, No.1, 2005.

[4] ZHU Bo. Method to Select the Optimal Web Services, *Mini-Micro Systems*. Vol.28, No.4, 2007.

[5] XU Guang-xia. Seamless integration of isomerous system based on web service, *Computer Engineering and Design*. Vol.28, No.6, 2007.

[6] Hu Ping, Design and Realization of a Web Service Bas ed Enterprises Information System, *Control and Automation*. Vol.23, No.9, 2007.

[7] Zhong Huiling. A Data Exchange Platform bas ed on Web Service, *Control and Automation*. Vol.23, No.9, 2007.

[8] HU PING. Design and Realization of a Web Service Based Enterprises Information System, *Control and Automation*. Vol.23, No.9, 2007.

In: Network Protocols
Editor: Geng Liang
ISBN 978-1-61470-821-6

Chapter 9

COMPREHENSIVE AUTOMATION INFORMATION PLATFORM IN POWER PLANT BASED ON FIELDBUS PROTOCOL

***Geng Liang*[1] *and Wen Li*[2]**
[1]School of Control and Computer Engineering, North China Electric Power University, Beijing, China
[2]Beijing GUODIANZHISHEN Control Technology Co. Ltd, Beijing, China

ABSTRCT

The important significance of comprehensive automation information platform (CAIP) and the implementation by means of FCS are elaborated. Several solutions to implement CAIP in power plants in different condition are researched on and analyzed. The network architecture of CAIP based on fieldbus is proposed, functions and the roles of each part in the architecture are elaborated; two schemes for the implementation of the communication subsystem between management level, supervision level and field level , which is the key part in the implementation of CAIP in power plant , are proposed, merits and problems are pointed out for and the selection principle of the schemes is expounded. Operation practice with the proposed solution showed a good result and improved production efficiency in power plant. Significant economic benefit is achieved.

1. Introduction

Computer, information technology and computer network have achieved great development. Computer, automation and communication technology have been used to implement comprehensive automation in enterprises to improve the efficiency in manufacture, management and decision-making. To implement the information fusion for the whole manufacturing process and to implement comprehensive automation, a communication and control system, which is running in field, reliable in performance and low-cost, is necessary for the implementation of data exchange and information sharing among the field intelligent devices and between the network for field control and the upper network Digitalization for the transmitted signal is the foundation for the digital communication. Traditional architecture in the lowest network of DCS is changed by FCS. Peer to peer connection is adopted in field in traditional DCS and interconnected respectively according to control loop and only unilateral transmission for digital signal is allowed. Field intelligent devices are used in FCS which enables the embedding of field module into field intelligent devices. Meanwhile, field intelligent devices communicate with each other completely digitally. Digital information can be transmitted directly between transmitters in field and computers in supervision level; analogue signal has been replaced by digital signal and multi digital signal can be transmitted over one line and full digital communication in field and the distributed control are implemented thoroughly.

The implementation of full digital communication based on fieldbus technology makes its advantage over traditional DCS. The amount of data exchange between field level and supervisions level increased greatly. Not only process related data and information but also the running parameters and status of field device, fault information, which is not achievable in DCS, transmitted to supervision level. Fault playback and coordinate control in process level and resource rating in management level can be implemented by these valuable data. Therefore, information platform architecture based on FCS is very important for the implementation of comprehensive automation in power plants.

2. ARCHITECTURE OF COMPREHENSIVE AUTOMATION INFORMATION PLATFORM

Hierarchical architecture is the main feature for process control in power plant. Network architecture of CAIP in power plant based on fieldbus is shown in Figure1.

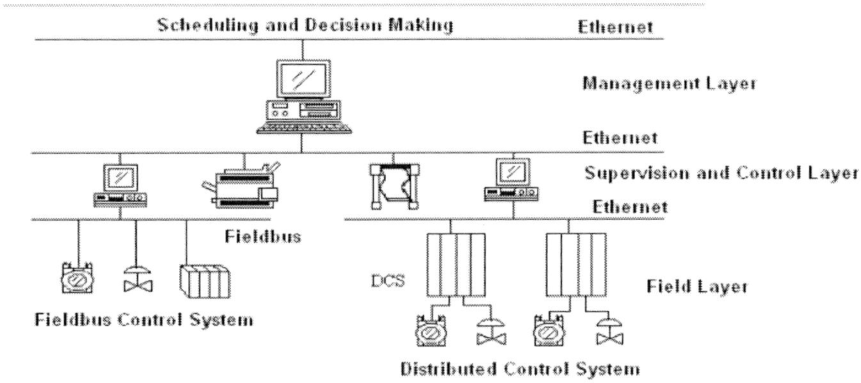

Figure 1. Network architecture of CAIP in power plant.

DCS field level consists of not the traditional analog instruments intelligent devices with complete digital communication ability, which is the key element in implementation of comprehensive automation

Field level is the lowest level for the integration of information network in plant and is the foundation level in the network of enterprise production.

The first-hand information is transmitted to supervision and control level and put into real-time database and used in advanced control, optimizing calculation, integrated display. Inside the supervision level, other computers except the master computers for supervision and control play role of slave computers to share the work of master computers. For instance, the parameters to be supervised and controlled in upper-level is often in great number in some large-scaled system, which were heavy load for the master computers if all the work including displaying and operating is done by them.. If some slave computers are used to assist the work of the master computers, such as display, data-storing, spread-sheeting while the key operations such as data-acquisition, execution of control program, downloading of control parameters are executed by master computers, the efficiency and reliability of system can be improved greatly and the system can operate more smoothly. Supervision level is often made of Ethernet which has higher bit-rate.

3. Implementation of Communication between the Field Level, Supervision Level and Management Level

3.1. Two Solutions for the Implementation

In view of network connection, the computers in supervision level and management level are on the same level in network. Therefore, the essence of communication between the computers in the two different levels is the same and the problems dealing with data exchange are to be solved properly. 2 implementation schemes for the data-exchange and information-sharing are available.

Solution 1: Implementation with independent programming. Data exchange is implemented by programming in the master computers and other computers in supervision level by user on a software platform such as VB and VC++ independent of upper level. The downward connection by the applications or software is implemented by the interface between the applications and the operations system and the TCP/IP or IPX/SPX protocol supported by Windows. Winsock control can act as the programming interface in VB; Winsock control in ActiveX controls and CSocket class can achieve this as well in VC++. Dynamic linking library (DLL) or dynamic data exchange (DDE) can be used in the connection between the application communication module and the real-time database in management level. Connection is implemented with Ethernet card and cable in hardware. The communication architecture is shown in Figure2. This scheme is a desirable choice to meet some special demands such as the control of the time interval in data-acquisition and data-storing, the control of spreadsheet generation, access of database.

This independent programming scheme is very flexible in development, easy to transplant. It is a general-purposed solution. However, it is necessary to programming by users which increase the complexity and work load. Besides this, communication program runs independently of the upper-level management system, which will affect the coordination of whole system.

Solution 2: Implementation of communication by the network function embedded in supervision level. Supervision and control level connecting field level with management level is indispensable in the transmission of digital information top to bottom. It is not only the hub in the data-exchange between field and management level but also responsible for the real-time data acquisition, storage. and the download of instructions and data to field level. Generally, supervision and control level possess powerful network function. Therefore, implementing the data exchange and information-sharing between field and management level with the network function of supervision level is a good choice.

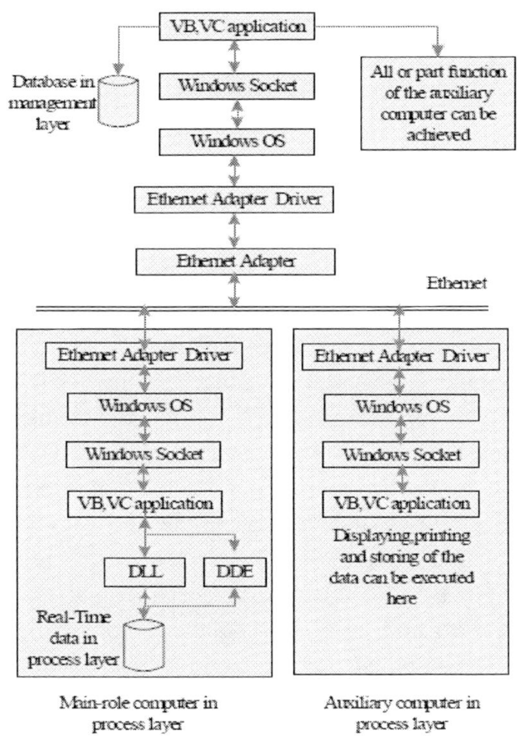

Figure 2. Implementation of communication between supervision and management level by independent programming.

It is desirable to utilize the network function of supervision and control level to achieve general-purposed communication function. Supervision and control software play a key role in the implementation. This solution is expounded with a instance, in which a supervision and control software AIMAX for Smar System302 fieldbus control system is used.

Network communication function is powerful in AIMAX. It is necessary to establish AIMAX network before implementing communication in the AIMAX system. Physical level and data link level in AIMAX system are standard according to Ethernet protocol. Media for data transmission and network adapter are standard too. TCP/IP protocol supported by Windows is adopted in transmission level and network level; session level, representing level. Application level above the transmission level is customized to meet some special demand in accordance with international standard. Above the transmission level, "network node" is used in AIMAX to identify AIMAX system process, which differs from IP address which is used to identify the computers on network in which AIMAX system is installed. The master or slave computers running AIMAX system in supervision level can access the real-time database in the controlling master computer in supervision level. AIMAX LAN driver is necessary when the node computers in AIMAX network send data to or modify the data in the peer computers.

Following setting-up is needed to use AIMAX network: (1) TCP/IP setting-up (2) AIMAX network nod setting-up. It is up to 255 nodes in AIMAX network. Local node and remote node are to be configured. It is up to 254 remote nodes and 1 local node. (3) Real time data points in database of remote node computers' database is added to the local node computer's database. When all above are properly configured, the data exchange and information sharing between different levels can be achieved when AIMAX system started. The implementation of communication between the computers in the same level or different levels is simple and easy to understand. No special communication program is needed and the reliability for data transmission is high. Besides this, the data can be put into the database in management level off-line with the database converting application by AIMAX system. Development of extra converting program is not needed, which maintain a very good integration for the whole system. However, it is required for each node computer to have AIMAX system installed before AIMAX network can be used, which will occupy more resource in computer. The ability of transplantation is limited and the flexibility is lowered for that reason.

3.2. Applications of Two Solutions

For the construction of CAIP three choices for the implementation of subsystem for communication between different levels are available:

(1) By Solution 1 Only

The lowest level control network can be constructed with 1~4 fieldbus segments in the case that the scale for field level is small and no many loops to be controlled. The connection between field level and supervision level can be achieved by 1 supper-level master computer acting as gateway. The master computer in supervision level is responsible for the supervision and communication with field level. It can also exchange data and communication with the master computers in management level. Slave computers are installed to do some slave work such as the display of data from field, printing, spreadsheet generation, data storing and forwarding. They can also provide information to the master computers in management level to relieve the workload of the master computer in supervision level. The network structure for this system is shown in figure 3 a. In this case, it is desirable to program independently to implement the data exchange in supervision level and between supervision and management level. The main feature for this solution is its clearness in network architecture and well-defined distribution of workload among different computers, which can lower the fault rate of whole system greatly.

(2) By Solution 2 Only

The lowest control network is often constructed with multi fieldbus segment in the case that the scale for field level is large and there are many loops to be controlled. In this case, it is desirable to implement the connection between field and the supervision level with multi master computers. The master computers in supervision level are mainly responsible for the supervision and communication with field. They can also communicate and exchange data with master computer in management level, display of data from field, printing and spreadsheet generation. They handle data storing and forwarding, providing information for the master computers in management level at the same time. The network structure for this system is shown in figure 3 b. In this case, it is desirable to implement communication and data exchange in supervision level and with management level with the network function in supervision computers if no special demands are raised. In this solution, the resource of system is used fully. Good coordination between the master computers in supervision and management level can be achieved and the efficiency for the whole system is high. However, the main disadvantage in the solution is its worse flexibility by which some special demands can not be met.

(3) Combination of Solution 1 and Solution 2

Combining solution 1 with solution 2 can achieve a good balance between the advantages and disadvantages from the single adoption of solution 1 or 2 in the case that the scale of field control and the number of loops to be controlled are relatively large. This solution is the most desirable for communication and data exchange in large-scaled system. It can meet demands on general and special purpose. The network architecture for this solution is shown in Figure3 c.

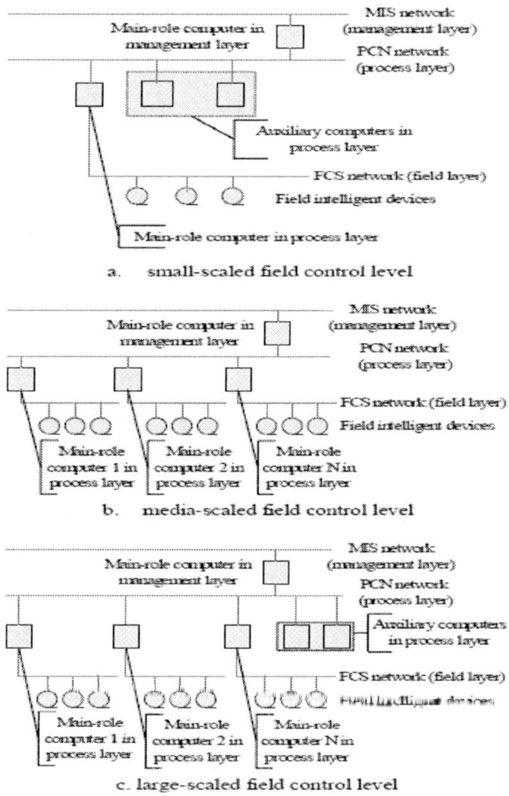

Figure 3. Three network architecture for CAIP with different scale of field control level.

Many cases such as operational effect in production should be put into consideration in choosing which solution can be used and more suitable for control and management. The final solution for implementation can be chosen until several solutions are compared and analysed.

CONCLUSION

The implementation of CAIP in power plant is a key factor in improving production efficiency in power plant. The fast development of fieldbus technology makes the last preparation for the CAIP in power plant ready. The final design and implementation and field operation are the result of combing technologies dealing with system configuration, network communication and programming. The implementation and selection of different solutions for the subsystem of communication between management, supervision field level are two important problems to be considered. Proper solution to these problems is very important in the designing of feasible and highly efficient CAIP in power plant.

REFERENCE

[1] Zhu, XQ. Process information acquisition based on fieldbus ICIA 2004: *Proceedings Of 2004 International Conference On Information Acquisition* , 2004.

[2] Liu Dan. Application of FF Fieldbus Control System in Coking Gas Production Industry, *Process Automation Instrumentation*, Vol.26, No.3, 2005.

[3] Zhang ji. Comprehensive Automation System based on Fieldbus Technology in Thermal Power Plant, *Power System Engineering,* Vol.14, No.1, 2005.

[4] Fu Hua. Research about Multi-fieldbus Integration, *Microelectronics and Computer,,*Vol.24, No 1,2007.

[5] Treytl, A, Sauter, T, Schwaiger, C. *Security measures for industrial fieldbus systems - State of the art and solutions for IP-based approaches.* WFCS 2004: *IEEE International Workshop On Factory Communication Systems, Proceedings* : 2004.

[6] Kanai, S, Kishinami, T, Tomura, T, et al. Object-oriented design pattern approach to seamless modeling, simulation and implementation of distributed control systems. *INT. FED. INFO PROC.*, 2005.

[7] CAO Wen liang. Status quo and development prospect of plant level supervisory information system of power plant, *Electric Power*, Vol.35, No 9,2002.

[8] [8] Zhang Fengdeng. Fieldbus and Integration Technology of Comprehensive Automation System in Power Plant, *Power Engineering,* Vol.21, No 3,2001.

[9] [9] Zhou Yilin. Improved Method for Monitor and Control Software Based on Field-bus Foundation, *Instrument Technique and Sensor,* Vol.18, No 2,2007.

In: Network Protocols
Editor: Geng Liang
ISBN 978-1-61470-821-6

Chapter 10

NEW NETWORK PROTOCOL ARCHITECTURE FOR A DISTRIBUTED MEASUREMENT AND CONTROL SYSTEM WITH ITS APPLICATION IN NETWORK EXTENSION

***Wen Li*[1] *and Geng Liang*[2]**
[1]Beijing GUODIANZHISHEN Control Technology Co. Ltd, Beijing, China
[2]School of Control and Computer Engineering, North China Electric Power University, Beijing, China

ABSTRACT

A network protocol architecture based on software components integration-OFC is introduced in this chapter. The layered architecture, structure and features of OFC are expounded. Its function in network extension is analyzed.

1. INTRODUCTION

With the rapid development of computer and network technologies, more completed production process need to be designed in the hot competition of modern automation market to meet users' various requirements. By means of commercial data communication system, most manufacturers of measurement and control equipments are committed to research and develop the field instruments with better data access performance and safety insurance. However, international norm is not be finalized as yet regarding these requirements.

To break the limitation from the proprietary technologies of manufacturers, it is necessary to make these instruments interoperable and interchangeable. Integrating OLE (Object Linking and Embedding) with some widely used industrial norm, such as Foundation Fieldbus, based on Client/Server architecture and Windows O/S platform, a new network protocol architecture OFC (OLE for Foundation Configuration) is formed. A typical control system for heterogeneous computational environment based on OFC is shown as Figure 1.

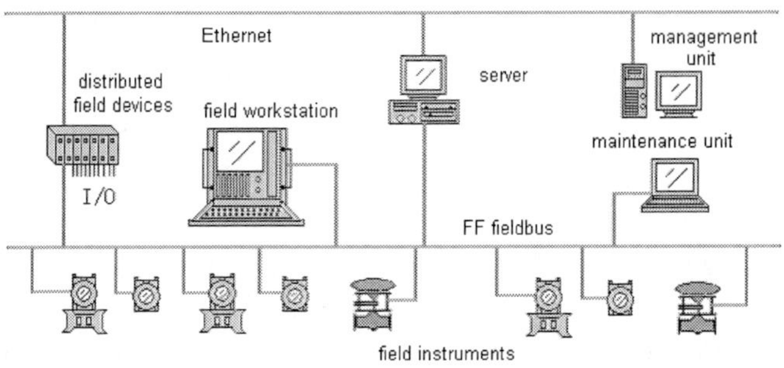

Figure 1. a typical control system for heterogeneous computational environment based on OFC.

The main advantages of this architecture are: (1) heterogeneous computational environment adaptability (2) high data transmission efficiency (3) easy to meet the requirement of manufacturer (5) remote addressing ability.

2. Layered Architecture of OFC

2.1. The Ground Layer: Foundation Fieldbus Protocol

Foundation Fieldbus (FF) protocol is interoperable among many manufacturers. It is a newly network oriented norm, composed of 8 parts. Its main advantages includes complete digital signal instead of 4~20mA analogue signal, distributed control and processing, interoperability and interchangeability.

FF architecture is developed based on OSI/ISO model. Layers 1,2 and 7 in the model, i.e. physical layer, data link layer and application layer, are adopted. Layers 3~6 is not used out of consideration of time critical application. The simplified structure enables higher data transmission rate and easier implementation. Physical layer of FF involves features of several fieldbus technologies. Token passing, access detection, error control and data packaging and synchronization are used in data link layer to ensure reliable data transmission. Application Process (AP) is used to realize application layer. AP is composed of a set of function blocks with sequential organization, and system management kernel (SMK). Some algorithms are used to implement the transmission of data from input to output. Users can configure the AP. SMK can provide users with functions such as address allocation, device identification, clock synchronization and function block scheduling.

Each fieldbus can be viewed as a link. Devices on the link can be basic devices, link masters and bridges. Basic devices can receive passed token and response to it. Link master can act as scheduler. Bridges can connect each links to form a more wide-area link tree. The identical link medium and transmission rate is applied to devices on the link.

2.2. The Second Layer: OLE

Object Oriented Programming (OOP) has ever been a solution to constructing complex software architecture. Although it is powerful, a practical problem always exists, that is to say, a standardized architecture has to be constructed to inter-connect software components from different manufacturers in such heterogeneous computing environment. Object Link and Embedding (OLE) is the best solution to the problem.

OLE is implemented by means of dividing commercial software into binary components, just like Integrated Circuit (IC). Software updating can be achieved with the original functions maintained in OLE mode. Component Object Model (COM) is the kernel of OLE. COM provides user with a powerful, extensible architecture for software development and design. Under the guide of such concept, software manufacturers can pack various functions into the reusable component, just like the mechanism in IC design.

2.3. The Third Layer: OPC

Various HMI necessitate the development of drivers for each data access to each kind of hardware, which make the development redundant. Besides, multiple application can not access the same hardware simultaneously by means of traditional drivers. OLE for Process Control (OPC) is composed of a series of standardized interfaces, properties and methods for use in process control and manufacture antomation.. ActiveX/COM defines how industrial software components can inter-act and share data. Supported by Windows NT architecture, OPC can provide user with a common interface to multiple devices for process control. The interface is independent of the control software or devices. Essentially, interface only need to be developed once while used many times. OPC construct a connection between hardware and software manufacturers and improve software compatibility greatly. Seamless integration of various application is improved consequently. OPC also enable the application to take full advantage of interoperability from FF devices to realize supervision and control for the field data. OPC client based on OLE and COM call the OPC server provided by hardware manufacturers during operation. Multiple clients can simultaneously access to the same OPC server.

OPC server implements data acquisition function. It provides user defined interface conforming to some specification. The architecture of OPC is shown in Figure2. OPC server is composed of Server, Group, Item and I/O DLL for devices from different manufacturers.

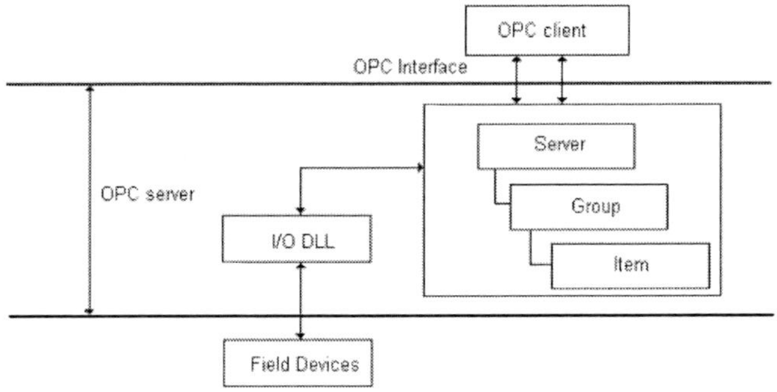

Figure 2. OPC architecture.

Only access to physical medium and interconnection between different applications are specified in FF norm. Implementation of user layer is not defined, resulting in different data supervision and configuration schemes. FF has its own advantages. Although OPC can meet users' requirement in data supervision, some configuration system is still required to serve as the media to utilize these advantages.

3. INTEGRATION OF FF, OLE AND OPC: OFC

OFC realize the integration of FF, OLE and OPC, solving many problems which can not be solved by each of them independently. OFC combines the merits of FF and OLE and construct a new network architecture based on fieldbus for heterogeneous computing environment.. By applying OFC, the configuration of FF become easier and simplified in that configuration of devices from different manufacturers can be implemented by one kind of software.

Components of OFC is managed based on client/server architecture. As the data access interface of physical layer in FF, OFC server works as the bridge between configuration software and the field devices. Standarization of interfaces makes the data transmission and sharing between each components easy and simplified. OFC Client can access to the field data by means of one or multiple OFC servers, as shown in Figure 3.

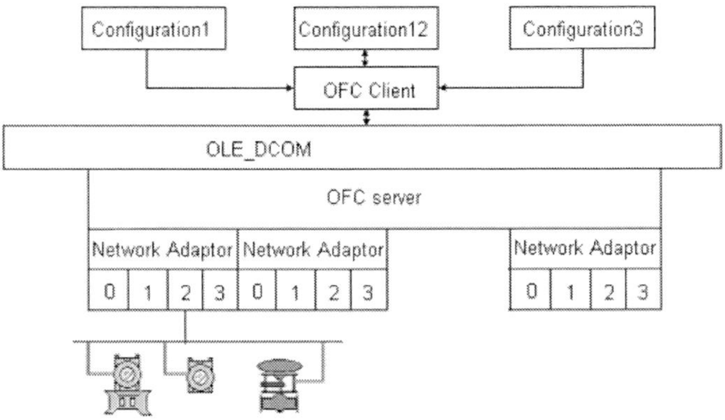

Figure 3. OFC client, server and field devices.

User can choose local connection or remote ones according to practical requirement. Using DCOM, destination node must be specified by clients in remote connections. Local connections have higher efficiency than remote ones.

4. STRUCTURE AND FUNCTIONS OF OFC

OFC has its own special norm for interface configurations, mainly orienting client program written in C/C++. Interfaces to new protocol objects are provided and managed by OFC server components as shown in Figure 4.

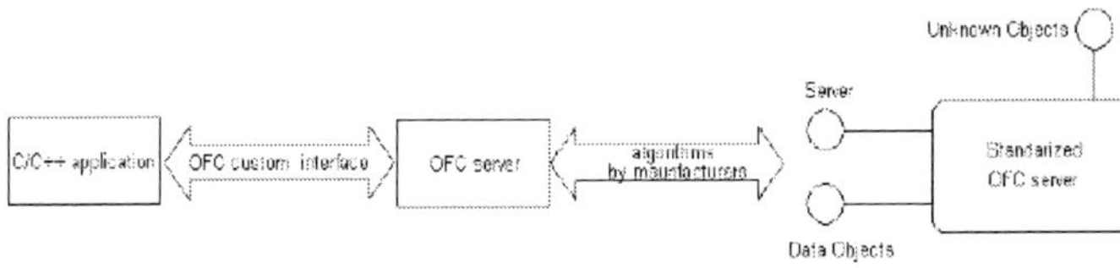

Figure 4. OFC with its interfaces.

In many applications, this new architecture and interfacing technology is used directly or indirectly. OLE base configuration interfaces, events adopting OLE interfaces, and DCOM are generally included in these functions. A OFC server can also be constructed to enable the client applications deployed on different network nodes to use the same objects, which enables network protocol developed by different manufacturers to access the data on servers. This distributed mechanism ensures the transparency in data access.

Data access is implemented with asynchronized communication between clients and servers, enabling the ground layer of protocol identify the sequence in data access. Server can optimize the data access in synchronized mode to obtain higher efficiency in communication. Although a transaction is required for each request to waiting for response from server, synchronization mode can be chosen by clients freely to waiting for the request to be processed. Transaction to be processed must be acknowledged by server and returned to clients. User data and acknowledgement are processed at the same time and returned to clients. Servers and clients receive data by means of a common channel created between them with virtual handshaking protocols.

Applications can access data in devices with OFC interfaces that support access to data chunk and system configuration. Application instance is created in server by OFC. FF configuration can be started from design of topology (offline configuration) or loading function blocks (online configuration). OFC-based configuration allocates tags for all devices and control strategies can be constructed by connecting function blocks in the same or different devices.

Conclusion

With the rapid development of network technologies, higher and higher demands are advances for industrial automation. Network based distribute measurement and control will develop further orienting open and universal norm. Network interconnection and system integration in heterogeneous computing environment is the trend in future. OFC ,the new components interconnection technology based on FF, will also play more important role in network extension and system integration.

References

[1] David A. Glanzer and Charles. Interoperable fieldbus devices: a technical overview, *ISA Trans*,35(1996),pp147-151.

[2] Fieldbus Foundation, *interoperability Test System- user's guide*,2001.

[3] www.fieldbus.org.

[4] Berge J. Fieldbus for process control: Engineering, operation, and maintenance.*Research Triangle Park: ISA Books*. 2002.

[5] Smar International Corporation. *Fieldbus tutorial:* A FOUNDATION fieldbus technology overview. Sert„ozinho: Brazil. 2004.

[6] International organization for standardization. ISO/IEC 7498-1: Information technology open systems interconnection basic reference model: *The basic model*. Switzerland. CD-ROM. 1994.

[7] Fieldbus Foundation. FF-890-1.3: *Foundation specification function block application process, part 1*. Austin, USA. 1999.

[8] Fieldbus Foundation. *Foundation specification function block application process Part 3*: FF-892 FS1.4. Austin, USA. 1999.

[9] Fieldbus Foundation. Foundation specification function block application process Part 5: FF-894 DPS0.95. Austin, USA. 1999.

[10] N.P. Mahalik, *Fieldbus Technology*, Springer, 2003.

INDEX

I

L

N

O

P

S

T

U

V

W